voice & vision

voice & vision

A Guide to

Writing History

and Other

Serious Nonfiction

STEPHEN J. PYNE

HARVARD UNIVERSITY PRESS
Cambridge, Massachusetts
London, England
2009

Library of Congress Cataloging-in-Publication Data
Pyne, Stephen J., 1949–
    Voice and vision : a guide to writing history and other serious
nonfiction / Stephen J. Pyne.
        p.   cm.
    Includes bibliographical references and index.
    ISBN 978-0-674-03330-6 (alk. paper)
    1. Authorship.   2. English language—Rhetoric.   3. English
language—Style.   4. Historiography.   I. Title.
    PN145P96 2009
    808'.02—dc22   2008043403

For Sonja
who ever reminds me that
life is still the best editor

and

for Lydia and Molly
my two best editions

acknowledgments

I want to express publicly my gratitude to Geri Thoma, Joyce Seltzer, and Maria Ascher. Geri saw that the manuscript got a good home, Joyce that it said what it needed to (and avoided saying what it didn't), and Maria that voice actually met vision on the page and that I would be able to talk with others, not just with myself. My thanks to you all.

contents

▓ Part III. Doing It

And further, by these, my son, be admonished:
of making books there is no end.

—Ecclesiastes 12:12

"Captain, there are always alternatives."

—Mr. Spock, chief science officer,

USS *Enterprise, Star Trek*

Packing Prose

Don't think I invented any of these tangled-up con-
glomerations of wood, leather, rope, and metal thing-
a-ma-jigs herein described in my crude way. . . .
There've been adaptations and whimsical changes,
and maybe fancied improvement, but mainly it's
what has been used from the shadowy long gone
procession.

—Joe Back, *Horses, Hitches, and Rocky Trails*

It has become commonplace these days to speak of unpacking texts. This is a book about packing that prose in the first
place.

I'm speaking of a prose that often gets left behind. Fiction has guidebooks galore; journalism has shelves stocked
with manuals; and certain hybrids such as creative nonfiction or New Journalism have evolved standards, aesthetics,
and justifications for how to transfer the dominant modes
of fiction to topics in nonfiction. But history and other serious nonfiction have no such guides. Nonfiction—apart
from memoir—is not taught in writing workshops or MFA
programs, and its standards and aesthetics are not discussed
on freelancer listserves. Neither is it taught as part of professional training by academic guilds. While scholarly historians are eager to discuss historiography, they ignore the

craft that can turn their theses and narratives into literature.

This curious omission places beyond the pale of taught writing whole realms of serious nonfiction that do not rely on reportage or segue into memoir. It dismisses scholarship based on archives and printed literature. It ignores writers who do not make themselves the subject, overt or implied, of their work. It relegates texts in the field of history, in particular, to the status of unlettered historiography or unanchored prose. They exist only as conveyers of theses and data or as naïve exposition.

This book is for those who want to understand the ways in which literary considerations can enhance the writing of serious nonfiction. In their search for new texts to deconstruct, literary theorists have in recent years seized on nonfiction to demonstrate literature's critical primacy over all kinds of texts. It's time for historians, especially, to reply. History is scholarship. It is also art, and it is literature. It has no need to emulate fiction, morph into memoir, or become self-referential. But those who write it do need to be conscious of their craft. And what is true for history is true for all serious nonfiction. The issue is not whether the writing is popular, but whether it is good, which is to say, whether it does what it intends. Here are my thoughts on how to make this happen.

Since much of what follows will ponder the internal shape and architecture of books, I should explain why I organize this text as a roster of topics like beads on a string—a choice that on the surface might seem a violation of yet-to-come pleas for integral designs.

My reason is that this is a text whose subject is style, and that if I picked one or several books and analyzed them in depth, the content of those selections would interfere with my treatment of how they present it, and would inevitably alienate some readers. (Why choose one topic rather than another? Why analyze that specific book?) Keeping the topic of style separate allows readers to project the particular lessons onto their own material. But why, then, not make this book more integrated, less episodic? My reason here is that a critical book, in its self-consciousness, can overwhelm its holdings—can redirect attention to itself and away from the purposes for which it was nominally created, much as public buildings (e.g., modernist museums) too often quarrel with the duties assigned them and the display of materials within. I wanted instead to highlight the selected texts and what we might glean from them and let readers reassemble the pieces for their own purposes. A collection of commentaries can do that. A master design based on some other organizing principle might too easily slide into theory, could distract by its own ostentatious presence, and would certainly demand a significant fraction of the overall text to support its internal heft. There would be more rope than pack frame. Few readers might fight their way past the virtuoso knots to get at the goods actually carried.

That is not the purpose of this project. Its pattern more resembles a string of pack mules, each lugging some useful item of gear or foodstuff. Their arrangement is not wholly arbitrary; some critters show preferences as to which of their companions they want to follow or lead, and a good packer will array them with a sense of how contentedly (or submissively) they line up. But in the end they remain a string, tied by a single rope and a wrangler's will, if occasionally left for a while to loose-herd along a confined path.

The point is to get the goods to camp; the craft lies in packing those pieces securely; and the art consists in moving that ornery mob along. Writing, after all, begins as a verb.

A good guide will furnish lots of examples and demand endless exercises. See, then show. Study, then do. The examples vary in scope and intent. Particularly for a book about books, some samples need space to develop; not everything need be, or should be, distilled into Emersonian epigrams. While the excerpts presented here come from real sources, they mostly reflect my own tastes and thus are biased toward history. Still, in the end, there is no substitute for writing; and no writing for practice can compete with writing toward a genuine project, which argues for getting into what you want to do as soon as possible. Even apprentice work should be real work.

So get on the trail. Reading about writing isn't writing. And remember the wisdom of fabled packer Joe Back: when you come to the end of your rope, *"Tie a knot in it and hang on."*

Part I
Arts

chapter 1

In the Beginning, Words

In which we sample some texts and consider why they
might belong with literature, and where, for that
matter, serious nonfiction might belong

In the beginning should come the word. Consider these:

Count Alfred von Schlieffen, Chief of the German General Staff from 1891 to 1906, was, like all German officers, schooled in Clausewitz's precept, "The heart of
France lies between Brussels and Paris." It was a frustrat-
ing axiom because the path it pointed to was forbidden
by Belgian neutrality, which Germany, along with the
other four major European powers, had guaranteed in
perpetuity. Believing that war was a certainty and that
Germany must enter it under conditions that gave her
the most promise of success, Schlieffen determined not
to allow the Belgian difficulty to stand in Germany's way.
Of the two classes of Prussian officer, the bullnecked
and the wasp-waisted, he belonged to the second. Mono-
cled and effete in appearance, cold and distant in manner, he concentrated with such single-mindedness on
his profession that when an aide, at the end of an all-
night staff ride in East Prussia, pointed out to him the
beauty of the river Pregel sparkling in the rising sun, the

General gave a brief, hard look and replied, "An unimportant obstacle." So too, he decided, was Belgian neutrality.

—Barbara Tuchman, *The Guns of August*

My great-great-great-great-great-grandmother Elizabeth Scott was born in 1766, grew up on the Virginia and Carolina frontiers, at age sixteen married an eighteen-year-old veteran of the Revolution and the Cherokee expeditions named Benjamin Hardin IV, moved with him into Tennessee and Kentucky and died on still another frontier, the Oil Trough Bottom on the south bank of the White River in what is now Arkansas but was then Missouri Territory. Elizabeth Scott Hardin was remembered to have hidden in a cave with her children (there were said to have been eleven, only eight of which got recorded) during Indian fighting, and to have been so strong a swimmer that she could ford a river in flood with an infant in her arms. Either in her defense or for reasons of his own, her husband was said to have killed, not counting English soldiers or Cherokees, ten men. This may be true or it may be, in a local oral tradition inclined to stories that turn on decisive gestures, embroidery. I have it on the word of a cousin who researched the matter that the husband, our great-great-great-great-great-grandfather, "appears in the standard printed histories of Arkansas as 'Old Ben Hardin, the hero of so many Indian wars.'" Elizabeth Scott Hardin had bright blue eyes and sick headaches. The White River on which she lived was the same White River on which, a century and a half later, James McDougal would

locate his failed Whitewater development. This is a country at some level not as big as we like to say it is.

—Joan Didion, *Where I Was From*

When at approximately four o'clock that afternoon the
parachute on the radio had failed to open, the world
had been immediately reduced to a two-and-a-half-mile
gulch, and of this small, steep world sixty acres had been
occupied by fire. Now, a little less than two hours later,
the world was drastically reduced from that—to the 150
yards between the Smokejumpers and the fire that in
minutes would catch up to them, to the roar below them
that was all there was left of the bottom of the gulch, and
to the head of the gulch that at the moment was smoke
about to roar.

Somewhere beyond thought, however, there was an
outside world with some good men in it. There were a
lot more men sitting in bars who were out of drinking
money and also out of shape and had never been on a
fire before they found themselves on this one. There are
also times, especially as the world is blowing up, when
even good men land at the mouth of the wrong gulch,
forget to bring litters even though they are a rescue
team, and, after having gone back to get some blankets,
show up with only one for all those who would be cold
that night from burns and suffering.

—Norman Maclean, *Young Men and Fire*

What do these passages have in common? They all read
well. They are vivid; they inform; they make us want to read
more; and if you have the instincts of a writer, they make

you want to write something as good. (If they don't strike you that way, then you should close this book now.) Equally to the point, they are all grounded in fact, and don't exceed the bounds of their evidentiary sources. They ponder; they judge; they characterize; they appeal to figurative speech, such that each passage must be unique to its author. But they are not works of fiction. They are nonfictional texts, and unlike those that serve as dumb barrows to hold data, these carry their information with a style that amplifies their meaning. Facts become words, and history—for all of these selections are historical in intent—becomes art. They are literature of a sort different from fiction, creative nonfiction, journalism, or scholarly exegesis.

This, at least, is how I understand the issue. "Style" is not merely decorative or ornamental, any more than are feathers on a bird. Style performs work. Whatever its loveliness or ostentation, it is what allows the creature to fly, to attract mates, to hide from predators, to be what it is. Those feathers, moreover, are only as good as the wings they fit to, and the beak and claws to which they are indirectly joined, and all the rest. The parts have to connect; they have to work as a whole. Getting them together is what makes good writing.

So what writing isn't "stylish" or "literary"? Or, to restate the issue, how does the genre of writing we're discussing here differ from any other species? It differs from fiction in that it isn't made up: its imagination is tethered by rules of evidence and sources. It differs from creative nonfiction in that it tends to be less explicit about the author; generally speaking, it isn't memoir, at least not of the confessional sort. It differs from most journalism and travelogue in that it relies on sources other than interviews and personal experience, and can't pretend to emulate the immediacy and dialogue of fiction. It differs from most scholarly writing in that it is willing to adapt existing genres to its own ends, and to look beyond the conventions of a journal article and the template of a dissertation. But it shares with all good writing the fact that it relies on a craftsman's skill and an artist's sense.

The literary element is thus a matter of nuance. Most writing depends on prepackaged designs that merely require you to assemble and color them correctly. But when those packages can't hold what you want to say, you have to reshape the project, and that redesigning—the job of synchronizing structure, voice, character, framing, narrative arc, and the like—is what I understand to be the literary task of serious nonfiction. You come to resemble the packer who must find a way to stuff hunting gear into panniers fashioned for bread loaves, or to discard those containers altogether and heap the goods around a frame in ways that won't unbalance or overburden a burro, or to replace that burro with a mule, and make sure that what looks securely lashed at camp won't shake apart on the trail. Since each choice demands others, writing must rely on an extra dose of craft, and on what can only be called art. That's what makes narrative out of facts, drama out of data, and history out of dates and artifacts.

chapter 2
Art and Craft

In which we distinguish between the art of writing
and the craft of writing and determine why they
matter

Ours is a good age for nonfiction, and the case for it, always solid, is strengthening. To some extent this reflects, particularly in America, the recession of literary fiction, which seems unconcerned with anything but itself. But nonfiction has its own claims, too. Explaining why the *Atlantic* was trimming back on fiction, Cullen Murphy, its departing editor, wrote: "In recent years we have found that a certain kind of reporting—long-form narrative reporting—has proved to be of enormous value . . . in making sense of a complicated and factious world." What had once been the peculiar domain of fiction was passing more and more to nonfiction. Elements that had once been "standard" in serious literature—like "a strong sense of plot and memorable characters in the service of important and morally charged subject matter"—"[are] today as reliably found in narrative nonfiction as they are in literary fiction. Some might even say 'more reliably' found." Revealingly, the scandals of contemporary fiction tend to involve novelists who are passing off fiction as nonfiction (the most notorious recent example is James Frey's *Million Little Pieces,* but comparable revelations occur almost weekly). Novelists recognize the dominant genre and are writing to it.[1]

The range of genres easily scales up from the long essay to the trade book. But there also exists a genus which for lack of a less awkward label might be called *academic trade,* a book that is based on solid scholarship and that aspires to reach beyond an ever-narrowing circle of specialists—a book that, quantum-like, hovers between two states, something that might appeal both to university presses and to trade publishers. "It wouldn't be a monograph, it wouldn't be a text and it wouldn't be twenty-five walks in New Jersey," explained one university-press director. The ideal text would be "serious nonfiction written for a high-level general audience. It would have some course use after its initial year. It would have book club potential because it would be at that level. These are books on major topics of general interest written to satisfy scholars but at a level that pulls in everyone else." He concluded: "You would have consensus on this issue. We all know what the perfect book is. The problem is that there are precious few scholars writing them and we all want them."[2]

The topics vary: history, science, biography, politics—any nonfiction work could qualify, for the issue is not the subject in itself but how it is treated. "Calliope and Clio are not identical twins," as Wallace Stegner once observed, "but they *are* sisters." So while the principles behind literary expression may apply more readily to history and biography (which rely on *narrative,* or storytelling) than to physics and engineering (which typically employ *exposition* or *discourse,* a setting forth of information)—it may be easier to write a dull textbook than a dull story—there is no excuse for dullness anywhere. And there is no need to falsify to enhance effect. There are always other ways to express what you want.

Those ways are the art and craft of writing. They, not fictionalizing, are the true acts of literary imagination.[3]

The *art of writing* is the act of matching substance with style. This is not something that scholars in general give much thought to. They use off-the-shelf formulas or the house styles of target journals. Paradoxically, even as novelists adopt the devices of nonfiction in order to gain some gravitas and an aura of authenticity, nonfiction writers are urged to "borrow" from fiction to acquire some élan. There is no reason to do either.

Preferences have their fashion. Most historical writings today emulate the publication styles of the sciences except that, in place of hypothesis and data, they advance thesis and evidence. The prevailing formulas are the means to convey this material as succinctly as possible. The common use of such expressions as "the historian" or "a historian" (as in, "It is the concern of the historian to . . .") only reinforces the sense that the design is a collective formula, not unique to the writing at hand. Writers of books, like writers of journal articles, tend to accept a genre and conform to it. This is a prudent practice, for the genres exist because they represent the evolutionary experience of historical writing; they work. Most experiments fail, which is why successful writers play at the periphery of genres rather than try to remake them. (Even in the case of dissertations that follow the thesis-evidence-conclusion schema, where the process can be numbing for both writer and reader, the strategy will work in that it satisfies the relevant audience: the student's committee.) Most hybrids, like mules, prove sterile. They can carry the particular burden assigned to them but can't propagate. They fail to become a breeding genre.

Like software templates, however, the genres and formulas can be tweaked. Every part can be modified, and to be an effective writer you will need to reexamine those parts and decide where and how the particular material at hand might demand alterations to the pattern. Perhaps most fundamentally, you must choose where to begin, where to end, and how to connect those two points through some arc of narrative or exposition. This framing cannot be separated from all the other choices you must make, such as voice and plot, since the positioning of the endpoints helps to determine how the story will be interpreted (for example, whether it is ironic). This can be tricky: reconciling style with substance demands an artist's eye, a craftsman's discipline, and something of a gambler's daring, for the cost of not writing to a formula is the need to choose or contrive another design. You have to recognize (and admit) that something isn't right, that the words grate or the transitions stumble, that the theme is outfitted with clothes too baggy or tight, that the voice is too ponderous or whimsical to suit the body of the text; and then you have to commit to inventing a solution, and believe, perhaps against rational odds, that you can get it right. This recalibration is how I define the art of writing.

The *craft of writing* is the business of actually matching your words to the chosen design, whether it be a received template or an architecture of your own fabrication. Choices abound. You need to decide such elements as voice, character, plot, setting, rhythm, tone, and the way to show rather than tell your story, or evoke as well as logically explain a character or event, or dramatize an argument or idea rather than declaim it. Scenes are recreated. Understanding comes, as with a painting, through the artistry and craft of the text, not solely from the data or evidence or thesis that can be plucked out of the words and held aloft, like a collector's bird shot out of a tree and stuck into a specimen bag. The bird should live. The context helps to convey its real meaning. The craft of writing can be learned, and probably taught. It's a skill, like building a workbench or planting tulips. Its techniques are those of literature generally. The art of writing is more mysterious. Like Xeno's Achilles chasing the tortoise, one can approach it ever more closely without ever catching it. At some point there must be a germ of genius, a talent that might be planted and pruned but can't be concocted out of the ether. My guess, though, is that many scattered seeds fail to germinate because they fall on stone rather than loam, that insight improves with understanding, that knowing more helps to solve the interminable problems of putting words on the page, that unstudied writing, like the unexamined life, may not be successful or satisfying. What books like this one can do is try to demystify and make conscious what is often subconscious and intuitive. Beyond that, practice may not make perfect, but I doubt any degree of perfection will come without it.

One further caution. Writing with literary considerations in mind is not simply writing popular nonfiction. It is hard to imagine popular writing that does not read well, but serious and even scholarly writing may be beautifully conceived and crafted without finding a broad audience. The subject may be too arcane, or the treatment too technical, however interesting it might be in principle or however brilliant the clarity of its explanations. Popular books, academic-trade books, serious nonfiction books, scholarly monographs, theses, dissertations—the principles of conscious writing apply to them all.

Each of those genres has its formulas, exemplars, and

aesthetics. When they don't quite fit your topic or intention, then you need to modify them. This is where the literary imagination comes into play, which is a fancy way of saying that you need to identify the parts and practices that make good writing, and then apply that understanding to make your writing serve your purposes more effectively. Bad writing tends to survive when the text is little more than a means to convey data, opinions, or familiar stories, as is generally the case with theses, celebrity biographies, and aiming-for-TV histories. (As a rule of thumb, popular writing tends to favor plot and narrative, such that the writer uses evidence to support the story, while archival research tends to make the information itself the story.) But there is no excuse for bad writing. Scholarly writing can be done well or poorly. So can popular writing. The point is to make writing better regardless of the genre that shapes it.

The flip side of conscious writing is conscious reading. The art embodied in a text means that its medium conveys much of its message, and it has become commonplace to do close readings of nonfiction texts, even to deconstruct them, as species of literature. The practice is certainly legitimate: understanding *how* something is said is vital to understanding *what* is said. Knowing how elements of style can advance your purpose as a writer will equally improve your ambitions as a reader.

But just as naïve writing can create confusion by presenting data as if they can stand alone, so can naïve reading by assuming that meaning lies solely in the style, that identifying genres or rhetorical tropes is a sufficient exegesis of the text. The essential point is that style and subject so intertwine that one cannot be disentangled from the other. Substance has no meaning apart from its expression; we cannot understand unformed stuff. Likewise, we know style by the work it does: it has no reality apart from its action on stuff. Style, as René Daumal has noted, is "the imprint of what one is on what one does." So, too, how a text does its work says what it is.[4]

chapter 3

Rules of Engagement

In which we lay down the laws of serious nonfiction,
both of them immutable, as distinct from nonfiction's fashions, which change with cultural fads and
aesthetic taste

There are only two rules specific to nonfiction, and a raft
of recommendations that pertain to writing overall. The
rules are nonnegotiable: you can't make anything up, and
you can't leave out something that really matters—meaning
something that, if included, would alter our fundamental
understanding.

The usual outcome of research is to have too much material, or too little, or both. You are either inundated with
data, records, exhibits, transcripts, and observations; or you
have almost nothing on the topic at hand; or, too often, you
have both conditions at the same time. Your shelves bulge
with documents, yet you cannot extract the vital item that
resolves, thematically or aesthetically, the issue of the text.
Or this elusive evidence may simply not exist. The temptation is either to invent what you believe you need or to discard what you find inconvenient. The rules say no to both
urges.

Rule 1 is simple. It means you don't include details unsup-
ported by the evidence; you don't tinker with the chronol-

ogy to simplify the narrative; you don't introduce characters or scenes that have no documentary basis; you don't conjure up a person's thoughts when these are unknown; you don't invent dialogue. It means you don't put quotation marks around words that were not actually said, or were not said in that precise way. Especially if you are working from written sources rather than interviews, it means, by implication, that you cannot indulge in the dialogue-and-drama devices favored by fiction.

In practice, hewing to Rule 1 should cause no inconvenience, even of a minor sort. It's like learning how to fell a tree properly: refuse to consider all the bad techniques and wrongheaded styles, and you won't get hurt. You'll do the work the only way you know, which is the right way. The sole reason to dabble with "fictional" techniques is that you want the work to feel like fiction. If that's the case, then just write fiction and be done with it. Write historical fiction. Write science fiction. Write fictional memoirs. Don't muck up nonfiction.

There are ample ways to enhance plot, setting, character, moral punch, and drama without inventing so much as an apostrophe. Showing some of these ways is the particular aim of this book. There is no justification for inserting what isn't really there.

Much trickier is deciding what to leave out. This is the dominion of Rule 2, and it calls for judgment based on evidence rather than aesthetics. You can't leave something out in order to "make a better story" or sharpen the scene or quicken the pace. This is simply the converse of inventing material for the same purpose and is equally wrong. The argument for leaving out or putting in is murkier, since it demands a decision that simple invention doesn't. Lying—making stuff up—is a straightforward choice; it's an error of commission. But resisting the temptation to shade an issue requires integrity of a more subtle sort, for it is possible to come up with different interpretations that are all legitimate. The error will likely be one of omission, out of a desire to support a particular interpretation or create a preferred effect.

In this case, the critical concern is not aesthetic—how conveniently or pleasingly a part fits into the whole, how smoothly it can slide into the existing text. Rather, the correctness of the choice depends on how the item's presence or absence affects our understanding of what is said. Would removing it change how we assess a character? Would it affect our conclusions about why an event went one way and not another? Is it surplus information, offering more of the same, and hence disposable? Is it an outlier fact which is so bizarre and disconnected that it bears no discernible link to the topic, and whose inclusion can only encumber understanding? Or is it decorative, a bit of textual embroidery that enriches appreciation but does not change the fundamentals?

This is a call that you as writer must make, and must make with a bias toward substance over style. If including that ungainly fact upsets the narrative flow or blotches a passage with an ugly stain of prose, but the item is essential—then the fact stays and the text gets rewritten. This is where real artistry comes into play: not adjusting substance to fit style, but altering style to suit substance. If your imagination can't work this way, then do fiction. There is no single way to tell a story or explain a phenomenon; but there are good and bad ways to do it, some that stay within the rules and some that don't, and there are ways that read better or worse. True imagination lies in bringing richer literary expression to what must be said. Evidence trumps aesthetics—that's what makes this sort of writing nonfiction. But another consideration also argues the case. The nature of documentation, and of evidence generally, pleads for a literary pragmatism because there is always the possibility that you have overlooked a vital item or that fresh data will arise. (This is why erecting a design out of the latest scientific evidence is dangerous: data are like so much sand ready to be swept away by the next flood of information or paradigm shift.) Locking in your judgments strictly on aesthetic grounds—ignoring stuff because the prose will be brisker, the text more self-contained, the ending more emphatic—or plucking evidence selectively to strengthen a case is unwise because our conclusions are always tentative. Besides, other people have access to the same information and can verify it, unlike the facts that obtain in a novelist's world. Far better to use literary techniques, guided by aesthetics, to shape a text that can absorb new revelations or accommodate varied conclusions. Here again, the choice between a "good" story and a "right" one is false, a chasm that exists only where literary fancy or skill is too feeble to leap over its own shadow. There are always ways to bridge the gap. There are, as *Star Trek's* Mr. Spock liked to say, always alternatives.

Violating these rules is not simply bad writing. It is corrupt writing, and it is inexcusable, not least because it is unnecessary. Thematic closure is your duty to scholarship: it's what logically bonds evidence to argument or story. Aesthetic closure is your duty to art: it makes the theme manifest. You need both. But in nonfiction, substance must rule, and style must support, not determine, theme. Adjusting the evidence to fit the form almost always causes grief. Rather, the relationship goes the other way, with the closure promised by aesthetics supporting that proposed by theme. Falsifications to make a text "read better" are the result not of too much literary imagination but of too little.

By way of example, consider two decisions, one an act of authorial prudence and one a piece of foolishness. Since I wrote both, I have some inkling of what at least the author thought he was doing. The manuscript was intended to be a biography of G. K. Gilbert (1843–1918), a founding giant of American geology. But what kind of biography was it to be?

Gilbert did it all—he discovered two types of mountain building, devised flume experiments, penned essays on the philosophy of science, founded astrogeology with his study of the Moon, served on two major expeditions to the American West, became the first chief geologist of the U.S. Geological Survey, served as president of the Geological Society of America (the only person elected to two terms), etc., etc. He was also unusually reticent and self-contained—personable but private. When not in the field or at the office, he stayed home. It is said that he avoided going to the theater for fear of losing control of his emotions. He studied the Moon from a telescope in his attic. What was the story here? How best to tell it? My solution was to write the biography of a mind.

Gilbert's domestic life is largely a blank to us. He grew up in a warm, closely knit family, and always sought similar circumstances; this much is evident. But we know little about his wife, Fannie, or their marriage. One fact, however, is that their first child, Bessie, died of diphtheria at age six. The horror and grief caused Gilbert to slough off the personal religious sentiments he had inherited from his father, and must have affected Fannie as well. She also suffered, official memoirists say, from coal-gas poisoning and occasionally had to recuperate away from home. My biography of Gilbert went to print on these terms.

Years later, I learned some scuttlebutt left by Gilbert's contemporaries, to the effect that Fannie had been an alcoholic. It would take little imagination to interpret the child's death as a probable cause of Fannie's drinking, coal-gas poisoning as a euphemism for her substance abuse, and her recuperations as a periodic drying-out. I don't know the truth of the rumor, but it makes sense. After Fannie's death, for example, Gilbert, seemingly liberated, decamped for a new life in California, and at age seventy-five spoke of plans to remarry. But is the issue critical? And how might it affect the already published biography of Gilbert, even as rumor?

That would depend on the purposes and design of the book. I had originally decided that the documentation of his personal life was too sparse to support an intimate biography, and that I would craft a biography of ideas instead. I would sketch my portrait from his published writings and the facts of his expeditions and experiments, in the belief that such material would reveal his sense of nature and establish his place in the history of geology. My Gilbert would be the one he had chosen to present to the world; it would read him through his public presentations and speak of his personal life only where it poked through the public one. So the existing biography can accommodate either outcome. If true, Fannie's alcoholism would explain and glue together many shards of Gilbert's home life and career. But those same items can exist in the story without that particular clustering. The revelation of alcoholism would upend an intimate biography; an intellectual one, as constructed, could take it or leave it. What mattered was the reality of a private life that, regardless of source, projected itself onto the greater world. Gilbert perceived a nature that was in many ways a reflection of his own character.

That was the prudent decision. The foolish one came when I decided that, to make the conclusion stronger, I ought to place Gilbert within contemporary enthusiasms, presenting him as an epitome of a dynamical geology that was challenging historical geology. I wanted to show that his conceptions of laccoliths and his views on the structure of the basin-range had endured, and that this accounted for his significance (and hence the value of my biography). While the facts were true, my strategy was dumb because those trends would pass and because, even within the text, I had argued for Gilbert's capacity to transcend particular times. Fortunately, prudence prevailed; aesthetic closure did not depend on whether Gilbert was still in vogue and his theories dominant. But the book came close to foundering.

In brief, resolving an argument or thesis on the basis of evidence and theory is different from resolving the question of how to express it in a book or essay. The first requires a reasoned conclusion; the second, an artistic one. For the first, rely on the best data and concepts around, although if you are not doing science or reporting on how it is done, it would be wise to hedge your understanding on the particulars rather than place all your bets on the dicey roll of the prevailing theory. For the second, build on the rocks of philosophy and aesthetics rather than on the sands of scientific paradigms and contemporary fashions.

Two rules: Don't invent, and don't leave out what needs to be in. Beyond these, rely on prudence, humility, boldness, wit, common sense, and a recognition that theme and design have to support each other. If one is wrong, it will pervert the other. A theme at odds with its expression will be unconvincing, even ridiculous. But a desire for aesthetic closure can't be allowed to overrule or substitute for thematic closure. Substance and style are not intrinsic competitors, such that only one or the other must prevail. They must both be harnessed to a common sled.

chapter 4

Nonfiction as Writing

In which we mull over the differences between
fiction and nonfiction, and see why some kinds of
nonfiction might be dubbed more literary than
others

The essence of enlightened writing is to match what you
want to say with how you say it. This applies to all categories
of writing, from novels to business letters to biographies. Introduce fictional techniques into nonfiction? Why not introduce nonfictional techniques into fiction? Both have
been done; both have flourished and flopped; both have
suffered from misuse and fraud. Today's paradox is that
nonfiction is the far stronger realm, yet fiction (and memoir) get taught in writing classes, while history gets sidelined
into historiography, and hence techniques closely identified with fiction and the aesthetics of contemporary fiction
have become the established norms of writing. The apparent infection of nonfiction by fiction involves more than a
slipperiness with facts; it entails judgments, grounded in
contemporary taste, about what makes good writing.

Yet when Coleridge said that the reading of fiction required a "willing suspension of disbelief," he spoke for
all imaginative literature, not least many domains of self-
consciously literary nonfiction. For when you profile a personality, track an expedition, trace the genealogy of an idea,

sketch the terrain of a battlefield, or otherwise plunge readers into a place beyond the here and now, and do so with the techniques of literature rather than with logic alone, you are inventing an imagined world, and you should do nothing to shatter the illusion of that evoked time and setting. The conjured-up world needs to be believable. It must convey the sense that it is complete and coherent, though both qualities are illusions, for only a minuscule portion of it can be known or described. In order to read smoothly, the text should avoid breaking the imagined world being created, whether in the form of a sustained argument or an evoked landscape or an adventure tale. Its believability does not derive solely from the massing of data about it, but depends also on the techniques by which it is evoked and implied. We can't visit nineteenth-century Alaska, watch the 1939 Black Friday fires in Australia, or enter the courthouse at Appomattox with Grant and Lee, but we can build up and communicate a sense of such places that allows the reader to enter into them, or that permits us to guide readers through—unless factual errors, sloppy prose, and a confused voice or point of view shatter the illusion. What John Gardner, in describing novels, referred to as a "fictional dream" has its analogues in literary nonfiction.

If we say that there is one set of techniques for fiction and another for nonfiction, we are wrongly framing the whole issue. The only sound advice is, adhere to the Two Rules for nonfiction, and then sculpt a text to express your understanding of the subject at hand.

Still, some styles slide naturally into one or the other camp. Novelists and short-story writers like to use dialogue, to dramatize scenes as though these are being acted out in a play, to explore the thoughts and feelings of characters, to use, often, a first-person narrator. It's hard to imagine doing this with, say, the Emperor Constantine as a toddler, the Laurentide ice sheet, or the last dodo as it contemplated the extinction of its species. Fiction often relies on richly figurative prose. Try that in a report on sedimentation in the Colorado River or the economic causes behind America's entry into the Great War. Fiction writers are urged to show, not tell. Nonfiction writers are generally exhorted to explain clearly by extracting critical parts out of the inherited narrative and analyzing them explicitly.

Yet such distinctions disguise the deep commonality behind all good writing. Finding the right word. Varying sentence cadence and prose tempo. Fashioning a narrative arc. Highlighting the moral drama. Crisp prose can make settings sharp, scenes vivid, characters alive. In the case of narrative, especially, simple telling—letting the action unroll, permitting a confused conflict to unfurl—is better than endless telling *about*. Nonfiction writers can change point of view. Can select voice. Can slow or quicken the pace. Can, within limits, impart character and agency to natural processes. Can heighten or dampen the drama of one incident relative to another. They must, in brief, do what all good writers do: they must match form to content, and to context. Good writers know not only which techniques to use but which to shun, when accomplishing the task at hand.

Much of what passes for accepted fictional technique, moreover, is really fashion. Today's fiction prefers some devices over others—or at least some styles get canonized and propagated in classrooms, and in venues like writing workshops and manuals. This, we are led to believe, is how we must write. The fact that contemporary fiction survives so poorly outside hothouse settings like campuses and workshops suggests that a writer of literary nonfiction might think carefully before deciding to adapt the methods of fiction into his or her text. Just which styles? For what effects? To which purposes? If the style of contemporary fiction is what attracts you, then write fiction. Simply transferring techniques from contemporary fiction into nonfiction topics may lead you to violate the Two Rules, or to confect an unconscious parody.

Some points of crossover are worth highlighting, though, because these seem to be where the temptations to violate the rules are greatest and the breakdowns most frequent. One is dialogue. The insistence that dialogue should carry narrative is a contemporary convention of both fiction and journalism, and seductive in its bid to convert scenes into conversations. In fact, there are circumstances where something along these lines can be done in nonfiction—where soliloquies based on speeches, letters, or diaries are possible, or where transcripts exist, as with court proceedings, congressional hearings, or oral histories.

This is a favorite technique of journalists. Consider the effect of quoting from transcripts drawn from South Africa's Truth and Reconciliation Commission, as Antjie Krog has done.

> *Ms. Gobodo-Madikizela:* Baba, do you have any bullets in you as we speak?
>
> *Mr. Sikwepere:* Yes, there are several of them. Some are here in my neck. Now on my face you can really see them, but my face feels quite rough, it feels like rough salt. I usually have terrible headaches.
>
> *Ms. Gobodo-Madikizela:* Thank you, Baba.
>
> *Mr. Sikwepere:* Yes, usually I have a fat body, but after that I lost all my body, now I am thin, as you can see me now.

Ms. Gobodo-Madikizela: How do you feel, Baba, about coming
here to tell us your story?

Mr. Sikwepere: I feel what—what has brought my sight back,
my eyesight back is to come back here and tell the story.
But I feel what has been making me sick all the time is
the fact that I couldn't tell my story. But now I—it feels
like I got my sight back by coming here and telling you
the story.[1]

Why not simply quote Mr. Sikwepere within the text? Why
not, indeed? In this case, the theme is about letting people tell their experiences in their own words, and longish
quotes from transcripts do that nicely. The story is the telling, not the event told about. That the quote is actually an
exchange quickens the tempo. Though sometimes a lengthy
excerpt can give everyone a breather and help to recenter
a narrative, in most contexts too-frequent or overly long
quotations upset the narrative flow, and reading becomes a
broken trek, like constantly climbing hedgerows to cross a
field.

Of course, there are plenty of examples from fiction in
which authorial description—straight narrative without quotation and drama—achieves its purpose. Here is Jack London's profile of a minor character in *White Fang*.

It was about this time that the newspapers were full of
the daring escape of a convict from San Quentin prison.
He was a ferocious man. He had been ill-made in the
making. He had not been born right, and he had not
been helped any by the moulding he had received at the
hands of society. The hands of society are harsh, and this
man was a striking sample of its handiwork. He was a

beast—a human beast, it was true, but nevertheless so terribly a beast that he can best be characterized as carnivorous . . .

After this, Jim Hall went to live in the incorrigible cell. He lived there three years. The cell was of iron, the floor, the walls, the roof. He never left this cell. He never saw the sky nor the sunshine. Day was a twilight and night was a black silence. He was in an iron tomb, buried alive. He saw no human face, spoke to no human thing. When his food was shoved in to him, he growled like a wild animal. He hated all things. For days and nights he bellowed his rage at the universe. For weeks and months he never made a sound, in the black silence eating his very soul. He was a man and a monstrosity, as fearful a thing of fear as ever gibbered in the visions of a maddened brain.[2]

The prose is hardly the most exquisite, and violates nearly every fashion of contemporary fiction by declaring rather than dramatizing; but the passage creates a vivid portrait and establishes Hall as a human-turned-wolf, ready to confront White Fang, a wolf becoming domesticated. The showing and telling lie in the images, not in the setting. Here we see not an intrinsic difference between fiction and nonfiction, but a shared style turned to different purposes.

Another instance of common cause concerns the use of detail. This has become a standard device among novelists, for it makes the fictional world more convincing. It is the particulars that impart believability to scenes, whether invented or recalled. The extreme illustration involves the slippery case of recovered memories, in which purported experiences, repressed deep in the subconscious cortex, are "restored" through promptings. What reason is there to believe such stories, especially in the absence of any tangible supporting evidence? They succeed on the same grounds that texts do—namely, their capacity to evoke a believable world; and this depends not only on internal logic but also on gripping details. The glint of sunlight off a mirror. The rustle of eucalyptus leaves near a second-story window. A pointy eyebrow with a streak of white hairs. Such things, it is assumed, must be correct because their vividness could come only from experience. And so they may, though perhaps not from the event under investigation. What nonfiction writers can learn from these oft-misused episodes is the power of a defining detail to make an imagined world seem real. On this point, both realms of writing converge; they merely do so with different standards for evaluating proper use.

Does this mean fiction and nonfiction emulate each other? Yes and no; the question itself is the problem. Nonfiction no more emulates fiction than a forest fire does logging. That both may strip a forest does not argue for their common identity. That both fiction and nonfiction involve prose does not make them interchangeable; and mixing their literary DNA, as it were, might only yield chimeras and monsters.

Before we can chew on this theme further, we need something with more substance than tidbits of textual tofu. So consider two efforts by a prominent man of letters. In one he uses factual sources to strengthen his fiction, and in the other he creates a compelling narrative flow from nonfictional sources. The details get pushed along like suspended sediment and river sand by the rush of prose, which has a momentum that a fiction writer might envy.

In its attention to believable details, fiction often extracts material from the real world or documentary archives, or even borrows text, just as nonfiction does. Usually such borrowings either remain in the realm of historical fiction or are culled from multiple sources and salted into the text where they may prove useful. But what happens if the borrowing comes in bulk? Just this question animated the curious controversy over Wallace Stegner's Pulitzer–prize winning *Angle of Repose,* a historical novel whose central character, Susan Burling Ward, is a simulacrum of a real person, Mary Hallock Foote. Foote's letters and writings constitute, under the guise of fiction, perhaps 10 percent of the text. Ward's letters (actually Foote's—or their close paraphrase), quoted extensively and at length, shepherd the overall story.

This rich tapestry of detail, tactile and felt, could have been invented—the book is a novel, after all. But writing a story set in the past, Stegner drew on a source from the past, which conveyed an aura of authenticity that a modern mind might never have matched. The prose acquires through a kind of stylistic transfer some of the attributes of its source, like a limestone cliff colored by the downwash from a layer of red shale above it. There is a mundaneness of expression that helps to make Stegner as author seem remote, an impartial chronicler of this imagined past. Most good fiction writers search out sources (which may be themselves or other people or various texts) to get the right palette of details, to make their invented scenes believable. Stegner's technique evoked comment because he took so much from a single source, and one perhaps not adequately attributed.

Some of Foote's descendents felt that Stegner had, in effect, plagiarized her legacy—that despite obtaining permis-

sion from the holder of the documents, he had used them
without sufficient public acknowledgment, and that he had
invested Susan Burling Ward with characteristics and experiences quite different from those of Mary Hallock Foote.
The latter charge is bizarre: it could hold only if he had
named his protagonist Mary Hallock Foote, in which case
he would have been verging on biography and could not
have changed the contents of the letters he used. And the
former charge is a rare example of a novelist accused of
tacking too close to the facts. In the end, the episode may
testify to the hazards of hybridizing genres.[3]

Now turn to a passage from another Stegner book, *Beyond
the Hundredth Meridian,* in which he reconstructs from actual journals and letters the saga of the first boat trip
through the Grand Canyon. Here Stegner's vision allows
him to pick and choose the right medley of facts and quotes,
while his voice imposes the kind of stylistic coherence usually identified with novels.

> Above them, where they camped below the cataclysmic Y
> of the canyons, the walls went up three thousand feet—
> the highest they had yet measured. From the rim Powell
> saw that to the westward they were even higher. Their
> campsite afforded no decent water, no game. It was
> "filthy with dust and alive with insects," and they killed
> three rattlesnakes the first morning. Anyone camping
> on the river learns to shake the scorpions out of his bed-
> ding and shoes before dressing in the morning, but
> Bradley (and others, he observed, were in the same fix)
> did not even have a pair of boots to catch scorpions in.
> For lack of footwear that would let him climb the cliffs,
> he went around camp barefoot, saving his one remain-

ing pair of camp moccasins to put on when the sand got too hot or the rocks too sharp.

Few fictional accounts could hope for so rich a broth.[4]

Each literary realm has its peculiar pathologies. Many of fiction's recent disgraces come from its efforts to masquerade as nonfiction; typically, this takes the form of an ostensible memoir. The author claims the authority and gravitas of nonfiction, stating that what he or she says is true, but in reality fictionalizes the story or in some cases invents it out of whole cloth. (The practice has become so common that the *Economist* actually lumped fiction and memoir together in its best-books roster for 2006.) Nonfiction's offense is to plagiarize. An author passes off as his or her own what someone else has written. This is simple cheating, unlike the more complex case of fiction writers who transgress whole borders. A nonfiction author who falsifies part of the text, either by putting something in that doesn't belong or by omitting something that does, will likely be found out. The matter is provable. A fiction writer's assertion of truth can be tested only against the believability of the text.

Such considerations yield a lesson that might stand as Rule 3. Writing involves choices, a ceaseless chain of choices, ranging from the location of a comma to the placement of a narrative's entry and exit. Some of the choices are a matter of morals—whether or not to break the Rules, for example. Some are matters of logic and evidence. Most are matters of personal preference, the artistic inclinations of the writer. And on this, as Horace reminds us, there is no accounting for taste.

chapter 5
Voice . . .

In which we read with our ears, and the way a text
sounds decides who should be listening

The time-honored admonition is to begin with an understanding of the readers you are addressing and how you
propose to do it—that is, to start with an audience in mind
and an outline in hand. I would restate *audience* and *outline*
as *voice* and *vision*. By *voice* I mean how the text is mentally
read and heard. It explains who is talking and to whom. By
vision I mean the sense of what this text is—what it is about,
how its shape embodies its purpose. Crudely put, voice describes how a text sounds to the reader; vision, how it looks
in the mind's eye of the writer. Like two poles of a bar mag-
net, they hold all the particles of a manuscript within their
mutual force field.

All writing employs a voice; but as a studied element of style,
voice typically gets shoved to the margins. Either it inheres
in the genre, and hence is used without conscious thought,
or it is considered decorative, and thereby optional, like excessive punctuation. It may even be suspect, a kind of literary narcissism, because it would seem to shift focus from
the audience to the author. The assumption is that voice

should be something that flows out of the basics, not something that is itself foundational. Voice is a means; voice is an outcome, not an origin; voice follows, like everything else, from audience.

All this can be true, yet I think it entirely possible to pick up the other end of this rhetorical stick and, with equal justification, begin with a voice bonded to authorial vision. I myself cannot separate them, and often find that devising a voice, combined with whatever large theme I have in mind, is necessary before I can fashion the designs and details that collectively constitute vision. Is the text an exercise in academic High Seriousness? Is it playful, self-mocking, comic, irreverent? Is it dutiful—the drudge prose by which data are conveyed through text rather than by tables? Is it ardent, shrill, demanding? Does it have an elevated note of the epic? More than a synonym for tone alone, voice affects diction, sentence structure, the bulkiness of paragraphs, the impression of scale, and claims of significance. There is nothing that does not convey voice, or that voice does not itself convey. All this relates directly to the traditional concern over audience.

Voice thus goes beyond how you say something. It also implies to whom you are saying it. If you write from a template, these issues come precoded in the formula. If you are determined to tweak the existing templates, or must adjust genres out of necessity, then the choice of voice will be among the most fundamental decisions you make. Get it right, and your prose will glide over minor potholes and bumps. Get it wrong, and the entire enterprise will limp and lisp, as if you had a rock in your shoe or a tongue numbed by novocaine. For voice involves more than audience: it becomes itself a medium.

Most writers aspiring to write serious nonfiction wish to

reach a general audience, one well beyond the realm of those specialists whom they regard as their colleagues. The "general reader," however, may be the Bigfoot of contemporary publishing—always sought, never seen. The market for books is both expanding and fragmenting, as it is for other media such as radio or cable TV. While whopping bestsellers do come along, and someone always does win powerball lotteries, the odds are formidable. Most writers do not live off their writing; they have a day job, increasingly one in a university. They write for people like themselves. Their imagined general reader is their circle of colleagues, students, and acquaintances writ large. Just as they read works on topics beyond their specialty, yet not in a style too unfamiliar, so they imagine like-minded readers poring over their own texts.

But however conceived, your voice will reveal just what sort of audience you have in mind.

Like every aspect of writing, voice has its maladies and distempers. Severed from hard evidence, it can become mere attitude or incantation. It can flutter in ostentatious display, the rhetorical equivalent of sexual selection, or it can sink into private soliloquies and public rants. It can, as in the ironic mode, impose itself on material that might well be interpreted differently if cast in another voice. The academic voice, so often solemn, constipated, and inbred, constitutes almost a genus of its own, and a writer addicted to it after many years of schooling may need a literary detox program to escape from it.

Often the voice of a novice writer wavers and cracks, like that of an adolescent boy who is unable to project consistently in one pitch or another; or it substitutes loudness and bluster for conviction and authority. In this regard, one

might recall Aesop's fable that tells of a competition between the wind and the sun; whichever of them can induce
a traveler to shed his coat will be considered the stronger.
In the end, the gentle radiance of the sun prevails, while
the blustery wind evokes only resistance. In writing, an exaggerated voice often leads to satire, loud becomes shrill,
and ostentation seems silly. Reading a rant or exhortation
can be bracing, but will leave many a reader reaching for a
protective wrap.

The bad solution is to adopt a pose, and assume that voice
can by itself substitute for structure, theme, evidence, coherence. The good solution is to acquire substantive authority in a field so that your preferred voice is not something assumed or thrown over words like a cloak, but a
presence that fuses mind and heart. Voice is not merely rhetorical coloration: it carries the text in its lilt and rhythms
and tenor and pitch, and in the way it encourages a reader
to catch those same waves. It speaks with authority or appeals for empathy. Its haunting tone or blunt sentences can
challenge convention, its wry wit can deflate pretense and
persuade by indirection, its spunky colloquialism, touched
with satire, can force a stalled discourse out of its rhetorical
ruts. Whatever its effects, it is always there.

So get it right. With the proper voice, you'll have an easier time navigating around or sliding over the innumerable
questions that check and gag fluid writing. It makes the
quest for the right word simpler. It proposes transitions.
It will help you decide where to begin and end passages.
No one armed with voice and vision should suffer writer's
block. Voice establishes as nothing else can your authorial
presence. It provides for the reader a prism of tone and
nuance—a literary context—by which to interpret the text.

Voice, rather than topic, is what generally induces a reader to pick up your next book.

Time for a few examples: voices strong, voices gentle, voices pitched with emotion, nuance, conviction, and—we can't help it—irony. We need to hear how they variously bespeak an author's presence and perspective.

Consider three historians' voices; wry, sardonic, and empathetic. First, a passage from Hans Zinsser's offbeat biography of typhus, *Rats, Lice, and History,* in which he reviews the history of epidemics:

> Jehovah seems to have been pretty hard on the poor Philistines. In I Samuel IV, there is an account of a battle in which the Philistines overcame the Jews, slaying about 30,000 of them in what appears to have been a perfectly fair fight. The victory of the Philistines was facilitated by the fact that the Hebrew army ran away, and tried to hide in their tents. The conquerors then took the ark of God (I Samuel V) into the house of their own god, whose name was Dagon, and who was a sort of half fish, and consequently more or less helpless. The Hebrew God then smote Dagon, cutting off his hands and throwing him off his pedestal, so that his face was on the ground. This threw a terrible scare into the Philistines of Ashdod, so that they sent the ark to Gath. Thereupon, "the hand of the Lord was against the city with a very great destruction: and He smote the men of the city, both small and great, and they had emerods in their secret parts," and "the hand of God was very heavy there. And the men that died not were smitten with the emerods." This is the sort of thing, of course, which—

throughout the ages—has led to what in modern terms we may speak of as "Nazi movements." But the Lord only knows what an "emerod" was. Literally, it is a hemorrhoid—the etymological relationship of these two unpleasant words being obvious; but it is hardly likely that even the Philistines could have had a fatal epidemic of hemorrhoids.

The argument continues into a possible identification (or misidentification) of "emerods" with the swellings associated with bubonic plague, the controversy turning upon "whether it was the hinder end or the front end which was affected."[1]

Now a matched (or mismatched) set, this time speaking on a common subject, Christopher Columbus. Carl Sauer has little good to say about the Admiral of the Ocean Sea, while Samuel Eliot Morison can't praise him enough. That Sauer was a historical geographer, interested in the fate of indigenous flora and peoples, and Morison a proud historian-admiral attracted to his own professional lineage, only partly accounts for the differences. Sauer, like most contemporary authors, has a voice meant to be seen, while Morison's is a voice that can be spoken. One is read with the eyes; the other, with the ears. One is better for arguing, and the other better for storytelling.

Begin with Sauer:

> The last voyage retained the preconceptions of the first. Columbus had forgotten nothing and learned little. His letter adds almost no information about native ways. At Cariay he considered the people to be great wizards and noted in two lines the tomb his brother had visited, fol-

lowed by fifteen lines about a fight between an Irish dog
and some captured animals.

His knowledge of geographical position and celestial
navigation had not improved. He discoursed on the cos-
mography of Ptolemy and Marinus of Tyre, and reduced
the ocean to a seventh of the earth's surface. Josephus
was authority for the source of the wealth of Solomon
and David. His image of the world experienced little re-
arrangement.[2]

Now Morison, on the occasion of Columbus' second voyage and its aftershocks.

Columbus frequently "wrestled with God" to find out
why things turned out so badly for him. He performed
his religious duties regularly and did his best to convert
the Indians to the True Faith; so why did Providence
frown on his undertakings? He had served the Sover-
eigns faithfully, respected their every wish and guarded
their interests, and had won for them a new empire overseas; why, then, did they listen to his enemies and send
out a low fellow to insult him? He had made all practical
preparations, kept his ships staunch, his people healthy,
and his powder dry; but now, it would seem every Span-
iard's hand was against him. Why? Why? Why? The Book
of Job afforded consolation, but no clue. Perhaps it was
because he had embraced the deadly sin of pride after
his First Voyage, had worn excessive apparel (as befitted
the rank of admiral), had consorted too much with high
company, partaken of rich viands and rare vintages?
Pride, to be sure, is a deadly sin. So, upon arrival at Cádiz
and ever after, Columbus assumed the coarse brown

habit of a Franciscan as evidence of humility, and instead of accepting invitations to castles and palaces, he put up in religious houses with rough quarters and coarse fare.[3]

The differences go beyond the fact that Sauer thinks Columbus a dangerous fool and Morison views him as an intrepid (if inflexible) mariner, or that Sauer lays out his case with the methodical rigor of a lawyer's brief and Morison with a kind of avuncular chattiness. Sauer's prose keeps its edge: his voice hones it constantly, each declarative sentence stropping against the recorded facts. Morison's prose wanders and softens, his judgment clear but his voice forgiving, for what came out of the enterprise was greater than the personality that went into it. What each author says carries less conviction than how he says it.

Finally, bring into view two big-screen histories with very different voices, one used to explain by evocation and the other used to analyze by enumeration. Both make intellectuals into important protagonists; both portray protagonists made slightly or seriously mad by the ardor of their ideas.

The first is Simon Schama's *Citizens: A Chronicle of the French Revolution,* in which ideas are refracted through their purveyors and adherents. There is plenty of empirical history in the form of dates, places, and events, and ample analysis of contributing causes; but ultimately the study is one that examines how people and ideas interact, as melded in character. In an odd but satisfying way, Schama looks at the historical record as he might a gallery of art, judging how theme and medium mesh, or not. His capacity to evoke becomes a means of explanation.

The long text concludes with a series of profiles that assess the meaning, ultimately moral, of the Revolution. The last word (or image) belongs to Théroigne de Méricourt, whose life experiences reflected the tumult of those years— beginning with fiery political speeches, proceeding through mob beatings, and ending with hospitalization at a facility for "the poor and the deranged" in the Faubourg Saint-Marceau. Here is Schama's rendering of her in her final days, naked and demented, a portrait that conveys, equally, a judgment of the "revolutionary fever" from which she was diagnosed as suffering.

> Oblivious of all visitors, concerned or callous, who saw her, Théroigne, it seems, now lived entirely inside the Revolution and the Revolution inside her. Sympathy seems out of place here, for in some sense the madness of Théroigne de Méricourt was a logical destination for the compulsions of revolutionary Idealism. Discovering, at last, a person of almost sublime transparency and pre-social innocence, someone naked and purified with dousings of ice water, the Revolution could fill her up like a vessel. In her little cell at La Salpêtrière, there was at least somewhere where revolutionary memory could persist, quite undisturbed by the quotidian mess of the human condition.[4]

Here is the Revolutionary Ideal personified. Having se-lected his subject, Schama's authorial voice exists to shade and make vivid, but otherwise avoid marring, the portrait with his presence.

A contrasting approach is that of William Goetzmann in *New Lands, New Men,* a survey of America's role in the Second Great Age of Discovery. The towering figure of the era was Alexander von Humboldt; and in his retelling of the age's achievements, Goetzmann assumes for himself the role of historian as Humboldtean. The febrile empiricism, the reliance on maps as an integrating device, the delight in the picturesque, the odd, and the peculiar, the appeal to a romantic grandeur that somehow holds the pieces together—all echoes a Humboldtean ethos. Goetzmann has seemingly absorbed that vision, and emulates it with his overflowing catalogues of wonders found, deeds done, places visited, books published, maps reproduced. Heroes abound, but few deeds can match for charming eccentricity the wacky treks of Thomas Nuttall, dubbed *le fou* ("the madman") by French Canadian *voyageurs*. His was a madness that motivated, and a madness that perhaps saved his life on the prairies, since the Indians shunned him as one possessed.

In 1819, he set off on an expedition to the Arkansas country which took him through the Ozarks and the Arkansas River bottoms—among rude Indian villages and gangs of cutthroats and river pirates. Ill with malaria, he pushed on up the Arkansas halfway to the Rockies before he gave up and headed back to "civilization." But perhaps his grandest expedition came in 1834, when he accompanied the Boston ice dealer Nathaniel Wyeth up along the Oregon Trail all the way to the Pacific. On this trek he and Wyeth were accompanied by another naturalist, John Kirk Townsend, and the famous missionaries Henry Spaulding, Jason Lee, and Marcus Whitman. Townsend's diary is replete with references to Nuttall's hardy if otherworldly dedication to natural science. And when he researched the Pacific, Nuttall did not stop. He went to Hawaii and then down the California coast as far as San Diego, where he was spotted, thin and spindly with his trousers rolled, collecting in the Pacific tide pools, by one of his former students, Richard Henry Dana. In fact, Nuttall returned to Boston around the Horn with Dana aboard the *Pilgrim* (of *Two Years before the Mast* fame). Dana remembered that as they rounded the Horn in furious gales, Nuttall wanted to stop and collect specimens on the remote Patagonian shores. The captain pushed on for home.[5]

For our purposes, the difference between Schama's portrait and Goetzmann's is not simply one of theme and judgment—the fact that the former is tragic, the latter comic. The issue is the *way* each composes his profile, and the voice behind it. Schama selects the most revealing details (the refusal to wear clothes, the eremitic isolation), and shades them into significance. Goetzmann lists the events of Nuttall's life, one after another, much as Nuttall might register bird sightings for his *Ornithology*. He declaims, and then illustrates with rosters of examples. The vividness and coherence of the narrative result not simply from his stated theme—that a "romantic horizon" beckoned to the age—but from his capacity to animate that insight. In the end, the details add up because of Goetzmann's conviction that they do.

Such differences go beyond the usual hermeneutics of historiography. They involve more than thesis or counter-thesis, or schools of thought. Each author conveys a theme, rich with unique perceptions, but neither develops it by logical argument alone. Instead, each conveys the characteristics of an age through a particular character, and relies on the force field of his authorial voice to help make his portrait believable and persuasive. While the more extreme illustrations might suggest that voice is merely atti-

tude wrapped in clever language, it isn't. Voice shapes, voice
shouts, voice whispers, voice separates those who want to
hear from those who don't. It is the transtextual persona of
the author.

One mode of voice demands special consideration. It is so
common that pointing it out is like identifying crab grass
or house flies. For a century, irony has been the customary
medium of the modernist perspective, whether of art, literature, biography, history, or culture generally. While critics
will harp on someone who shuns it, no one is ever criticized
for adopting it. Yet irony is not something that falls naturally out of the sources like stringy bark from a eucalypt. It
results from the sculpting of that material, from, if you will,
a preconceived (or preternaturally understood) voice and
vision predisposed to see matters a particular way. The converse is equally true: an ironic voice must inhabit a text that
suits it—must find a story, or construct one, that will end
with a properly ironic ring. A conviction that irony is inevitable will—must—shape a text in which the ironic voice can
reside. Part of the modernist style is a preference to have
irony not merely present but to have it inform fundamental
design.

Irony requires distancing. Literary irony results from an
incongruity, a distance, between what a speaker says and
what he means, a gap perceived by the reader. Historical
irony involves an incongruity, or distance, between what is
said (or thought, believed, or expected) and what actually
happens. But such gaps depend on the scale of the frame
used. Move closer, and the ironic distance may become in-
finitesimal. Move back, widening the span between opening
and closing, and even vast ironies may be swallowed up in a
broader narrative.

Take the case of the Dust Bowl in 1930s America. An interpretive voice could assume many forms: it could be elegiac, a study in a lost time or place or childhood; it could be tragic, the collision of forces or destinies uncontrollable by the protagonists; it could be satirical, the outcome of collective foolishness and pretense; it could be didactic, a roster of lessons learned. But it is a good bet that the prevailing interpretations will be ironic, and that irony will likely dictate the larger narrative frame. The story will acquire tension from the distance between what people expected and what nature provided. Open a historical survey with optimistic but naïve settlers, and deluded (and venal) politicians. Show them advancing from more humid landscapes into the High Plains and plowing up the ancient sod to push the old frontier westward. Drought then sets in. The prospective civilizers die or flee. Anchored in this way, the episode could be a textbook definition of historical irony.

But expand those horizons to include the Hypsithermal, the Maunder Maximum, the Little Ice Age, and prosperous late twentieth-century America, and the Dust Bowl might seem an accident of timing. Of course the Great Plains can be droughty, as most of the West is; of course the climate changes, as it does everywhere, all the time. What caused catastrophe was the exquisite coincidence of drought, sodbusters, and imported ideas: the fact that they came when they did, as they did, outfitted with an intellectual apparatus that could not cope with what they found. If they'd come earlier, they might have had a stable society planted before the great drought struck. If they'd come later, they would have had access to more powerful technology, broader government assistance, and an infrastructure and economy to better spread the risk. If they'd had more humble aspirations and self-conceptions, irony might be swallowed by tragedy. The long history would then contain ironic moments, but it might not be itself defined as fundamentally ironic.

The restricted historical span of the first requires an ironic voice; the broader scope of the second does not. Or to reverse that relationship, a preference for an ironic voice will shunt a text into the first frame, while a preference for the nonironic will nudge it into the second. In a celebrated essay, "A Place for Stories," William Cronon examined the conflicting historical interpretations of the Dust Bowl experience, centering his intellectual concerns on the intrinsic nature of narrative. The choice of an ending determined the choice of narrative structure, and that, like a massive star bending light, warped the narrative geometry of spacetime, which accounted for the differences in the chronicles. But one could as easily lay the charge before modern historians' addiction to the ironic voice. If the nineteenth century was partial to progressive histories, told with providential confidence, the twentieth and twenty-first have favored declensionist versions, told with ironic condescension. Is the reason for the latter that historical facts demand it, or that a preference for irony, diffused widely throughout the culture, suggests it? Which comes first, narrative or voice? Or are the two inseparable?[6]

Whatever the case, irony is pervasive in today's intellectual culture, and such is the depth of this philosophical fashion that no serious rival is on the field. To carry the Western story beyond the hundredth meridian, consider a passage from Patricia Limerick's book *The Legacy of Conquest* in which she explores the case of Louis L'Amour, who was the author of "eighty-eight books about life on the American frontier" and whom Limerick describes as the "mid-twentieth century's successor to Zane Grey, a writer still intoxicated with the independence, nobility, grandeur, and adventure of the frontier." L'Amour wrote paeans to a "process of progress through conquest" that had no end. "We are a people born to the frontier," he wrote, "and it has not passed away." It is a heritage that will, he has insisted, eventually carry us into space.

The Legacy of Conquest is relentlessly ironic: for every past action (or idea or ambition) there is a contemporary reaction, in which rhetoric stumbles over reality. In L'Amour's case, a giant power line was proposed that threatened to mar his view of the mountains from his Colorado ranch. He fought back "with the conventional Western American weapon—the lawsuit—not the six-gun."

> If L'Amour recognized the irony in his situation, he did not share it with reporters. The processes of Western development do run continuously from past to present, from mining, cattle raising, and farming on to hydroelectric power and even into space. The power line is a logical outcome of the process of development L'Amour's novels celebrate. But in this particular case the author was facing the costs of development, of conquest, and not simply cheering for the benefits. "People never worry about these things until it's too late," L'Amour said of the power line in 1985. Eighty-eight books later, he was at last hot on the trail of the meanings of Western history.

Perhaps by the time the L'Amours of the space age get to Mars and the moons of Saturn we will have expanded geography, and even mind, beyond the reach of irony, and history will follow. For the present, however, irony continues to rule the historiography of Earth.[7]

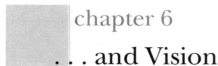

chapter 6

. . . and Vision

In which voice finds its complement, and medium
and message merge, as the way a text sounds joins
forces with the way it looks

The vision thing—it's obvious, it's attractive, it's insistent,
and it's elusive. Once valenced with voice, though, vision
provides the second strand of a text's DNA. If voice answers
the question, "Who needs to hear this, and how?" vision answers the question, "How does this book look, and why?"
It establishes an intellectual point of view: the sense of the
text as a whole. Together voice and vision code the literary
proteins that allow the text to do its work.

"Vision" is shorthand for all of what might be loosely
termed a book's general design, which is to say: Just what
is this text about? And what form—what genre—should it
take? Vision goes well beyond concerns over thesis or theme
to embrace the whole sense of how an idea is given expression and a form. Vision identifies where a book might sit on
a shelf, what cognates and peers it might claim, what dimensions it should assume—in brief, what kind of text it is. Is
this a big-screen history, an extended essay, a braided narrative of ideas, or a collage of biographical sketches? Look to
vision, which serves as a pole star and allows you, when un-
certainties about topic or style arise, to realign your prose

with your purpose. William James once observed that "a man's vision is the great fact about him." This is certainly true for authors.[1]

A sense of vision pivots around the project's Big Idea. If the text is truly to work, it must be inseparable from some kind of informing purpose or organizing principle, which may be a master metaphor, a thesis or argument, a narrative—something that gives shape to the theme. The theme as organizing idea should emerge from the material (my personal preference is to abstract that theme from the sources themselves). The Big Idea might thus translate into such capsule descriptions as: It's a biography of a founder of American geology, told through comparative biographies of his contemporaries. It's an account of a historic fire bust —what led up to it, what happened, what resulted—told month by month through various characters. It's an argument for the continuity of Australian fire practices as tracked by human use of the firestick. It's an evocation of Antarctica, told through a hypothetical journey in which every attribute and experience relates to ice.

Vision informs, gives internal shape to, the text. Just as voice helps you to negotiate around practical glitches like word choice or sentence transitions, so vision, by keeping the whole before you, suggests a realistic range of options, smoothing decisions about proportion and purpose and about selection of material. It is all too easy for writers to get deflected into side issues, puttering about the historical countryside, chasing thematic rabbits, burrowing into curious archival middens. It's particularly easy—notoriously so for beginners—to sink into a mire of introductions, continually packing and repacking, always getting ready and never getting on the trail. Before long they've forgotten what they started to do and why they cared. Rather, your vision should always be before you or around the margins of the text, like an insistent collie keeping a flock of sheep on track. It reminds you where to go next, how long to linger, what to pick up and what to discard. It keeps nipping at your heels and nudging you along in the right direction.

But it doesn't say how to do that, exactly. So vision must grapple with framings, foundations, spans, and design—structural concerns that collectively get us from a Big Idea to an outline. Those architectural analogies suggest a working metaphor: the shapes of texts might be likened to bridges. At one extreme, some resemble a pontoon bridge or a freeway overpass, one boat or decking linked to another, until the span reaches the necessary length. Only the beginning and ending parts differ in style from the rest, and the ends tend to be mirror images of one another. The text is simply longer or shorter. No internal part requires a redesign of the others. The counter image is that of a suspension bridge, in which every part must integrate with every other. Alter any dimension—length, shape, materials—and all the others must adjust. An example of a pontoon bridge would be a book in which the spanning chapters lay out, in sequence, illustrative cases or evidence; or it might be an anthology of loosely linked essays. Chapters could be added or deleted without structural collapse. A suspension bridge would be the type of magisterial work in which every element is organically connected with the rest. The scale of the suspension cables fits precisely the narrative arc; the materials and colors merge motifs with theme. This is the book as Golden Gate Bridge. No part can be changed without affecting every other part.

Vision should sketch what the bridge will span and what kind of bridge it will be. That style and subject should match is the one imperative. To throw a soaring cabled arch over the humble Skunk Creek diversion canal would go beyond indulgence into parody. To pour an elevated concrete corridor, bland as a parking-garage ramp, over the baroquely eroded Salt River Canyon would be to mock the subject. Beyond that rough bonding, however, lie matters of taste. A Golden Gate book may awe by its grandeur—I confess that I regard such productions as aesthetically more impressive and satisfying, and aspire, where the theme and material allow, to write them. (The tendency thus encourages me to look for subjects that lend themselves to this kind of project.) But I've written pontoon books and enjoyed the crossing. What matters is that the structure can bear the traffic put over it.

These are the poles, but the actual options are many and do not align themselves neatly along a spectrum, with the proportional features of the one waxing or waning in sync with the other. The field of possibilities more closely resembles an evening sky, arrayed with potential constellations given shape by the perceiving eye. Real books will be hybrids. Labeling them as mostly one type or the other may (or may not) help our sense of what the manuscript might be and where it needs work. Alternatively, we might characterize them through a textual-tightness index that assesses the consequences of changing or deleting passages. How widely will an alteration ripple outward? Will rewriting a paragraph force the rewriting of a chapter? Can one chapter switch with another without causing the collapse of the whole? Is a revision quickly quarantined, or does it force a cascade of further revisions that extend to the foundation pilings themselves? Some projects will have a lot of slack, with plenty of room for commentary or languid scene-setting and an elastic rhythm of sentences, while others may have limited tolerance for meandering, and rivet must follow rivet remorselessly, the tempo itself communicating an urgency to the argument or the narrative from which the reader can be granted little opportunity to muse or wander. Most books will exhibit parts of each, as authors adjust the purity of their design to the hard contours of the material at hand.

It should be obvious by now that the elements of writing do not parse themselves into convenient units for critical analysis, any more than one can take blood from arteries or arteries from blood and expect the creature to live. Vision does not disentangle from voice, or design from prose. A few examples—some representative patterns—can help root these ideas, and if they reach beyond their stride into other topics, consider them foreshadowings of analyses to come.

The loosest of book organizations is the collection of essays. Some are no better than a proverbial bag of marbles—a volume of conference proceedings would be a work of this type. Some find internal orderings that are more or less arbitrary; think of Joan Didion's *White Album,* in which the groupings could be rearranged without much dislocation, or Donald Worster's book *The Wealth of Nature,* containing sixteen of his personal essays, in which the opening and closing pieces probably need to be where they are but the others could be shuffled without altering the outcome. Other books are extended arguments in which the order of middle chapters might also be rearranged unnoticed—say, Shepard Krech III's *The Ecological Indian,* with its separate chapters on buffalo, deer, and beaver that might as readily be sequenced as deer, beaver, and buffalo.

Others seek some kind of internal structure, perhaps even

development. Aldo Leopold's *Sand County Almanac* groups essays by theme; a fuller gathering of Leopold's essays, *The River of the Mother of God and Other Essays,* arrays them in chronological order. The first clustering emphasizes topics; the second, the evolution of idea and style. In some texts, the theme may suggest an organizing concept. *World Fire,* which I published in 1995, arrays its essays into thematic categories that conform to the stages of wildland-fire suppression. The part entitled "Smoke Report" announces the problem. "Size-Up" examines how fire might fit into historiography. "Hotspotting" includes nine essays on fire in various countries. "Control" embraces six essays on fire management in the United States. "Mop-Up" offers a synoptic history of global fire. And "After the Last Smoke" presents a concluding essay that grounds universal themes in personal experience. The arrangement allowed for an internal ordering, one inspired by the subject although certainly not mandated by it.

Two books by John McPhee, each based on three "encounters," display contrasting degrees of structural tightness. *The Control of Nature* describes humanity's fight against a flood, a volcanic eruption, and a dynamic mountain. The order of the first two could be reversed, but the final story, "Los Angeles against the Mountains," works to synthesize and hence deserves its summary and valedictory position; the book's design is somewhat flexible. More rigid is *Encounters with the Archdruid,* a triptych of engagements between the ardent environmentalist David Brower and three of his "natural enemies": a mining geologist, a land developer, and a dam builder. Each of the episodes stands alone, yet together they form a tight geometry that could not lightly be altered without collapse. In principle, the number of episodes could vary, though two would not be enough and five would almost certainly be too many. What links the three encounters, however, is not just their shared protagonist but a subtle narrative between them that develops Brower's character. As the stories unfold, Brower diminishes as a person, appearing ever more petulant and self-absorbed, stuffing everything into a single formula just as he places every meal, from beans to steak, into a Sierra cup; at the same time, the idea he represents, wilderness, grows ever larger and more significant. The narrative becomes one of a flawed man in a noble cause meeting good men in flawed causes. While slack exists at the level of paragraphs, there is little leeway in the overall design. The equilateral triangle is the simplest and most stable of structural forms, capable of absorbing stress from any point. So the book's design is rigid, yet capable of carrying a narrative over its compounded trestles.

For a study of more complex designs, consider two histories by Bernard DeVoto, one focused on a single year and the other arching over three hundred years, both dealing with the same theme: the imperial saga that became the national saga of American expansion from Atlantic to Pacific. *The Year of Decision: 1846* weaves together many strands into a collective cloth, a Bayeux Tapestry of America's westering. All the dramatis personae are present, both the main movers and shakers and the bit players, and as the narrative advances chronologically DeVoto cuts between them to highlight the critical events. Whether his chosen characters understood their collective fate or not, they shared a grand narrative of Manifest Destiny that would set them separately in motion and join them at the book's conclusion. *The Course of Empire* expands the dominion of that narrative, beginning with Columbus and ending with Lewis and Clark. The narrative is less a quilt than a relay race, as one imperial power surges and then falls behind, to be succeeded by another—the Spanish, the French, the British, the Americans; the westering launches in Europe and concludes with the promised passage to India. The movement from Atlantic to Pacific is the great arc that unifies the text. In both of these large books, there are ample opportunities to add or delete people, places, or incidents, but the vision behind them, like a strange attractor, decides which will go and which will stay and how they will meet at their crossing.

Very different kinds of books; yet all are serious, all nonfiction, all informed by literary artifice. They speak to different topics and in different ways, but their varied themes and styles are in each case suited to their purpose. Each book has behind it an original vision, a sense of what it should be, and hence what belongs in it and how. Each does its task so well that it might become an exemplar, such that one can imagine wanting "to do" an *Encounters* but with philosophers or trail crews, or a *Year of Decision* for Samoa, or a *World Fire* for contemporary Florida.

Strict imitation, however, is not the same as writing to a genre, and identifying a genre is not by itself vision. When I was a high-school sophomore, my English class spent the better part of a year writing pieces in careful imitation of Washington Irving's *Sketch Book,* an exercise that sensitized us to matters of (archaic) style but that also yielded endless parodies as we substituted baseball players, pizza parlors, and dual-carburetor Chevys for Irving's poltroons, picturesque dales, and carriages. It was an ordeal that drove half the class to look longingly toward third-period algebra. If this was vision, it was one best left to Dante's Ninth Circle.

Vision is not one thing among many: it is everything. It is your conception of what the book is about, of what you are trying to do. Some visions will be etched and immutable from the outset with clearly conceived destinations and all the trails well marked. Some will be misty, even murky, but with a firm sense of where they are going, and why, and what the journey is about, ready to crystallize when research turns up the right precipitant.

Few experiences are more common than "not knowing" what you are writing until you have written it—not appreciating exactly where you will end up until you arrive. But without vision you wouldn't get there at all. The details will always surprise. It's your grand sense of purpose and design that prevents those surprises from toppling your heavily laden packhorses. Without it you would wander and founder. If you are lucky, you'll arrive at a certain point and will have an epiphany: a sudden sense of what your book is about that can shock you into action. If you are unlucky, the project will crawl and sprawl and may get written but will never cohere very well. The difference between those two scenarios is what I'm calling vision. Call it whatever you like. Just be sure you have it.

chapter 7

Designing

In which visions acquire shape, ideas structure, and
writing a strategy, so that voice becomes more than
musing and vision moves beyond mental mirage

Between a vision and a working outline lies the domain of
designing. Here an informing principle gets a structural
identity; the rough architecture gets blocked out. Here the
structural pieces and their connections come into alignment in ways that allow a text to tell a story, move information, and create effects. Designing identifies and arranges
the foundations; it lays out the frames; it places the corner-
stones, the pillars, and the spans. It establishes the whole
infrastructure of the text. In a narrative work this process
will bear a close relationship to plot, in a thesis it corre-
sponds to the development of an argument, and in books
organized in other ways it's whatever device bonds theme
with style. Here is where voice and vision actually have to
make each other seen and heard.

Design, then, means more than a sequencing of parts,
one after the another. It refers also to the proportions of
the whole those parts occupy, as well as to their shape, their
color, their dimensions. It is the way they are arranged: the
full effect, the gestalt that conveys the vision, but also those
connections that, as it were, allow the built text to speak and

not merely be seen. These are matters of style, though of style usually best left hidden. The stylistic flourishes that readers see are the moldings, the paint, the trim, and the fixtures. The frame simply is. The grand design that informs the whole text, done right, is something a reader will not see or, if evident, will appear so integral and obvious that no other arrangement can be imagined. In sum, *designing* is how the text gets known. An outline is the action plan to put that conception into words. You may go through outlines like tissues; for complex books, I've sketched and tossed away scores, at every level of production, from the book as a whole to fragments of subchapters.

There are dozens of ways to describe what is here called design. Every critic will have a quiver of idiosyncratic terms; every book on writing will restate the issue in the conceptual (and more or less eccentric) language the author finds most congenial. This guide is no exception. Probably because of a cyclical construction boom, architectural imagery springs most readily to mind. What matters, though, is not this term or that, much less scholastic quibblings over where one concept ends and another begins or how much weight to grant each. What's essential is the deep awareness that all these concerns are aspects of style and that there's only one true rule: style must reconcile with subject. That said, consider the following cluster of concepts as pieces of a working metaphor.

Framing determines where the text will begin and end, and how deep or thick its description will be. A book on the Civil War might start with the firing on Fort Sumter, or it might begin with the election of Abraham Lincoln, or with one of a series of political compromises over slavery. Where it begins, however, will decide where it ends—at Appomattox

Courthouse, or the mourning of Lincoln's assassination, or Reconstruction. That choice, of course, depends on what the book is about. Is it a military history? Is it a study in politics? Is it about the intractability (or not) of racism? What is the tone of voice? Is it critical, elegiac, didactic, admonitory, acerbic, judicious, hortatory, dispassionate, ironic? And so on and so on.

The frame's blueprint should specify dimensions: it should speak to depth and width. Is the book a comprehensive survey, or an extended essay? Is the target two hundred pages or eight hundred? This consideration is not strictly a matter of source material; one can fluff up parchment fragments into mighty treatises (as studies of the pre-Socratic philosophers have done), or reduce an inquiry into life itself to a slender essay (as Erwin Schrödinger famously did). Vision will determine the length of the text—and a sense of that length will influence the text's design and voice. Rough-framing the pages suggests, for example, how long a prologue or introductory chapter might be, or the shape of an internal chapter. A professorial voice might sound pompous in a quick survey; a playful and witty voice might grate when chattering over hundreds of pages. A long narrative history of the Napoleonic wars might have room for fascinating digressions on, say, literary offshoots of the conflict, while a summary distilled into 150 pages should resemble a miniature figurine, its prose chiseled and precise, its purpose exact and unwavering. To allow a digression on one topic would suggest the prospect for digressions on others, and the text would violate its organizing premise, crack its voice, and dissolve its sense of wholeness and authority.

The frame determines where the foundations go—or, more properly, framing and foundations jostle about until they acquire an equilibrium. To hold the frame together, you need some kind of connecting arch or literary span. It may be narrative, in the classic sense of a story with an internal life cycle that joins beginning to end with people and plot. It may be a chronological unfolding of events, in which characters and events collide and disperse under the rubric of a given period of time. It may be an argument built piece by piece, each new pairing of thesis and evidence fitted smoothly to the last. Or the arc may be the force of a magnetic metaphor that gathers particles around it in a great field, an organizing image or person or idea that gives coherence to all the elements the writer wants to include. The narrative might be the saga of the United States Exploring Expedition (1838–1842), a journey full of events and people told in rough temporal sequence. By contrast, an organizing conceit might be the shaking given American society by the San Francisco earthquake of 1906, in which many people, places, and events, each nominally independent, converge during the quake and fire.

Normally the choice of genre will come with the frame, prepackaged, ready for adaptation. But some means must exist to move readers purposely from the opening to the ending, and that spanning arch cannot carry the weight demanded without clear foundations and frames. Moreover, a complex, Golden-Gate-type project comes with serious design costs. More and more of the text must go to support its own weight, to carry the burden of the design. Even if a book is not big so much as complex, a goodly portion of text must be invested in the internal connections. (Two examples from my own work. The quasi-epic scale, and voice, of *Vestal Fire* demanded extra wordage to uphold its elevated tone; and because it was built out of separate "books," each of which had its own prologue and epilogue, it required still more text to grout those tiles into a coherent mosaic. By way of contrast, the eccentrically intricate, and troubled, structure of *Fire in America* forced me to commit an estimated 15 percent of the text to the task of holding its fractious parts together, since I had to explain in words how the separate pieces fit together because the book's design did not intrinsically do so.)

The literary minimalists for whom smaller is always better and less is more can point to such commitments and denounce it all as bloat, a stylish extravagance. This misses the point. The style is doing work, by sustaining an elevated text; if it is done properly, its very character tells us about the nature of the topic or theme. Ubiquitous minimalism is no more attractive in prose than in buildings. A literary landscape formed only of glass-and-steel cubes and no Taj Mahals might be more economical of words but would be a lesser, duller (if more utilitarian) world.

The rival danger is that the business of supporting and moving the text will consume everything else. Momentum and sparkle, the argument and its evidence, and ultimately a reader's interest—all will collapse under the weight of keeping the many parts together. If this happens, it reflects a failure of design. However elaborate or clever or gorgeous, the design is only a means to ends other than itself.

So far, this discussion has been a vision of vision; we need to give the idea some expression in actual texts. Here, I plan to go where critical angels fear to tread. I will use my own experiences and books as examples. For books by other authors, I can make reasonable guesses as a reader, but understanding design requires understanding intent, and while I can judge others' effects, the only causes I can understand are my own. Let me begin with two books that take the nominal form of traditional narrative, one the life cycle of the

fabled Big Blowup of 1910 and the other a big-screen history of fire in Canada. The first involves a single, galvanic
event; the latter, a long chronicle.

The Big Blowup—the central episode in an outbreak of
fires which consumed about three million acres in Idaho,
Oregon, Washington, and Montana, whose soot darkened
the skies as far away as New England, and which killed more
than eighty people—is the archetypal American fire story.
Like all such stories, it contains an internal order: the life
cycle of a fire. But the task of *Year of the Fires: The Story of the
Great Fires of 1910* (2001) was not simply to regale readers
with the raw narrative, but to establish the larger context,
mostly political, while relating the crisis itself in a suitably
exciting way. Ultimately this was a story in which events—
action—dominated ideas, yet the account of the burst of
firefighting could not be allowed to overwhelm our understanding of what the Great Fires meant when they happened
and what they continue to mean. Not least, I had ferreted
out new sources, primarily letters and military records, that
amplified and inflected the traditional narrative preserved
by the U.S. Forest Service.

The solution I chose turned on three hinges. One, since
fire season built up during the summer, climaxing in late
August, the book would follow a calendar year, announced
by the firing of Chief Forester Gifford Pinchot in January,
which set in motion the fires' subsequent political context.
The usual hero of the Big Blowup, Ed Pulaski, would be the
main protagonist during the fires' fury but could not shape
how the fires were understood by the larger culture, above
all how they were interpreted politically.

Two, various witnesses to the fires had left accounts.
These could personalize the perspective, helping to make
concrete and individual the torrent of flame that engulfed

the Northern Rockies. In particular, a man named William Morris had created a running commentary in the form of letters to his family in Chicago, a correspondence he later gathered and deposited with the University of Washington library. Will Morris would be a Little Big Man through the entire saga, even returning for the fiftieth-anniversary memorial.

Three, it seemed that the multi-stranded narrative typical of thriller novels could be adapted to the purposes of this history. The various strands, attached to individuals or institutions, could come and go, woven through the unfolding year. This design virtually abolished the usual transitions that normally demand so much attention to hold a narrative together, and it allowed for maximum tension surrounding the events of the Big Blowup. The text could describe the actions of each crew as the flames approached, cutting away from the moment of actual contact to focus on another crew, and then another; and after the fires had passed, returning, one after another, to give an account of what had happened. Since the climax of the Big Blowup consisted of Ed Pulaski's actions at the Nicholson adit (a mineshaft near Wallace, Idaho, where he sheltered his crew), the story could be divided into three parts: one leading up to the moment of contact, one giving an account of that climax, with Big Ed holding his crew at gunpoint at the adit entrance, and the third tracking what happened afterward. That structure would put Ed at the adit entrance at dead-center of the action.

What remained was to frame the calendar year itself. A short essay, "Before," did that; a longer essay, "After," reviewed the Great Fires' legacy. That still left, to my mind, the need for some kind of overall entry. A visit to the largely obscured Nicolson adit created a means to introduce the story, particularly for those to whom it is unfamiliar. The adit was often later referred to as the "Pulaski tunnel." It was not physically a tunnel; it actually resembled an elongated cave. But it could function as a tunnel for the text, transporting the reader from the overgrown entry, and so it was labeled.

The frames of the book would be several: January to December, snow to snow, political firing and political triumph, the hardening of fire policy from laissez-faire to all-out suppression, the many lives that would pass through the flames. The effect, however, was to provide cultural context for what would otherwise be (what is generally remembered as) an adventure story. When the fires came, acts dominated over words; but for a text, the words ultimately had to control the fire. The chosen design was one way to express that vision.

The long history of Canadian fire had different requirements. It needed to be something of a book of record that would contain the major events, personalities, ideas, and institutions, since it was unlikely the market could bear too many such histories. It would have to capture what I regarded as the central theme: the tension between the rhythms of a boreal environment and the cadences of Canadian society. And it had to express an important reality: that modern Canada addresses fire through institutions, yet the nature of Canadian political confederation prevents any single institution from integrating the parts into a master narrative. This sense reflected my larger reading of the Canadian experience, namely that its national story is the result less of an organic internal development than of outside pressures or threats that force the pieces into a whole. Canada's geography quarrels with its history.

How to hold this centrifugal saga together? My solution in *Awful Splendour* (2007) was to write a series of nested narratives, such that each nested group was contained within a defining outside force. The groupings clustered into three, thus echoing the fire community's predilection for triads. (The fire triangle serves this group as the water cycle does for hydrologists.)

The largest narrative was climate. That virtually all of Canada was under ice at the height of the last glaciation meant that its history was literally a blank page. The book would begin with White Canada, under ice, and end with Green Canada, as the last of the ice was rapidly melting and the country was edging toward greater environmental awareness. It was a dandy, obvious narrative arc. In the course of the span, fire and its favored creatures triumphed over ice and the denizens of its world.

The second frame came from Earthly fire history. It helped that the post-glacial recolonization of Canada had people as part of the menagerie. They provided the divisions that defined fire's appearance on the landscape. There was thus an era dominated by ignition (this part of the book would be entitled "Torch"), an era shaped by humanity's ability to create fuel ("Axe"), which mostly overlapped with European contact, and an era informed by combustion of fossil biomass ("Engine"), which usefully coincided with Confederation. Each of these eras, corresponding to parts of the book, reorganized the prevailing geography of Canadian fire. Each part opened with a description of how the era's defining process worked and concluded with exemplary fires, in order to give some historical specificity to abstraction. Each incorporated some on-site commentary from human observers. Loosely, the overall text resembled a historical geography.

The first era took the form of "fire rings," quasi-concentric circles of biota and burning. The text moved, ring by ring, from the incombustible Hudson Bay to incombustible outliers at Cape Breton and Queen Charlotte islands. (As a narrative, this was pretty feeble—but without an identifiable human group or person, and attendant conflicts, it at least provided some movement.) The second part of the book followed the progress of swidden agriculture and then European contact as they broke down and reassembled fire landscapes. It assumed the narrative form of fire frontiers. The third part was the most complex, for there was far more information available and the story was more convoluted. When, in 1930, the Dominion government ceded its western lands to the provinces, it ended an embryonic national narrative. The provinces would henceforth oversee fire. Canadian fire history fragmented into a confederation of narratives, spread among the provinces and those federal institutions that had an interest in fire management or research.

How could I move the story in an interesting way that would not resemble building a corduroy bridge over muskeg, log by log? There were of course many possible strategies, but I chose to break up the chronology into three phases (using the 1930 event as one marker). Each would incorporate provincial histories (east, west, and fringes); each would tell the national story in whatever form was workable; and each would include a pair of biographies that would distill critical themes into the experiences of two competing men. The provincial histories had the character of cameos; they were less mini-histories than profiles that highlighted the critical events and themes that made each distinctive. The parts of the book would plait into a narrative braid. All this, I hoped, would enliven the text beyond pure institutional history, would ground abstruse discussions in the particulars of personalities, and would keep readers (and myself) from nodding off. In this way I hoped to hold true to the reality of Canadian experience while still offering something that might resemble a master narrative.

All in all, a complicated, composite structure. If I had been willing to relinquish my goal of approximating a book of record, or to simply summarize the prevailing scientific literature, or to leap from major fire to major fire and use each to distill what had happened in the intervening years, I could have had a more compact and spritely narrative. I didn't, because that was not my purpose or my reading of Canada's fire history. The design was intended to embody my sense of how Canadian fire had come to look the way it did. Of course, other writers could see it differently—will see it differently. They will want another design.

Now turn to two texts that evoke very different continents, one (Antarctica) where everything is related to ice and the other (Australia) whose epic history revolves around fire. The problem was to transform ice and fire into informing principles.

In its original conception, *The Ice: A Journey to Antarctica* (1986) treated Antarctica as a unit within a larger historical survey of earth science and exploration. Three long months on the Ice itself scotched that idea. Antarctica did not fit into inherited narratives: it was about ice, it was self-referential, it was sui generis. An honest book would move beyond the borders, where most people clung, and advance into the interior, which people as well as ideas shunned. An honest text would confront Ice—ice as reductionism, ice as isolation, ice as a modernist nature. This would be a journey to the underworld, and after arrival there, a journey to the ice source through the concentric shells of ice terranes, one terrane after another. The tale would be told in a series of paired chapters, one on the kind of ice manifest at that terrane and one on humanity's encounter with it.

The structure would begin at the outside and move in. It would open with a prologue in the realm of the extra-Antarctic icebergs and conclude with an epilogue at the cold core of the East Antarctic plateau. A suite of "ice" chapters would carry the movement inward, past the iceberg to the ice pack to the ice shelf to the glacier to the ice sheet to the source region. A parallel suite of "history" chapters would describe what happened to Western civilization as it encountered the Ice. Since the pack ice was the great barrier to wooden-ship exploration, a study of exploration would follow the pack chapter. The shelf would spark an inquiry into art and literature. The glacier would prompt a survey of earth science. The ice sheet would lead to geopolitics.

Each of those two chapter types had a template. The ice chapters began and ended with an account of this particular ice—where it comes from and where it goes. Then would follow a detailed description of that species of ice, drawn from the scientific literature. Additional sections could tap other relevant natural features. Then would come an art essay, an attempt to create an aesthetic for each ice terrane. Each ice chapter would thus begin and end with the geography of ice, and within that frame the text overall would inflect from science to art. The history chapters would track historical developments, roughly organized around the concept of three great ages of discovery, or—since the first age never reached the Ice—the change from the second age to the third. Exploration, art, science, and politics—each history chapter conformed to this loose design, as the Ice worked on institutions and ideas to similar effects.

The normal structure for such a travel book would have it open and close with people. They would come, they would be changed, they would leave. This, in fact, was the traditional pattern of human encounter with the Ice. But *The Ice* proposed another design, one that would not obscure the depth of the Antarctic experience: it would have the place transcend the people. The text would open and close with ice, letting the people come and go in between. In this underworld, there would be no guide—no Tiresias, no Sybil, no Virgil, no indigenes. There would be no persona inserted into the text to assume that role. There would be no single vantage point. There would be no time; the descriptive passages would be written in the present tense. The journey would end at the source region, a place of icy solipsism. Terrane by terrane, the Ice would reduce whatever was brought to it. The world would simplify to a single mineral as high as Mount Whitney and as broad as Australia. Under its impress, even the self would begin to dissolve. The usual organizing devices of understanding—time, space, perspective, persona, contrast, context—were absorbed within the Ice. The book would attempt to express that experience.

It made for tough sledding. Antarctica is a place perhaps best characterized by what it lacks, by the things that normal places have and it doesn't. Instead, everything relates to ice. So, too, *The Ice* removed many of the devices that make a text accessible. They became noticeable by their calculated omission. This was a text informed by ice.

Burning Bush: A Fire History of Australia (1991) applied a similar vision to Antarctica's Gondwana twin, Australia, but evoked a world informed by fire. The result was an environmental epic in which the reader, by seeing how Australia looked when viewed by flame, could appreciate fire's role as a defining trait.

But a Big Idea is not a vision until it can be expressed in

a suitable design. The project stalled when I realized how thoroughly Australian historiography polarized into "Aborigine" and "European." I wanted the bush to intervene, or, to express this differently, I wanted to have Australia's natural features capture and redirect that history. The breakthrough came when I realized that I could frame the prevailing polarity with another. I could begin with the Eucalypt, the "universal Australian," as a first colonizer, and conclude with the New Australian, the postwar demographic shift that led to a reformation of values.

What emerged was a simple design. A prologue would introduce the positioning of Australia on the Earth and convey the principal events that shaped the natural history of its bushfires. An epilogue would close the saga, focusing on the Ash Wednesday fires of 1983. Although Australia is not a religious country, an epic should at least contain echoes of elevated language, and this suggested religious phrases if not imagery, or, in the case of a burning bush, a formative image. The prologue would begin with "dust to dust"; the epilogue, with "ashes to ashes."

Each of the four eras in between focused on a primary agent of Australian fire, and each followed a common if loose template organizing a suite of internal chapters. This design argued for dividing the book into parts and devoting each one to a separate era. In each part, an opening chapter would introduce the dominant character of fire and themes for the era, serving as an internal prologue or preamble. A second chapter would sketch a fire profile of the principal actor. Another chapter would describe the resulting fire regimes of Australia under its influence. A concluding chapter, or internal epilogue, would provide a brief interpretation of that era. Parts I and IV were limited to those four basic chapters. Parts II and III expanded to include other topics relevant to the study, as needed to sustain the theme and as they could be supported by sources.

The end result was a narrative bridge with four grand spans, each of which described a fundamental reorganization of Australian fire and each of which obeyed a subtle symmetry. The overall design suggested that Australia had powerful continuities, that even as new eras crystallized out of old, similar themes persisted, and above all, that bushfire was both defining and ineradicable. The book would demonstrate, with particular force, that Australia is a fire continent just as Antarctica is an ice continent. Of course not everything in Australia has connected to fire, but it is possible to devise a history of Australia in which fire acts as an ordering principle, a kind of central bonfire, around which the more familiar elements of the Australian experience dance, and in this way to show, not merely state, fire's powerful presence.

Enough of my stuff. It's time to ponder more deeply some other properties of traditional narrative. To simplify, we might consider two general strategies, again informed by an architectural analogy. One, the classic narrative, might be likened to a load-bearing wall that can rise only as high as its base allows and that builds stone by stone. In order for it to reach higher, the base must widen to support that weight, but proportionately more of the bulk goes to width than to height. The second type of narrative resembles a modernist grid. The walls can be airy, could even be made of glass, because they don't support the reach of the structure; only the grid does. Such a narrative can leap from node to node—detail to detail, event to event—shedding lengthy transitions and lightening the text. The downside is that it might have a matrix of "telling details" but lack the heft that the topic requires or the continuity that a reader craves. Sometimes you need muscle, not just ligaments. Sometimes you have to feed prose carbohydrates, not just vitamins.

Which option is better? That depends on the purpose of the book, and on aesthetic taste. Contemporary critical fashion favors the modernist approach, though plenty of readers savor the load-bearing narrative if it treats one of their favorite topics. Besides, the grid-narrative has its dark side, for it requires that much be left out. It captures the defining details, but leaves out the vast quarries from which they come. These particulars may, for scholarship, be what the text is about; or in those cases where the details are not mandatory, they may still do work and enlighten by their enriching presence. One aim of the text may be to collect, in a single format, information that would otherwise remain diffused throughout an archival sea. There is a place for scholarship that accumulates, organizes, gives shape to, and explains without resorting to breathless prose and piledriver verbs. Most of a giant sequoia is, after all, nominally dead wood, with only its outer cambium and needles alive; but that seemingly inert cellulose has a function. It makes the tree what it is.

Besides, a book that merely cherry-picks the juiciest details may read well and sell well but fail to prove its case and may destroy the market for a book that can do both. Or not. A good bad book can go either way. If, say, you wrote a book about historic forest fires and plucked out only the most garish, tragic, and gripping events, and wrote stories centered on strong and quirky personalities, high-grading only the choicest human-interest episodes, a fable of firefighter heroes and fire-breathing dragons, and had at least the verbal skills to put subject nouns properly together with verbs, you would probably come up with a fairly popular book. If it sold exceptionally well, another trade publisher might want to publish a copycat version, and general interest might swell sufficiently to sustain a more comprehensive survey. Yet if you tried something equivalent with an academic study, not really doing the hard intellectual work and not getting the context right by careful literary designing, the text might get published but the market could wither away because no other publisher would want to publish on the topic again; what was only a niche would become saturated, perhaps ineptly, but saturated nonetheless. The original might sell maybe 1,000–1,500 copies. A successor, even it if were a much better book by any measure, might struggle to find a publisher at all. By cynically culling the topic, the author will have clear-cut the market; another version probably wouldn't find an outlet for at least a decade, unless the topic became front-page, above-the-fold news.

One premise behind a literary approach to nonfiction is that the choice between doing a popular hack job and a kludgey academic book is false: you can merge the best of both. But if you do it badly, it may be tricky for someone else to do it well.

What might seem, from an aesthetic perspective, to be textual debris that clutters the purity of the human-interest drama might in truth be what makes the whole work, much as junk DNA, which for protein-coding appears to be so much biotic deadwood, still seems essential for the active DNA to do its job. What may get lost in minimalist design is the full shape, bulk, and context of the topic that from a thematic perspective the subject requires. If scholarship is what you want, then a sensible fraction of the text must go to support it, even at the expense of a general readership or a gazelle-like rush of words, or the addition of a thematic buttress here and there. A command of literary understanding should reduce the trauma of such choices— should make a serious book sit lightly in the hand if not in the mind, should keep the flow of interest brisk, should make ideas and settings as gripping as personalities. But in the end, scholarship is not to everyone's taste.

The fitting of spans and load-bearing walls to foundations is what moves the words beyond a spectral voice and a rhetoric that can display but do no real work. Such performances can suffice in realms of literary fiction, where critics may praise a writer for a "delicate" or "distinctive" voice or for "exquisite" prose, on the assumption that aesthetic pleasure alone is adequate. It is never enough in nonfiction, where the style must carry a burden beyond itself. Poorly organized texts force readers to leap across the narrative stream by mental boulder-hopping that is guaranteed to leave a good many of them, if not most, floundering in the author's prose, a drenching that few will likely enjoy.

Vision and voice, the elements of design, the framings, the foundational pilings, the linked spans—all converge on a working plan. Or at least that is how I conceive an outline. Until the manuscript is done, I regard outlines as mutable, heuristic, disposable. They—and an outline is always plural—are the action plans that identify what must be done.

Typically these decisions already come, coded and hidden, with the chosen genre or template, such that designing, while strenuous and often imaginative, becomes a gigantic exercise in analogizing and adapting. This is the wisest, the conservative approach. But as the analogies stretch and the metaphoric chasms widen, it may be necessary to abandon the general exemplar and devise something that will carry the particular burden at hand.

In his classic essay "Politics and the English Language," George Orwell railed against clichés, dying metaphors, verbal false limbs, pretentious diction, worn-out phrases, and other flaccid devices. They cause both "staleness of imagery" and "lack of precision," an amalgam of vagueness and incompetence. "The writer either has a meaning and cannot express it, or he inadvertently says something else, or he is almost indifferent as to whether his words mean anything or not."[1] Such failings are the stock fare of writing manuals, and provide much of the fun of reading denunciations by editor-evangelicals as they denounce and damn particular passages. What is less appreciated is that the same considerations apply to features of design as fully as to phrases and sentences. Tired, hackneyed structures bespeak tired, hackneyed ideas and arguments. If you have something truly new to say, you may need to devise a new way to say it.

The fewer the modifications of existing forms, the less disruptive the outcome will be for most readers, and the less likely it is that the structure will collapse, like a Tacoma Narrows Bridge, as the critics bluster. Novelty must speak to the evidence, not simply to literary experimentation. In the process, the strains will be felt most acutely in the outlines, less so in the designs, and least in the vision, if the vision is something that can be given expression; or so it should be, if the project is to work. The give-and-take of envisioning, designing, and outlining, of moving from Big Idea to working blueprint, repeats over and over until it turns on itself, like a Möbius strip.

All well and good, but a pretty abstract explanation, with one metaphor holding up another like a crowd of drunks. We need some examples. We have already examined some coarse designs under "Vision" (it really is hard to segregate the pieces; a great passage will speak to many issues simultaneously). But consider here descriptions of two books, one of the modernist-grid variety and one of the Golden Gate class.

In *The Ecology of Fear*, Mike Davis argues that the identification of Los Angeles with disaster, so abundant in the popular imagination, has a material reality: the place really is prone to catastrophe, in recent years seeming to reinvent itself as "a Book of the Apocalypse theme park." But its "dialectic of ordinary disaster" hinges on properties like "deep Mediterraneanity," nonlinearity, and cataclysm-prone economies of both nature and people, for which averages mean little. Every element of Los Angeles displays this characteristic: fires erupt into conflagrations under Santa Ana winds; water comes in deluges or disappears into drought; earth cracks in savage quakes; air harbors violent storms and even tornadoes. On these eccentric and unstable foundations, American society has sunk its capitalist piles and pushed out its freeway-linked suburbs. It is a recipe for making natural eruptions into cultural catastrophes.[2]

The episodic nature of such disasters suggests that a book about Los Angeles might echo those same qualities, leaping from thesis node to node, or event to event, instead of cranking along in an even-paced chronicle during which, for long periods, very little happens. It's the extremes, which are really normative, that define the geography. The trick is to hit the crises without losing the connections between them, and for this a modernist grid is an ideal style. Davis exploits it within and among chapters. Topic after topic—earthquake, flood, fire, recession—assumes a similar form, and adds another span to the grid. In the end, where the text is well grounded in evidence, the book is practically unshakeable, even by the critical equivalent of a 6.7-magnitude Northridge earthquake.

Chronicling the advent of the Great War demanded a

very different architecture. The problem in this case not cataclysms rattling and flooding the foundation of a so ciety, but the accumulation of minutiae, individually trivial but collectively catastrophic, set off by a catalyst, the assassi- nation of the Archduke Ferdinand in 1914. Such an argu- ment called for a load-bearing narrative of the sort done magnificently by Barbara Tuchman in *The Guns of August*. She chose to begin with the flowery details of a funeral pag- eant, nominally of George V but in reality of an era, and to end with the emergence of a new age, shell-shocked, crawl- ing out of its trench-war paroxysm, this one without pag- eantry or panegyrics.

How Europe got from one point to the other involved choices, thousands of choices, by people; many choices, many people, the cumulative effect of many drips that be- came a trickle that scoured out a rut that became the trenches of the Western Front. The horror need not have occurred. The seeming inevitabilities were packed, one within another, like nested dolls, waiting for an improbable but in the end unstoppable sequence of events, as politi- cians and soldiers made one miscalculation after another, working out a destiny that no one really foresaw or wanted but that no one could stop, all the tiny pieces acting like a cascade of released U-239 neurons that led to nuclear fis- sion and explosion. It is entirely possible to distill such ob- servations into an essay, or even into the character of a sin- gle person or event. But somewhere behind that portraiture must lie a mass of historical detail; and where the tragedy evolved out of many details, a load-bearing narrative can show as well as tell.

Between the Grid and the Golden Gate—this is where most books reside. Some texts grow like vines, their thematic ten- drils held by a lattice that they subsequently cover over (and

:ader does not see). Some are tightly coiled,
it you see is what there is: the design is the ar-
most books will combine features; their au-
nt something more than stacked grids and
something less than isthmus-sized spans. A lot of designs
will be hybrids, like J. Tuzo Wilson's *IGY: The Year of the New
Moons.*

The book follows the eighteen-month International Geophysical Year from July 1957 to December 1958. As president of the International Union of Geodesy and Geophysics
during IGY, Wilson had the opportunity to participate at a
high level and, as a person eager for a revolution in earth
science, to comment on its meaning. The design of *IGY*
combines all three interests. As the months unfold, Wilson
travels to sites of significance and then uses his experiences to explain the current state of understanding, not
only of the science but of the often alien and mutually sus-
picious societies of the Cold War. Thus, he is in Communist
Romania when the Soviet Union lofts Sputnik I in October
1957. He then devotes a chapter to the variety of satellites
launched under IGY auspices, and later shows what they revealed, particularly in the upper atmosphere. Cosmic rays
then inspire a visit to the north magnetic pole in June 1958,
which segues into chapters on the Earth's magnetic field
and auroras. And so on. A graceful voice, the unpretentious
wit of a truly curious man, packs an enormous amount of
information into the course of these travels.

Which is to say, this is a variant of the travelogue, but as
a journey of ideas. It is also a design that could easily be
adapted to historical studies. In this case the "journey"
would be the larger narrative, and as it touches places and
personalities and topics, they could receive extra commentary. The narrative could be anything with a chronological

beginning, middle, and end; it could easily be, for example, a biography such as Peter Brown's *Augustine of Hippo,* in which each stage of Augustine's life triggers a discussion about some feature of the larger social setting that pertains to Augustine, from education to rhetoric to church administration and so on. The life is the journey; its critical moments, the places visited; and its experiences, the themes pertinent for commentary. A simple enough design, and one that manages to juggle narrative movement with lots of information. It certainly avoids the thudding organization of thesis-evidence-evidence-evidence-conclusion. But that, of course, is its purpose.

chapter 8
Plotting

In which we examine more closely the arranging of textual spans, such that beams and pillars get placed in a sequence that allows the text to move from a beginning to an end

Bringing coherence to words and ideas is what design is all about. The task of actually moving the text belongs to the realm of plotting or, to hold to our architectural metaphor, spanning. No single or simple formula covers all the ways to do this.

Since Aristotle, critics have associated plots with stories, or, to express that concept in more formal terms, with narrative. Plots provide a particular kind of organization: they hold the pieces together according to an order in which one piece must follow some and precede others; the more complete the "unity" of the pieces, the more satisfying the outcome. But since nonfiction embraces more than story, its plots, or plot surrogates, can assume other forms.

For example, an argument. That is, the text begins with a premise, musters evidence for it, and then concludes. The progression of sources may be logical or chronological— might develop from one datum point to the next, or might unfold in some evolutionary progression in which the sequencing itself becomes the explanation. These are customary solutions for scholarly books and theses, and a chronological plot is the notional structure for biography. But other arrangements are possible: plot analogues might perform the same task. Finding, tweaking, or devising those devices puts plot into the domain of conscious literary choice.

One might, for example, organize the text by space rather than time. You could reveal a place's boundaries, contrast its periphery with its core, or move through it in ways that advance the argument or otherwise define the arc that grandly spans from opening to closing. Start at the periphery of Antarctica, amid its asteroidal icebergs, and advance to the immutable source regions on the East Antarctic plateau. Or begin at Hudson Bay and move broadly outward, ring by biotic ring, from inner tundra to the outer temperate rainforests at Vancouver Island and Cape Breton. Or build by dimension, order by order of magnitude, from quarks to galaxies, or mineral to Earth. Or have that movement occur through a character or an expedition in which plot segues into quest, in which case space and time converge. What all such movements convey is an ordered progression that does for your text what traditional plotting does for traditional narrating.

Another alternative is to adopt as an informing principle some master metaphor around which the shards of text can gather. Even the most powerful conceit, however, has a limited force field, and as a rule of thumb will not hold together much beyond a sketch or essay without being buttressed by a genuine plot.

With minimal rhetorical flourish George Orwell, in his essay "Shooting an Elephant," uses an experience he had in Burma when, as a minor functionary of the British imperial constabulary, he was called upon to destroy an elephant that had run amok but by the time he arrived had quieted down. He shot it anyway, unable to resist the power of the crowd that had gathered, and unwilling to lose face. In the essay, shooting the elephant becomes a powerful metaphor, one that organizes all of Orwell's other thoughts about the dirty work of policing the empire and the limits of British power, and in some ways stands for the empire itself. But the metaphor works because it takes the form of a story in which the arguments accompany the act of responding, shooting, and reflecting. Without the plot that animates the metaphor, the reach of the essay would probably not have exceeded that of an op-ed piece.

With far more gusto, Tom Wolfe develops the American folk metaphor of a young man going west and growing up with the country, and uses it to organize thoughts not only about the creation of Silicon Valley but about the moral capital on which that effort ultimately drew. "Two Young Men Who Went West" tells parallel stories: one a brief sketch of the Iowa lawyer, minister, educator, railway developer, and eventual congressman Josiah Grinnell, and the other a lengthy profile of the microchip inventor Robert Noyce, who grew up in the Iowa town founded by Grinnell and himself founded the Intel Corporation in California. The first of these lives was a product of a fierce moralism bonded to the driving technology of the day, the railroad; the second, of a drawn-down moral reserve applied to the electronic revolution. Horace Greeley's admonition, "Go west, young man!" becomes an organizing conceit to make Wolfe's case: that American settlement is not yet finished (or is chronically unsettled, as technology and opportunity allow), and also that the energy that powered the first Young Man had exhausted itself on the West Coast by the time the second one came along. To the claim that "Noyce is a national treasure," Wolfe replies:

> Oh yes! What a treasure indeed was the moral capital of
> the nineteenth century! Noyce happened to grow up in
> a family in which the long-forgotten light of Dissenting
> Protestantism still burned brightly. The light!—the light
> at the apex of every human soul! Ironically, it was that
> long-forgotten light . . . from out of the churchy, blue-
> nosed sticks . . . that led the world into the twenty-first
> century, across the electronic grid and into space.[1]

Wolfe could have simply asserted his argument as a thesis, at the opening, placing it within the existing scholarship, and then introduced Robert Noyce as an example,
perhaps using Noyce's youth in Grinnell as a daub of bait
on an otherwise bare hook. Instead he turned that observation into a master metaphor and outfitted that metaphor
with a structure in the form of a story, which is to say a plot,
without which he could not have carried his comments with
anything like the sustained zest he does. The research embedded in the piece is as well hidden as the Protestant soul.
Wolfe's conclusion, with its tangy pronouncements and
over-the-top exclamations, further distances the piece from
academic argument, and hence removes it from the proto-
cols of scholarly discourse and critical grousing. Wolfe dis-
penses his observations while coyly distancing himself from
them. Whether you accept this, and his Tabasco-sauce
prose, or believe that the argument works as well as the
story, is as always a matter of taste.

Enough of surrogates. Most plotting will occur within narrative as commonly understood. It will tell a story. The text
will relate some rivalry, decipher a mystery, undertake a
journey. There will be a point of departure, a trek, a conflict, or an extended experience, and a terminus. A casus
belli will prompt a war, battles will follow, and a treaty will

bring all to a conclusion. An expedition will launch from Lagos, sail down the coast of Africa, and return. A person, perhaps famous, or infamous, or perhaps undistinguished and unknown but revealing of the times, will be born, live, and die. The easiest narratives emerge from quarrels and quests, from overt conflicts and military campaigns, geographic expeditions and tales of survival, biographies of people or ideas or institutions, all circumstances in which a beginning, middle, and end are evident and a struggle or goal turns the gears of the plot. A story of simple survival might invite the simplest of structures, stark words shuffling mechanically along with as few stumbles and wanderings as possible toward a fixed end.

These are familiar formulas, and, as with other aspects of writing, they can be done well or poorly; where found wanting, they can be tweaked. As with other features, too, from character to setting, plot depends on the right mix of detail and revelation, on pacing and proportion, and on the relative allotments of telling-via-showing and telling-about. What details matter depends on the text's design: a load-bearing narrative demands lots of particulars and events; a modernist grid, only the telling detail at the node where beam welds to pillar.

Most of the customary techniques come hardwired in the genre. But a few are worth highlighting. One is the role of plotting in pacing, and vice versa. Just as sentences quickly bore if they all have the same shape and rhythm, so do scenes. Vary your narration. Let some scenes mature with stately grace, others rise and fall, a few zip quickly past. As always, the proportions and pacing must fit the design; or, to restate that imperative, design should include plot variety, not only in the sizes and ratios of its beams and walls but in the way the eye reads across them. The more extreme expression breaks the narrative flow altogether with flash-backs, foreshadowings, or sidebars. The story pauses, re-groups, then moves ahead.

Again as with sentences, the unexpected, by startling, can rekindle interest. Begin, say, with the nominal ending. What would be the effect, for example, of opening a book about the Lewis and Clark expedition with Meriwether Lewis' sui-cide? That would impart suspense to what is an oft-told tale, and would conclude the book not with Lewis' melancholy coda but with the Two Captains' triumphant return. The truth is, there is no singular or intrinsic way to treat a theme. A forest fire, for example, contains within its life history an informing narrative arc: it begins, it spreads, it goes out, and each moment breathes suspense. Any story of a fire would seemingly beg to follow that trajectory, and almost all accounts do, particularly in rendering fires that are unfa-miliar to the public.

But not Norman Maclean's *Young Men and Fire*. By the second sentence he has named and placed the 1949 Mann Gulch fire, previously obscure to all but a few partisans, and announced that thirteen smokejumpers died in it, appar-ently giving away the ending before he has started. He then explains why and how he came to the scene. In Part I he begins the first of many retellings, a nonlinear narrative in which he hovers and circles over the events. The point is not the factual story, which is both obvious and unknow-able, but the quest for storytelling and what meaning those deaths might have. Part II portrays "a world of no explo-sions, no blowups, and, without a storyteller, not many ex-planations." Systematically, Maclean explores different in-tellectual prisms by which to interpret the events as he has been able to reconstruct them: history, art, science, what-ever straws blow in the investigative wind. Each repeats the basic story, from a changed perspective. The circlings continue.[2]

The reason is that the correct conclusion is unclear. For a sure narrative arc, the ending must be known, but here the apparent endings—the death of the smokejumpers, the official board of review that examined the fires, institutional reforms—are not the "true" ending. The true ending must resolve the "moral bewilderment" left in the fire's ash. These involve transcendent matters, the meaning of life and death. For Maclean, they are resolved only by the storytelling quest itself; and poignantly, revealingly, Maclean himself died before he could complete the text. In another's hands, the text might have slumped into self-indulgence, or slipped its moorings from the concrete crosses on the hillside, or become a literary exercise in self-reference in which the writer writes about himself as a writer, the historical facts merely an occasion to experiment with literary expression, which is its own end. Maclean's finely honed voice—crusty woodsman, questing skeptic, dismisser of cant and pretense—keeps the text's feet on the ground. Although deeply inventive, the style serves the theme; the story does not serve the ambitions of style, as though the text were a literary Mr. Potato Head, there to amaze with exotic combinations.

The point is, this kind of narrative cycling is not inherent in fire as a topic. Previously, fire stories took other forms, mostly as adventure narratives. That changed because simple adventuring was not the question posed, so Maclean had to invent other devices to address it. What matters is that, in this instance, Maclean found a way to fuse subject and style so indissolubly that it is almost impossible to imagine the story of Mann Gulch told any other way. And this capacity to move a text from beginning to end in a way that blends vision with voice is what plotting is all about.[3]

Even less amenable to parsing is Simon Schama's *Landscape and Memory*, an inquiry into aesthetic imagination and place. In his introduction, Schama playfully hints at his method, recalling his delight in Kipling's *Puck of Pook's Hill*, a boyhood favorite infused with "potent magic." The premise is that with "Puck's help you could time-travel by standing still." On Pook's Hill, Dan and Una "got to chat with Viking warriors, Roman centurions, Norman knights, and then went home to tea." Something like this happens in *Landscape and Memory*. Stand at one place and its associations, notably with art, will transport you to other eras and times, implying that all are ever-present and merely require the right incantation to conjure them forth.[4]

The book has four parts. Three implicitly echo the ancient elements (wood, water, and rock), and then the three come together as Arcadia. At any single spot, however, the text becomes almost a free association of ideas and experience, of personal and collective memories, of art to art to art, from past to present and back again, as memories rise out of civilization's subconscious and sink back. A kind of invocation replaces simple narrative, the complexity too rich to pin into taxonomic categories like a collection of beetles, because the world outside is really a world within, or rather because the external environs are literally and figuratively shaped by people. Landscape is a work of art. Accordingly, the text appears to slip in and out of art history like the denizens of Pook's Hill.

This is not to everyone's taste. Critics who prefer a more linear narrative or a more explicit thesis have groused that the text is an overgrown jungle of allusive vines, strewn with classical roots ready to trip the traveling reader, and broken by cloud-strewn chasms awaiting leaps of imagination, landscapes all but impenetrable, better suited to an Henri Rousseau than an Alexander von Humboldt, a kind of aesthetic Freudianism in a tumble of recovered images. Reading is less analysis than immersion. All this suggests that Schama achieved what he wanted, although not what everyone else might have wanted from him. An author's prerogative, a reader's right—both sides are correct.

Looking forward and looking back, anticipating what is to come and recalling what has happened—these are among the most common techniques of plotting, and among the most easily fumbled. Call the first *foreshadowing*, since the reader sees the shadows of the approaching object before the substance, and call the second *backlighting*, since the object is present and the reader's understanding improves by having it illuminated with material recalled from earlier text.

Foreshadowing is everywhere, and everywhere embraced by authors. The point of historical development in particular is to trace and expose continuities, and anyone writing a chronological text, be it biography, big-screen history, or family saga, is eager to show how the boy solving a puzzle anticipates the man winning a Nobel Prize in physics, how the accidental encounter between two orphans is the germ of a later reform movement, how a mother's flawed ambitions get transferred to a daughter in ways that will disrupt the daughter's adult life, how a chance phrase or observation later reappears to inspire a famous song or novel. Foreshadowing is fundamental to the expectations that keep a writer clacking at a keyboard and a reader turning pages.

But it is often overused and can stall the flow of narrative, and too frequently it substitutes a clumsy gesture of suspense for genuine drama. After all, everything anticipates everything that follows. The trick is to find just those criti-

cal events and signs that augur the future and most inform
and propel the narrative or argument. Where the foreshadowing is dense, it is usually better to cluster those literary
omens into a single sketch or summary than scatter them
like seed amid loam and rock equally. Avoid the tendency
to follow one foreshadowing with another, such that the
text becomes all shadow and little substance. Watch for
overuse of the conditional voice: "She would soon know
what hiking this trail would mean. It would put her among
rocks that her new boots would turn into blisters. It would
mean that her eyes would focus on the trail rather than on
the mountains she told herself she wished to see. It would
involve awkward questions upon her return. It would put
her behind the wheel late at night with weak vision and impaired judgment." Consider instead the effect of leaving
the topic sentence in the conditional and putting the rest
into the active voice. "She would soon know what hiking
this trail meant. It put her among rocks that her boots
turned into blisters. It meant she saw the trail rather than
the mountains she told herself she wished to see. It involved
awkward questions upon her return. It put her behind the
wheel late at night with weak vision and impaired judgment." Or just state that there were unanticipated consequences. Or perhaps even better, let the story unfold without those knowing authorial comments about what is to
come.

An alternative strategy is to let the story evolve and then
reflect back at critical moments, recalling how the past
helps explain what has happened. This approach, too, can
stall the narrative, but it has some comparative advantages.
It builds on what the reader has already absorbed; it grants
a pause for reflection; and if done deftly it induces the
pleasant sensation of recognition. It's best handled through

careful attention to telling details and design, so that the reader needs little lecturing to see the connections. The observation is an echo, similar to but not quite the same as what happened before; the scene slyly recreates an earlier one, so that few authorial comments are needed to reset it. The structure carries the message.

Which is better? As always, that depends. Suppose you are writing about the American space program and want to discuss the controversy regarding whether the future lies with human or robotic explorers. Since the projects have been running in parallel, there are ample opportunities to compare them, and since the debate is a long one, extending back to the foundations of NASA, you have plenty of occasions to foreshadow and backlight. Suppose, further, that you focus on the Voyager mission, which was marked by three prominent incidents that demonstrated the intersection of the two traditions in a thematic way. One involved the original planning for Voyager, in which the decision to develop the space shuttle threatened to divert means and money from planetary exploration to the shuttle as a precondition to human colonization. A second occurred when Voyager 2 encountered Jupiter while Skylab was seeking to serve as a bridge between capsules and shuttle. A third came when, as Voyager 2 was concluding its spectacular 1986 near-encounter with Uranus, the space shuttle *Challenger* exploded during launch, a disaster that again threatened to redirect NASA.

In foreshadowing, each event would have a tag about how the intra-agency competition not only distorted the Voyager mission but would affect its future (note the use of conditionals, even in explication). Each competition seemingly lessened Voyager's role, although irony would prevail because the shuttle, by gutting NASA's budget, left the Voyagers and the sputtering Pioneers as America's sole explorers to the outer solar system. By contrast, a strategy of backlighting would simply tell the stories in sequence without undue commentary, and then during the *Challenger* debacle would look back and explain how the event was only the most publicly visible expression of a rivalry that had shaped the trajectory of the Voyager mission from its inception. The events of 1986 are the strongest, so it probably makes more sense to backlight rather than foreshadow. But either technique may be done deftly or clumsily, and the choice between them depends, as ever, on authorial taste, salted and sauced by thematic context and overall design.

The choice is similar to that between using the active or passive voice. In works of history, however, "did" is usually stronger than "would."

chapter 9

Transitioning

In which we segue into a discussion about how to make transitions—getting from one passage to another while keeping stride, along with a cautious hop, skip, and occasional jump

Just as every writer will have certain mannerisms (or tics), so every writer about writing has certain fancies that obsess him. The tendency is hardly unique to writing. Stock-market brokers, baseball scouts, dance critics, diet promoters—all reduce the complexity of their chosen spectacle to a few items that, for them, become an algorithm of understanding ("lock those wrists," "shun carbs"). Every one will point to some different feature that speaks with particular force. For one, this will be narrative; for another, argument, or audience, editing by elimination, designing, whatever. Know this, they will tell you, and you will master the game or fathom the critical tricks of the trade. The only constant is the evident need among everyone to identify one or two such items. My own fixations are several, but among them is the curious matter of making transitions.

Transition is not here a technical term extracted from literary lexicons. Rather, it is code for a number of stylistic issues, tiny and huge, that range from the sequencing of sentences to the grand architecture that determines where and how beams and pillars meet. It involves something more than plot, for it focuses on all the points in a text where something changes, where one part connects to another. A thesis extends through a further argument; one more character trait is added to a portrait; yet another event of plot unfolds. It may be abrupt or continuous, the leap minuscule or monstrous. But this is where the stress builds up and where the text will strain, bend, or break. Call those points transitions.

Transitioning occurs at all levels, in the movement from one sentence to another, one paragraph to another, one scene to another, one chapter or part to another. Good design can identify where these stresses will be felt, and, conversely, where an accumulating strain may force changes before a span deforms or breaks. A long passage may need internal pauses, the way sidewalks need expansion cracks. A complex plot may absorb the stress better through many small arches than through a single grand one in which much of the text must be sunk into scene-setting and background-informing pilings, taking away from the narrative arch itself. Standard handbooks on writing will rail about unnecessary adjectives and adverbs and about making nouns wrongly do the work of verbs; I am adding "transitions" to that rogues gallery.

The issue is not, however, simply to delete transitional words, phrases, and passages, but to design a text in which the transitions are neither too dense nor too sparse. This places the burden on design. The issue at all levels is how to link up the elements without either clotting the passage or collapsing the structure. That is, if connections are too fine or intricate, they can join passages but at the expense of flow. If connections are too coarse or elliptic, they may sacrifice any sense of coherence to a great leap. If they are too numerous, the narrative arch may sag or even sunder.

Critical fashion today favors the elliptic over the plodding. Many of the masters of literary nonfiction rely on light transitioning to keep their text from bogging down in the connective particles of the prose, like so much arterial plaque. When this is done well, the reader makes the transition; the proportion of information to text is high; the prose moves; the ideas connect. By contrast, many academics (particularly graduate student apprentices) pack each phrase and sentence with a connective padding of conjunctions and subordinate clauses that assures a logical sequencing but that demands exhaustive unpacking by the reader. This is the literary equivalent of micro-managing; and while there may be spots here and there that require authorial intervention, sometimes intense, they should be rare. As the adage goes, trust your story. Trust your reader.

There is nothing inherently wrong with a meticulously written text that moves steadily and completely through its paces in one sweeping narrative bound, marshaling all the parts into ranks and files, if the intention is to be consistent and comprehensive. There is nothing intrinsically right with a text that bounces from scene to scene, cherry-picking all the choice parts, zipping through what purports to be a full-bodied history as though it were a high-school reunion newsletter. Each style has its place, and most texts, being hybrids, will display bits of each. What matters is recognizing that transitions don't just happen. They are integral to designing; they occur at every level.

Consider samples that solve transitioning problems with grace and verve (okay, P. J. O'Rourke excepted). Beyond that, they are just good writing, worth reading on several counts (including O'Rourke).

Open with a passage from John McPhee, a master at compressing information by eliding transitions, as he sketches the domestic circumstances in which David Brower grew up.

> Brower's father taught mechanical drawing at the University of California. He was a small man (five seven), with a rock-ribbed face and stern habits. His first name was Ross. He never smoked. He did not drink, even coffee. One traumatic day, he came home with the news that he had lost his instructorship. Home was 2232 Haste Street, where the family had two frame houses, one behind the other, that had been partitioned into eleven apartments. For the rest of his life, Brower's father managed and janitored the apartments. Things became, in Brower's words, "pretty thin," and he remembers holes in his sweaters, holes in his shoes, and paper routes. His father's mother moved in to help with the apartments. She was a high-momentum Baptist who had seen to it that her grandson David was underwater when presented to God. She also saw to it that he always had plenty of housework to do. He washed clothes. She banned card games. She permitted the drinking of hot Jello.[1]

There is no chronology here, nor an overt conjunction between past and present, only interesting and (one hopes) vital information that helps to illuminate Brower's character. The connective links will emerge as Brower's personality emerges through his behavior in the later text.

Now consider a passage from Eric Rolls's essay on the environmental history of Australia, "More a New Planet Than a New Continent," in which he describes the propagation of rabbits. Each sentence belongs with the whole, but not in a necessary sequence. Avoiding transitional particles keeps the flow going, accents the ease and rapidity of the rabbit flood, and quietly emphasizes the cumulative disaster that resulted from the separate acts of many people, each generally pursuing some economic gain (the market in rabbit fur and, perversely, the bounty on rabbits, both of which gave incentives to keep rabbits on the land).

> In the 1880s and 1890s rabbits spread, and were spread over the whole of southern Australia. If a trapper caught a pregnant doe, he let her go again. Overlanders walking out of South Australia across the Nullarbor carried billies full of furred kittens to be set down at a good waterhole. Crates of rabbits, fifteen to a crate, were consigned by rail to Queensland for release on the Darling Downs. In the next drought of the 1890s millions of rabbits in the Riverina swarmed and ran in search of water. They ate everything moist in their path, even Kurrajong trees up to 17 centimetres in diameter. In the north of South Australia they climbed trees like possums, ate the leaves and stripped the bark. In the Centre they turned Mulga scrub into barren plains and they have kept them barren ever since.[2]

Similarly, Rolls emphasizes the disruptions that followed by drawing a parallel roster of otherwise disjointed effects, with their only common factor being the plague of rabbits. "Pastures over huge areas degenerated to plants that rabbits would not eat. Sand and red dust lifted in storms that blacked out towns like Broken Hill for a couple of days at a

time. Mothers hung wet sheets over their babies' cots to fil-
ter the air and they shoveled dust out of their houses by the
bucketful." Men driving carts laid poisoned bait along 150
million kilometers of roads and tracks, such that "grain-
eaters and flesh-eaters died in thousands. The rabbit population thrived. The poison killed enough to keep the breeding stock healthy." This method of telling has far stronger
effects than an attempt to join every fact to every other fact
or to indulge in an authorial rant.[3]

Now note how Mike Davis catalogues striking details from
the 1993 fire at Malibu without allowing his passage to emulate the road-jam he describes on the coast highway. Fanned
by Santa Ana winds, "the summit of the Santa Monicas was a
funeral pyre."

> At dusk that day, Malibu was a surreal borderland be-
> tween carnival and catastrophe. On the pier nonchalant
> crowds played video games while television news heli-
> copters hovered overhead and the Coast Guard cutter
> *Conifer* stood offshore, ready to evacuate residents. Be-
> neath the flaming hills, the Pacific Coast Highway was
> paralyzed by a hopeless tangle of arriving fire trucks and
> fleeing Bentleys, Porsches, and Jeep Cherokees. Hun-
> dreds more trekked out on horseback, by bike, or on
> foot. A few escaped on roller blades. Three hundred
> sheriff's deputies were brought in to guard against loot-
> ing. The chaotic exodus was oddly equalizing: panicky
> movie stars, clutching their Oscars, mingled with frantic
> commoners. Confronted once again with its destiny as a
> fire coast, Malibu replied in the vernacular. "This is hell,
> dude," one resident told the *Los Angeles Times*. "I'm ex-
> pecting to see Satan come out any time now."[4]

Sending those observations in quick succession to jostle against each other in semi-pandemonium on the page mimics the effect of the traffic jam nicely. Outfitting each with transitions and conjunctions would not.

Transitioning has its extremes of too much and too little. Once again, leanest is not always best. There are times when ideas, phrases, and attributes do not automatically self-adhere like laundry with static cling, when a line of reasoning requires some connective links, when unexpected associations or leaps of logic beg for handholds, and (shudder) when rhythm and pleasure, which can also contribute to sense, seem to cry out for it. As with any literary technique, transitioning can suffer the vice of its virtue. Removing too much can erase sense, or become the essence of satire. One thing comes after another without linking up in any logical or empirically necessary way.

So, conclude with this passage from P. J. O'Rourke, which follows from the observation that "the U.S. government has been a terrible steward of the environment."

> While the rest of America was hugging trees, the U.S. Forest Service was selling them at throwaway prices and allowing clear cutting in places where ecological damage would be extreme and reforestation almost impossible.
>
> The Bureau of Reclamation was damming rivers, turning scenic canyons into motorboat parking lots, and leaving salmon with no place to have sex. The electricity produced by these dams and the water collected behind them were sold at below-market prices, permitting cities to grow where cities shouldn't and allowing farmers to irrigate land they oughtn't. The land suffered salinization: The cities trembled, burned, and got covered in

mudslides. And disaster relief was paid with our tax dollars.[5]

The satirist's stock in trade is exaggeration, and O'Rourke's clipped construction serves that end. There is no effort to be logical or reasonable; the prose strips away the ties that bind, the normal context of understanding, and so reveals the absurdity or humor of the statement by itself. Okay for satire; not good for serious nonfiction, unless you want to slide into comedy or demagoguery.

These same considerations work on broader scales. Many particles (usually conjunctions such as "nonetheless," "yet," "although") are helpful, assuring the reader that what follows connects with what came before. Yet many can disappear without loss. The strength of the theme—the story, the argument, an illustration—can carry the reader along without clumsy prose prosthetics. (A bit of craft can also help. Try, for example, building a paragraph so that its last sentence, which seems like a conclusion, actually serves to introduce the paragraph to come.) A common technique is to signal a transition visually by leaving a spacebreak in the text (as I have done frequently in this book), so that paragraphs or sections resemble paving stones set slightly apart rather than laid edge to edge. This lets the text breathe. The reader takes the pause in stride and may enjoy the pocket of fresh air.

When a book is constructed of chapters, transitions are a design feature, part of what holds the entire text together. Our consideration here is to establish a house style and stay with it. This, too, is a kind of parallelism; when there is structural repetition, the reader not only mentally makes the transition from one chapter to another but links them.

The available techniques are many. Title your chapters in a similar way. Use epigraphs. Introduce legends, or authorial explanations. Begin each chapter with an anecdote, or a recapitulation of past events, or a new character. The point is, establish some formal order and stay with it. The reader will absorb and expect the pattern, as with shaped and colored highway signs, and will rely on it for guidance even if rushing through the text.

Which approach is best? You still need to ask?

chapter 10

Dramatizing

In which techniques transcend gimmickry by
conveying genuine human interest, which lies in the
portrayal of what William Faulkner called "the
human heart in conflict with itself"

Drama is what keeps readers turning pages. The slickest
transitioning, the wittiest voice, the most elegant phrasing
will not hold their attention for more than a few sentences.
What matters is their urge to know more, to see what comes
next, to understand how the narrative or argument works
out. If the text is not disposable—if it is not a curiosity or
a diversion intended to help pass the time or a reference
from which to extract data—it must engage readers in a
fundamental way. They must care what comes next. Why
did that happen? How? What's the point? So what? Getting
at this can take many forms.

It might mean informing. The prose tells readers something they don't know, or describes some practice or procedure or skill. We read on because we want to know how
things turn out—what the laboratory results add up to, how
the granite wall gets climbed, how the premise will be argued, how the bill got out of committee and onto the House
floor. It might mean entertaining; in this sense, the text tells
a story and we want to know how it ends. Or the drama is
genuinely moral and the action pivots around the kind of

conflict that demands hard choices. We read on because, in addition perhaps to informing and amusing us, the text strikes to the core of our curiosity about human nature, and does so not by bald declarations but through a plot in which characters must choose and act. We want to know not only what happens but how we should think about that outcome, because it speaks to our sense of who we are and how we should behave. It means showing, not stating. Moral drama can make a poor book passable and a good book great.

Not all dramatizing has a moral purpose, and not all moralizing has dramatic punch, and neither intrinsically demands a hard weld to the other. There are classic stories that, retold, add little to our moral sense. Often they recount familiar material in a fresh way, but we already know the outcome and neither writer nor reader has any wish to alter our fundamental understandings; the only desire is to savor the retelling. These are the nonfiction equivalent of fiction's genre literature, particularly the mystery novel. (Think Civil War battles, Robert Scott's polar expedition, biographies of historical celebrities, and so on.) There are also weighty meditations on moral issues conducted with high solemnity and almost no drama. They are not framed around human choice and conflict, not embedded in acts and decisions, but instead resemble the literary equivalent of a data table, a mathematical matrix, or a sermon. (See, for example, essays on criticism, exegetical discussions of rare texts, debates over historiography.) But where morals and drama slam together, the resulting fusion, as with atomic particles, can be explosive.

This is most easily achieved in narratives that revolve around quarrels or quests, narratives that put people in situations where they conflict, strive, and choose. (That these are also the favored elements of narrative fiction has tempted some observers to say that nonfiction should borrow from novelists as a means of getting more rhetorical leverage out of the material, though this is nonsense; nonfiction packs plenty of punch on its own.) Perennial favorites are military campaigns, exploring expeditions, blood rivalries (sports or politics, preferably). But any competition will do—within someone, between people, between people and the natural world. The narrative driver could be a crisis of conscience or of character, a riot or a political campaign, a great flood, an earthquake, or a fire. In all of these instances, the deep drama will lie not with the physical action of shaking houses and burning woods and overflowing rivers, however gripping and suspenseful such events may be, but with how the characters respond, the nature of the choices they make, what they say about the human condition. The conflict must be daunting, the circumstances serious, the characters' agency real if limited, the nature of the choices not just stated but shown; otherwise the outcome is melodrama, pedantry, or propaganda. This much, at least, great nonfiction does share with great fiction.

Fiction can invent the necessary parts, or (more often) adapt real-world incidents in ways that sharpen the circumstances, heighten the tension, and raise the stakes. Nonfiction must stick with its sources. But it is entirely acceptable—in fact, obligatory—to pluck out incidents from the vast welter of experiences and to present them in a way that remains true to the evidence yet allows the intrinsic drama to burst forth. Some selectivity has to occur, some shaping of the setting, some dramatic framing—this is where the artistry lies. It comes in recognizing where, amid the infinitude of events (Thomas Macaulay's "seamless web"), reside those moments and people that might convey some drama, and to present them without distorting their factual character.

Dramatic narrative is not the only form of drama, but narrative without what we are calling drama lacks the gravitas that takes a work beyond mere virtuosity and entertainment. That means not that every story must be about ultimate things, only that it matter, that the choices be real and the stakes serious, that the episode be something more than an intellectual puzzle or wordplay. Wallace Stegner once noted that "the postwar history of Berlin will not be properly written until it is narrated. A *good* book on Berlin may be a pastiche of communiqués, conferences, policies, ultimatums, and abstract forces. The *great* book on Berlin is going to be a sort of *Iliad,* a story that dramatizes a power struggle in terms of the men who waged it." That analysis, coming from the instincts of a novelist interested in history but imagining it in terms of characters, may over-accent the role of particular personalities as effective movers and shakers. But character, and choice, can be refracted through places and ideas and institutions, too, and bear the weight of the necessary drama.[1]

What matters is that it be somewhere. In discussing the core of fiction, John Gardner observed that "no fiction can have real interest if the central character is not an agent struggling for his or her own goals but a victim, subject to the will of others," and that the struggle must be "shown by action; the proof must appear in the plot." On this issue, fiction and nonfiction converge. Words holding data are not literature, and prose performing acrobatics is not drama. And into them might flow, as well, the sentiments of Jamesian philosophy. What makes a life significant? William James asked. Not, he thought, a Utopian "Sabbatical city,"

shorn of conflict. Rather, it is "the element that gives to ι.
wicked outer world all its moral style, expressiveness and
picturesqueness,—the element of precipitousness, so to call
it, of strength and strenuousness, intensity and danger." He
then nudges an essay on philosophy perilously close to melodrama: "What excites the interests of the looker-on at life,
what the romances and the statues celebrate and the grim
civic monuments remind us of, is the everlasting battle of
the powers of light with those of darkness; with heroism reduced to its bare chance, yet ever and anon snatching vic-
tory from the jaws of death." He concludes simply that what
"our human emotions" seem to require is "the sight of the
struggle going on." That could stand as a pragmatic definition of drama.[2]

Still, intention must translate into text. No less than with
voice or transitions, dramatizing is inseparable from designing, and, in the case of narrative, from plotting. Does the
text build out of many episodes, or does its movement in-
scribe one grand arc, the tension mounting, the stakes rising, until the climax passes? A book full of separate incidents and characters offers endless opportunities for
dramatizing—each scene allowing for some decision on the
part of its characters, and on the part of the author. Those
scenes may support a gridlike structure, or add, bit by bit, to
a load-bearing one.

Ideas, too, have their drama. Since people create them, the
simplest way to put them in conflict and force choice is to
identify them with their inventors or promoters. The theory
of evolution by natural selection can be distilled into "Darwin," and its hostile reception into formal debates, an intellectual trial-by-combat, as Louis Agassiz and Asa Gray, for
example, joust over the concept and its larger significance.

as might get refracted through institutions es-
promote a concept, perhaps one that appears
) one era and destructive to another (e.g., the
clamation and its determination to build high
dams). Or the idea might be given tangible form as a city
plan, a railway route, a felled forest, an atomic bomb, a
Schlieffen scheme for the invasion of Belgium. In this way,
the clash of ideas assumes material form and yields substantive outcomes. When big ideas represent big personalities
and confront major events, the shock can be powerful, and
rich in literary possibilities.

A quick example: in *Rising Tide,* John Barry matches the
ambitions of people against the dynamics of the Mississippi
River. Two engineers with outsized egos propose alternative
strategies for preventing catastrophic floods, ideas that then
get distorted into something neither approves.

> Although for very different reasons, Eads and Hum-
> phreys had both rejected the theory that levees alone
> caused a significant deepening of the channel. It was the
> only thing they had agreed upon. Yet, beginning a few
> years after both had left the scene, Mississippi River
> Commission engineers began to meld Humphreys' ar-
> guments for levees with Eads' arguments about the ef-
> fect of current. The result was a bastardization of both
> their arguments, and a theory that both Eads and Hum-
> phreys had not only rejected but condemned.[3]

Yet politics, local pressures, and constitutional quirks
about how the federal government might contribute all
forced the commission into a levees-only policy. Then, in
1927, the Mississippi rose, and the quarrel was no longer
between James Eads and A. A. Humphreys, or the Corps of

Engineers and the Mississippi River Commission, but between them and the river. The river forced them to choose
and to act; it broke ideas as fully as it broke levees; and it was
not susceptible to the kind of influence and character flaws
that human opponents might exploit in contests among
themselves. The river's current could scour out a levee's
base, while high winds and the waves washing out from passing barges could assault its top.

> But the biggest danger is simply pressure, constant unre-
> lenting pressure. Water, in seeking its own level, does
> not simply run over the top of a container; it presses
> against the side. A rising Mississippi presses against a le-
> vee with immense and increasing weight. The longer the
> river lies against the levee, the more saturated and
> weaker the levee becomes, and the more likely part of it
> will slough off. Such a slide increases the chance that
> the tremendous weight of the river can push it aside.
> Sand boils also result from pressure; the weight of the
> river pushes water underneath the levee. This water then
> erupts like a miniature volcano behind the levee, some-
> times 200 yards behind it. When a sand boil shoots up
> clear water, it is not dangerous. But when the water is
> muddy, the boil is eroding the core of the levee.[4]

People could cope with these hazards, at least in principle, and in practice if not too many happened at once. But
"since the river was relentless, men had to be relentless."
Here lies the value of using a natural agent to force decision: "Since nature missed nothing, made no mistakes, and
was perfect, men had to miss nothing, make no mistakes,
and be perfect." As of course we are not. Humans made
themselves known by their levees. The river made itself

known by its sheer weight: the implacable pressure of its waters. During the 1927 flood, some levees ruptured and some were deliberately destroyed in order to spare New Orleans at the expense of less populated parishes. What began as a conflict between ideas segued into a contest between people and nature and ended with people contending with one another directly.[5]

Just as a talent with words lies behind writing prose, so judgment lies behind moral dramatizing. Writing ceases to be strictly a matter of craft and becomes one of art in which the character of the writer, not simply of the individuals in the text, is critical. The moral universe of the writer matters. Slick prose in the service of bad morals—this is propaganda, nonfiction's equivalent of pornography. Being able to say something well doesn't mean you have something worth saying.

Much as fiction must ultimately be rooted in the character of the author, so it is with nonfiction, serious or otherwise. That is what moves writing beyond mere rhetoric. If moral vision is feeble, uncertain, or just immature, the text will probably be informed by intellectual consensus but will be the ethical equivalent of a cliché, and it is likely that the prose will be riddled with actual clichés as well, since it is hard to express a fresh vision with hackneyed language but easy to convey conventional values with well-worn phrases and garden-variety mores. The greatest writing reaches beyond: it bears a powerful moral sense animated by vigorous prose, both original. To the "So what?" question, it replies, "This is what, and why, and you will be fascinated to see it play out."

At the page's end, a text can still be no greater than its author. The most graphic scene will falter unless voice and vision convey it convincingly. A rant isn't an essay; anger isn't angst; angst isn't art. Yet while outrage and conviction can animate a text, can infuse passion into its prose, the morality they bring to life may be repugnant, a well-wrought obscenity. This is why technique cannot substitute for genuine vision, or posturing for voice, or data for understanding: a convincing text will require judgment that normally comes from maturity and from life, not libraries. So if nonfiction need yield nothing to fiction in terms of its ability to invoke a moral universe, it can claim nothing special in its capacity to transcend its creator. Nature unaided doesn't tell us who we are or how we should be behave, nor does history. That is the work of thought giving expression to experience.

chapter 11
Editing I

In which the question of how to get something down
evolves into how to get it right, which means not only
getting it down over and over but making each
revision better, which is a skill different from first-
contact writing

Good writing is made by rewriting, which is to say, by editing, which I understand to mean helping a writer say better
what he or she is trying to say. The only standard here is
meaning. The ideal editing improves the overall meaning
of the text by clarifying, making vivid, unencumbering, or
otherwise allowing the reader to comprehend the text. The
ideal editor is the writer.

Editing operates on all levels, from flaccid sentence to
wobbly passage to ill-conceived architecture whose design
features clash or fail to support the weight of written ideas.
Most books on editing and style—and there are many good
ones—harp on the sentence or maybe the paragraph because they believe these are the trenches where the battle is
fought and because sample passages are small enough that
they can be analyzed. That is not possible with larger pieces
such as chapters, much less with books.

What is the relation between sentence and structure?
Separate sentences don't add up by themselves to a larger
design any more than a pile of individual, if beautifully
crafted, bricks makes a building. It is not the sentence itself

that matters but the right mix of sentences and how they contribute to meaning overall. Too-tight sentences over a long text can be tedious and may numb a reader into insensibility. Too-fluid prose can leave a reader to wander and finally snap the text shut in frustration. What matters is getting the right sentence for the particular moment. Each sentence looks right because it fits the larger design, and it sounds right because it emerges from a convincing voice, not from the prescriptions of good-writing catechisms.

A text can surprise: it might push in directions that were unimagined when the project began. New ideas will arise; design features will suggest themselves; some sources may resist the thrust imposed by the plot, and others may wrench it onto a different path, conditions that become fully apparent only after the relevant passages are written. Most handbooks slaver over where and how to cut—the assumption being that draft prose is always overblown and that the only trimmer suitable for academic prose is a guillotine. While some writers seem to "write in final," fretting over every word and self-editing painfully through a complete text, most writers struggle, soar, and fumble their way through their thesis by actually writing, all of which leaves both heaps of excess or extraneous prose and of gaps where ideas popped up but could not flourish. (Gush writing is not a bad strategy for keeping the words flowing, for avoiding writer's block. It works, however, only if the writer is a disciplined self-editor.)

Pruning—trimming, snipping, shaping—is what most guides to editing promote and illustrate. The assumption, almost an axiom, is that there is plenty to shear off. It might be possible to substitute one word or phrase for another, but the gist is to cut. Snip out adjectives. Clip away adverbs.

Hack out ungainly clauses. Replace passive verbs with active ones, which also shrinks the word count. Shorter is better. Less is more. The implicit assumption in today's climate is that any word that can be scratched out should be. This, however, is a matter of fashion. Most guides to editing come from journalists who must operate under strict word counts and deadlines; this aesthetic does not translate directly to books, for meaning depends on more than length. Scaling from an article to a book involves more than piling up more of the same kind of sentences. Often a good solution requires adding a passage, or swapping out some parts for others. Sometimes the only sensible response is to reconfigure the overall design. (A different arrangement would allow a tighter packing ratio, as it were.) Regardless, you can compress only so much. At some point less becomes meaning-less.

Good editing requires knowing where to graft as well as where to prune. New data are uncovered, a character or incident clamors for more attention than the original conception allowed for, the leaf-supporting limbs are simply too feeble to sustain the planted trunk. Words must be added, sentences inserted, whole paragraphs or passages introduced. This, too, may require reconfiguring, and if the design's tightness index is high, changes in one part of the text may require changes in another. Since it is easier to destroy than to create, guidebooks tend to emphasize removing rather than adding. But in the end all editing must be judged by the criterion of meaning, which derives from the larger project. What to leave in and what to take out depend on a context greater than the sentence.

The hardest situation is that in which the flaws lie in voice and vision. The overall design doesn't quite work. The tone is wrong, or the informing principle can't span the range of sources, or the structure can't be translated into a working outline and real-world prose. At some point, well before the conclusion, and hopefully shortly after you begin, you realize that the gears don't synchronize. The text doesn't look right. It doesn't sound right. It doesn't quite make sense.

If you're near the beginning, the wisest solution is to start over. If you're farther along, some retrofitting may be possible in the form of a few braces and buttresses to keep the edifice from collapsing. But this can be cumbersome and disheartening, and the outcome may be obvious, ungainly, and distracting. A retrofit is never as good as a properly done original. The only way to avoid such a disaster is to get voice and vision right at the outset; and if you are uncertain, to experiment with sample pieces before committing to the project. If you sense a problem along the way, it's best to stop before that clicking sound leads to a blown rod or the U-joint falls off. The longer the problem goes on, the harder it is to fix.

It is doubtful that anyone knows, when starting, exactly where a text will end up. A few manuscripts seem to run unerringly from beginning to end without doubt or deviation. The vision is sharp, the voice steady, and passion and discipline are ample to keep the prose both moving and on the straight-and-narrow. Minor problems are no more than annoying potholes and speed bumps: the destination is fixed and the map clear. Editing involves wiping, polishing, straightening. Such projects do happen. That directness may be more apparent than real, however. It may indicate hackwork or formulaic writing, for example. And when original, it may reflect years of self-conscious writing during which the author has internalized sound principles of editing and semi-automatically corrects as the text unfolds.

But whether it happens during the writing or afterward, that surefootedness is generally the result of good trailwork, which is to say, unseen editing.

A period of fumbling and errantry is common. Expect it. Introductions are notoriously hard to get right, because they only set up the larger theme. Better to skip them—save that writing for the end of the project—and plunge into the central text. This will help firm up voice and vision. If difficulties persist, consult an editor for advice. Or if you are daring, complete the work and have it reviewed by a publisher and its outside readers.

Such advice seems a bromide. Of course you would do all this. But finding someone to advise in helpful ways can be tricky. Editing is a skill in its own right: it is not simply writing rewarmed and served up like leftovers. It is not the same as blank-page writing any more than coaching baseball is the same as playing it. Few great players make great coaches; few artists, good teachers; few writers, truly good editors. Not only the skill-set but the psychology is different. Worse, editing is a prickly business because few writers are as professional and distant from their material as they would like to believe, especially when a manuscript is a project that has consumed several years and commandeered a significant fraction of mind, soul, and wallet. The instinct is to turn to one's friends—what are friends for, after all? But having close friends read a manuscript is like lending them money.

In my experience, few writers want what they say. "Look it over," they will urge. "Just tell me if it works. Let me know what needs fixing." What they mean is: "I know it's brilliant. Tell me that it'll knock the socks off critics, gather awards like mussels, bring fame and even fortune. Yes, I know it needs work here and there. I don't have all the parts just right—that's what I want help with. But the conception is wonderful, the prose delightful, the energy quotient of its content astonishing. And you're going to tell me that."

Then you explain that, well, it doesn't seem quite that way. In fact, it needs a heavy overhaul. It just isn't that interesting, or that convincing, and the prose, while serviceable, doesn't sizzle; the voice slips and cracks here and there; the vision is hazy, at times more mirage than organizing conceit. The subject, and the style adapted to express it, seem out of sorts. Of course you can't say that directly—can't say what the writer asks you to say. You hedge. "That's how the text strikes *me;* but then this isn't really my field," or "This isn't the sort of book I normally deal with." Or you fudge and say it looks great, but maybe the writer ought to try for a second opinion, someone better suited. How do you say you just don't like it? Watch your friendship cool like old soup. You'll never see your money again.

If you are writing a master's thesis or a doctoral dissertation, your committee will serve as an editorial board. Don't expect too much. Some members will be distracted by their own affairs. Others will fuss over every word and concept. Most will have a menu of comments that they apply categorically to every thesis: simplify, clarify, reorganize. Being the product of a committee, the comments will begin to chase one another's tails. Each revision will satisfy one member but upset another. By the time the manuscript (or proposal) has made the rounds, it will probably look a lot like it did at the start. Paradoxically, the inattentive members may do less damage than the overly attentive. The only member who really knows what you want is yourself. The sooner you can begin to self-edit, the better.

An anonymous version is the "outside reader" solicited by

a publisher for comments. Generally advice is worth what you pay for it, and most reviewers work pro bono or for barter (a selection of books from the publisher's list), and everyone can conjure up horror stories of irrelevant, frivolous, or hostile reports; yet some reviews are excellent. Overall, the system can betray all the virtues and failings of the thesis committee system, save that most outside readers are even more distracted and inclined to review hastily according to individual catechisms of good and bad prose and whether the article or manuscript in question grants their own work the deference (they believe) it deserves. Peer review has its value, but I have come to doubt that the virtues of manuscript review exceed its vices; most comments, in my experience, tend to be ritualistic and unhelpful. (I confess, gladly, that the reviewers of this manuscript were exceptions to these sour observations.) Still, there may be good value even in lackadaisical observations, for if slovenly readers harp on the same issues, there is likely something amiss in the manuscript. The hope is that the text gets boosted along to credible editors who can do the work required.

Here—with professional editors at journals and publishing houses—is where the hard labor gets done. The advantage of such editors is that they have no particular commitment to the writer or knowledge of the topic: they can speak plainly from the perspective of an intelligent reader. A poor editor will not be able to resist the urge to remake the manuscript over in his or her own preferred style (it's always easier to tell someone else how to write than to do it yourself). They forget that the best editing serves to help the writer say what he or she wants to say, not what the editor wants said. But overall, a good editor is your best friend. (Better to make an editor your friend than a friend your editor.) The physician who treats himself has a fool for a patient. The writer who allows only himself to judge his text has a fool for an editor.

Good editors may not empathize with all of your intentions, or accept your literary innovations, but they can give you a frank assessment, and if they don't understand passages and give wrong reasons, they may still be right. The passage doesn't work—their intuition says so, even if they may not have reasons you credit or propose fixes you can stomach. Accept that something is wrong. The only one who can truly firm up that spongy prose and tighten that flimsy argument is yourself. A good editor alerts you that something is off kilter. That's enough. Better to be criticized by your associates than by your enemies.

The final edit belongs with you as author. Ultimately you are the only one who knows what you want and can say which changes help or hinder that ambition. My own calculus reckons that 90–95 percent of criticisms have some basis and are worth understanding, and a good editor is almost always right. Yet I resist. There are just some passages I want as written. *Stet.* I dig in my heels; we argue; the passage remains; and typically I later regret it, like those witty comments penned into high-school yearbooks that seem so clever at the time and so jejune later. Still, that call, the final judgment, belongs with you. Writing is choosing. You as writer choose.

But the sooner you learn to self-edit—the sooner you can see your prose as others see it—the better it is for everyone. This time it's the Golden Rule reversed: we should treat ourselves as we would treat others. This requires a distancing from the material. It requires seeing the words, not the anguish and sweat behind them. The best way to get that distance is to put the manuscript aside for a while and then return to it. Or pick it up in an unfamiliar place, a tent or a motel room, where the usual cues are missing. Otherwise, we tend to read and reread without really seeing the text as a first-time reader would. We read compulsively and obsessively but not with freshness, like glaring at a crossword puzzle that has us stumped and obsessively recycling the same failed entries. We aren't looking, really looking, for glitches or malapropisms. The words don't really bite; we gloss over the awkward transitions, knowing what is to follow; we can't imagine, and don't wish to imagine, another design. We're not editing, but ritually rereading, the literary equivalent of spinning our prayer wheels. Faith-based editing.

Put the manuscript aside. When you return to it, your problem may well be reversed. The text will rarely resemble the glowing document of your memory. You'll likely be shocked at how raw and misshapen it is, and maybe discouraged as the full clumsiness of your narrative and the awkwardness of your expression stare at you, the muck so deep that you're sure you can never extract your text from it and set out on the road again. But this is precisely the time to edit. Eventually, with practice, you may reach the point where you can see your work more or less as it would seem to someone else. All too often, however, the writer is the last to know.

If that happens, it is most likely because you failed to know at the start what voice and vision meant for the project at hand. Vision didn't crystallize out of a mist of wistfulness into genuine design. Voice never advanced beyond your mumbling to yourself. No philosopher's stone exists that can edit textual mush into lapidary prose, or that can bring timbre and tone to an inchoate voice. Most likely, it's not that you didn't know your project clearly; it's that you didn't know yourself—couldn't impose or elicit an authorial presence, which is why great nonfiction requires a degree of maturity. Only when the writer reconciles self and text can the undertaking achieve aesthetic closure, such that the text seems to be written in the only way possible by the only one capable of doing it. In that fusion lies the meaning of art.

Part II
Crafts

chapter 12
Prose

In which we attempt to sort out literary sheep from goats, matters of style from matters of taste, and rules of good prose from riffs against bad

Almost all writing guides begin with, or have near their opening, a register of good and bad prose. These correspond to the stretching exercises people do before advancing to strenuous calisthenics or pumping serious iron. Like genres, the guidelines represent hard-won wisdom and are best tweaked rather than discarded. They serve, also, as a testimonial to the guide-writer's membership in the legion of proper instructors, as a kind of pledge of allegiance to the writers' guild, and as a portal to the writer's particular aesthetic fetishes. There are precepts that are common to all such prose reviews: you could probably find more people willing to defend pedophiles than the passive voice, academic or jargon-clogged phrases are ritually humiliated, and clichés themselves elicit an almost clichéd denunciations. Beyond these ritual obeisances, the guides expound on matters that belong with literary fashion and personal preferences.

Still, the exercise appears to be required, and at least serves to clarify the special quirks of taste and judgment of the handbook's author. Most are aiming at a niche market.

What follows amounts to a handful of contrarian pennies tossed into this very deep well. A few topics, such as the use of figurative language, will be withheld for later. But the real counsel is nothing more than the golden mean: avoid prose fundamentalists. The only good advice is to say what you want and make sure that how you say it supports what you say. The rest is gingerbread and gossip.

Active and Passive Voice

Even Strunk and White's venerable book *The Elements of Style,* upon close reading, argues only a preference for the active voice as "usually more direct and vigorous" than the passive voice, but admits that the passive is "frequently convenient and sometimes necessary." What matters is the subject of the sentence, and what the subject either does or has done to it. The former leads to an active voice; the latter, to a passive.

Examples of an abused passive voice that misdirects the action or slows the pace are legion, a staple of composition textbooks. The serious charge is that the passive voice is used to disguise agency, and hence culpability ("mistakes were made," "actions were taken"). Almost never are examples given of a misused active voice or of the passive used in ways that identify responsibility. So in the spirit of curmudgeonly stylists, consider the following two sentences which say the same thing, one in the active voice and one in the passive.

> Layer by layer, rivals peeled away the Australian strategy of bushfire protection.

> Layer by layer, the Australian strategy of bushfire protection was peeled away.

Which is better? Neither, intrinsically. The first emphasizes the rivals, those active agents stripping away like sharks
at a vulnerable carcass. The second puts its emphasis on the
Australian strategy itself, a noble victim suffering through
bureaucratic ignominy. My preference in this instance lies
with the passive, followed by a litany of the predators that,
in a full-throated active voice, have come to strip it, since
the Australian strategy is the theme and its fate the larger
setting. Note that the passive-voiced topic sentence is followed by a string of active-voiced ones.

> Layer by layer, the Australian strategy of bushfire protec-
> tion was peeled away. National parks stripped away its
> lands and political base in state forest bureaus; emer-
> gency services absorbed rural fire protection; the Bush-
> fire Cooperative Research Centre usurped its role as an
> oracle of science; public corporations assumed control
> over the commercial woodlands on Crown land that had
> helped to underwrite its costs.

Or consider a reversed situation in which an agent, in the
active voice, sets events in motion, and the consequences
follow in the passive.

> On April 18, 1906, an 8.9 earthquake shook San Fran-
> cisco to its foundations, and indirectly kindled scores of
> fires. By the time the tremors and flames ceased, the
> bulk of the city was ruined. Much of its landscape, in-
> cluding some signature structures like the Ferry Build-
> ing, was leveled or gutted. Its water supplies were dis-
> rupted. Its economy was upended like an apple cart. A
> large fraction of its citizenry were driven into tents. Its
> democratic government was effectively seized by a cabal
> of plutocrats and military officers from the Presidio. The

city was not merely physically savaged but demoralized. Observers questioned only whether quake or fire had wreaked the greater havoc.

That string of passives is the kind of passage that can cause apoplexy in prose fundamentalists. Yet note the effect: the city has been hit, has had things done to it, and cannot respond. An active voice frames the paragraph, as the earthquake initiates and observers comment, but in between the city has been shaken to its roots.

Simplicity of Expression

There is a puritanical belief that simplicity, meaning the fewest and briefest words with the least flourish, equals truthfulness. The plain expression, unadorned, is always best. This, however, is an aesthetic judgment, although one granted a powerful boost by George Orwell's 1946 essay "Politics and the English Language," in which, following a long lineage of English puritans, he savaged a collection of wretchedly wrought prose, badly written because its theme is either poorly understood or deliberately obscured. In each of his instances, bad writing displays or disguises bad thinking, which is to say, faulty morals and flawed politics. This malady is manifested so routinely that we hardly recognize it from background blather (and is usually dismissed as "just a lot of b.s.").

The difficulty is that the proposition gets reversed to read: clear or plain writing must be inherently true. Not so. It means only that an author is able to say exactly what he or she intends. The bald statement, unadorned, bold, unencrusted with qualifiers, is also the essence of the Big Lie. Simplicity can be a rhetorical trick as devious as multilayered cant. Some material is complex by nature; some novel ideas are difficult to identify clearly at first light; some understanding requires metaphors rather than syllogisms. Simplicity of diction or structure does not equal clarity.

If the point of writing is to convey meaning, we would do well to remember that the mind often works figuratively and delights in occasional alliteration and rhyme, and tends to recall wordplay and striking phrases; and that what appears to the prose puritan as decoration may in fact assist understanding. A string of declarative sentences, with subject instantly linked to a vigorous verb, may make for good composition when standing by itself but may be so much telegraphic chatter when used serially or exclusively. Some devices work more often than others; some have a better shelf life; some accrue fewer traffic citations. In the end, the only pertinent criteria are the writer's good sense and the reader's understanding. In proposing his own prescriptions, Orwell concludes with the caveat: "Break any of these rules sooner than say anything outright barbarous."[1]

The following passage from George Dangerfield's book *The Era of Good Feelings* exploits a so-called periodic construction (in which clauses and cadences are echoed for balance, emphasis, and cumulative effect), a style once favored but now shunned. Here he uses it to sum up that mix of the special and the common that typified American diplomacy during negotiations toward the Treaty of Ghent:

> The humors were certainly distinct; they were also distinctively American. In their vitality and their suppleness, in the competitive methods by which they reached their decisions, in the optimism which was rarely banished even from their darkest hours, in their irritability and their sharpness and their intransigence, in the unity

of their determination and the disunity of their interests—they seemed to body forth, in some fragmentary
but effective way, at once the present and the future of
the young republic.[2]

Perfectly understandable, and a sentence that demonstrates
its argument in its very structure. Neoclassical rhetoric
seems, moreover, to emulate the late Augustan age in which
the diplomats had grown up.

Or consider this periodic summary from William Goetzmann as he describes the eighteenth-century travels of John
Bannister, "set down in the wilds of Virginia" yet joined to
an evolving global community, "the naturalist's network."

Thanks to the work of Continental scholars like Boer-
haave, Gronovius, de Jussieu, Buffon, Ray, Lister, and ultimately Linnaeus; thanks to the interest of institutions
like the Royal Society, the French Académie, and even
the Temple House Coffee Club (which by 1691 num-
bered some forty-one enthusiastic naturalists); thanks to
gardeners like Peter Miller and Capability Brown; thanks
to the enthusiasm of men like Sir Hans Sloan and Bishop
Henry Compton, whose gardens and collections were
the envy of Europe; and thanks most of all, perhaps, to
the new urge for scientific discovery around the globe,
the study of natural history began to develop dramati-
cally in tandem with the study of the cosmos in the late
seventeenth century. North America shared in this development as a great natural laboratory and hunting
ground for naturalists, who never failed to find something new and wonderful to add to the Great Chain of
Being.[3]

It's as though the Great Chain of Naturalists were being forged before our eyes.

Parallelism

Parallelisms are a venerable way to order unruly material. As we have seen, they can compress data, but they can also allow for systematic contrasts. The former matters because without some rhetorical organization, a manuscript may disaggregate like a dirt clod when squeezed. The latter matters because we don't know things in themselves—we know them in relation to other things; and parallelism of some variety is a dandy means to mass those comparative others together.

Today's tastes prefer the light to the tight. A nimble rhetorical touch that seems to fade into the background appeals to modern readers more than a highly wrought construction that packs its words tightly in its coils. The problem with emulating a Ciceronian style is that you may end up sounding like, well, Cicero. Still, it has its time and place. Take this testimony to the condensing power of Wallace Stegner's rhetoric, as he distills the early life of Major John Wesley Powell, who arose out of the frontier Midwest to become the fabled explorer of the Grand Canyon and, later, director of several national scientific bureaus, including the U.S. Geological Survey.

> It is worth looking for a moment at how he was made.
>
> It is easy enough to summarize: he was made by wandering, by hard labor, by the Bible, by an outdoor life in small towns and on farms, by the optimism and practicality and democracy of the frontier, by the occasional

man of learning and the occasional books he met, by
country schools and the ill-equipped cubs or worn-out
misfits who taught them, by the academies and colleges
with their lamentable lacks and their industry and their
hope, by the Methodism of his father and the prevailing conviction that success came from work and only
to the deserving. If there were not many opportunities,
if the cultural darkness was considerable, it was also true
that in that darkness any little star showed as plainly as
a sun.[4]

In this instance the roster of contributing causes briskly
follows the topic sentence ("easy enough to summarize"),
one prepositional clause after another ("by . . ."), like varie-
gated beads on a string. The concluding sentence reverses
the structure by using two parallel "if" clauses to lead to a fi-
nale. All together, a display of controlled rhetoric that com-
presses an astonishing amount of information in a way that
might otherwise require several pages of sluggish prose.

The powers of parallelism can go beyond description to
versions of narrative, as a means of compressing and highlighting otherwise complicated materials. Consider this passage from Felipe Fernández-Armesto's *Pathfinders* about the
many-flawed Bering expedition to Alaska.

He knew it was a mistake to sail for home so late in the
season, but there was nothing else he could do. He knew
it was risky to return by an unexplored route, but he let
his officers overrule him. He knew it would be fatal to
anchor off Bering Island—but, racked by sickness, he
was powerless to countermand his subordinates, submit-
ting to the madness of "minds as loose from the storm
as teeth from scurvy." He shared Cassandra's tragedy—

that of prophets proved right because their prophecies are disregarded. He followed "the shortest route but the longest manner, by bumping into islands," according to Georg Steller, the expedition's resident botanist, the smock-frocked scientist whose modesty is a counterfoil to Bering's ambition. The relations of commander and scientist were satisfyingly consistent with the canons of drama. When Steller presented a strategy based on local knowledge in the vicinity of the straits, Bering dismissed his views, muttering, "Who believes Cossacks?" The ill-matched pair were condemned to share a cabin, where Steller felt he "took up too much space" and forever feared the fate of the scientific specimens Bering contemptuously threw overboard for want of room.[5]

The repetitious contrasts at the beginning reinforce the sense of Bering's fatal vacillation, while the contrast between Bering and Steller suggests that alternatives did in fact exist; and because the two men are literally in the same space, the conflict of choices becomes inescapable. The dual parallel portraits ensnare Bering like the jaws of a bear trap.

Now, from the same work, ponder the value of parallelism for analysis, as Fernández-Armesto elaborates on the Pacific as "an arena of unbridled competition between Britain, France, Spain, and Russia."

The conclusion of the Seven Years' War in 1763 meant that all the European nations with interests in the region found those interests redoubled, while peace diverted to exploration ships and men formerly fully occupied in war. For Spain the Pacific was a dangerous frontier—the soft underbelly of an immense empire. For Britain it was

)f commercial opportunity. For the French,
rew from most of America at the end of the
rs' War, it represented the prospect of a new
npire building. For Russia, imprisoned in the
in immense country, virtually landlocked, ob-
structed by ice, and penned in and pinched by narrow
straits, the Pacific represented a unique route to sea-
borne expansion.[6]

The competitive Pacific becomes visible through contrasts,
and parallelism allows those contrasts to be made in a spry
way. They serve as ballast, helping the general narrative to
ride smoothly rather than bounce about or find the decks
awash with whitecaps of information.

And now to a recognized master, Francis Parkman, who
employs such rhetoric less as a tool of distillation than as
a miniaturization of understanding. In this passage from
Montcalm and Wolfe, he surveys the old regime with magisterial cadences that seem to evoke the majesty and concentrated energies that the French Revolution will soon un-
leash:

> The prestige of the monarchy was declining with the
> ideas that had given it life and strength. A growing disre-
> spect for king, ministry, and clergy was beginning to pre-
> pare the catastrophe that was still some forty years in
> the future. While the valleys and low places of the king-
> dom were dark with misery and squalor, its heights were
> bright with a gay society,—elegant, fastidious, witty,—
> craving the pleasures of the mind as well as of the senses,
> criticizing everything, analyzing everything, believing
> nothing. Voltaire was in the midst of it, hating, with all
> his vehement soul, the abuses that swarmed about him,
> and assailing them with the inexhaustible shafts of his

restless and piercing intellect. Montesquieu was showing to a despot-ridden age the principles of political freedom. Diderot and D'Alembert were beginning their revolutionary Encyclopaedia. Rousseau was sounding the first notes of his mad eloquence,—the wild revolt of a passionate and diseased genius against a world of falsities and wrongs. The *salons* of Paris, cloyed with other pleasures, alive to all that was racy and new, welcomed the pungent doctrines, and played with them as children play with fire, thinking no danger; as time went on, even embraced them in a genuine spirit of hope and goodwill for humanity. The Revolution began at the top,—in the world of fashion, birth, and intellect,—and propagated itself downwards. "We walked on a carpet of flowers," Count Ségur afterwards said, "unconscious that it covered an abyss," till the gulf yawned at last, and swallowed them.[7]

The contrast between elite and peasant, the roll call of protest from the top, the concluding image in which the heights collapse into an abyss—the structure of the paragraph embodies the action it describes; this is idea made flesh in words. That modern interpretations of the Revolution have changed is not the point: Parkman found a near-perfect way to convey his understanding. Modern critics might benefit from arguing less over his ideas than contemplating the means by which he expressed them, for any counter-argument they might make must not only challenge his evidence with more recent sources but must match his rhetoric in a more modern style.

All to the good, but consider the effect if every passage had a comparable degree of rhetorical compression. Francis Parkman and Edward Gibbon might be able to pull it off; most writers could not, and few modern readers would welcome such a nominal success. Parallelism, too, needs its pauses.

Varied Cadence

This is the flip side of parallelism. The power to compress comes at the cost of forcing everything into a few molds, where strings of declaratives march like ducklings behind a topic sentence. Even varying the parallelism—here with a train of clauses, there with a periodic eddy—is not enough. You have to break the mold, once and again. Insert an imperative. Use a sentence fragment. Change the rhythm of words or your diction, slipping in a colloquial expression now and then to roughen a somnolent flow, or letting a sentence run on occasionally, or hitching short sentences into a single, longer train.

Endless jazzing can be annoying and distracting. Commonplace rhetoric, if properly chosen, can do real work. But readers savor spice even as they feed on carbohydrates, at all levels of composition. So if you find yourself in rhetorical ruts, if your sentences march mechanically onward like toy soldiers, if your preferred constructions become your only constructions, if your paragraphs look like cords of neatly sawed firewood, then consider a change of pace.

You might even let a single sentence stand as a paragraph now and again.

On the Value of Clichés and Jargon. Selectively Used.
A Little. Maybe.

That's right: even clichés have their place, like flies and dung beetles, in the ecology of language. Without clichés, speech would drop in its tracks. If every sentence came loaded with novel expressions, the prose would tip over like a canoe piled with trophy souvenirs and would soon become unreadable. Who could read a narrative text comprising four hundred pages of haiku? The relentlessly inventive, the tirelessly active, a figurative phrasing followed by more figurative phrasing, a prose precipitated into crystals—such text becomes jumpy and jittery, unable to flow, and the novelty exhausts rather than inspires. Give the reader a pause. Connect passages with common understanding. Play with the familiar. Use a cliché now and then.

The point is, as with any literary convention, that clichés can help or harm. There are words fatigued into meaninglessness ("challenges," "sustainability"); phrases beaten to a witless pulp ("interdisciplinary"); jargon sprinkled over sentences like an oversalted carrot; politically correct pap inserted into text as a badge of membership, like the proverbial old school tie ("diversity," "contested"); bureaucratic babble that drips annoyingly in the text like a leaky faucet in the next room. The bad uses seemingly smother any prospect for good use. All this is familiar fare in composition manuals and deserves the scorn it receives.

But consider, in the opening paragraph above, the value of: "Without clichés, speech would drop in its tracks." The sentence is not essential; it could be deleted, and those figurative phrases and a string of virulent verbs could proceed unhindered. Yet by restating the thesis with a common expression—a cliché, though not a repugnant one—the reader has a chance to pause, to confirm the meaning of the argument, to ready himself for more. And it is even possible to use clichés creatively. One could, for example, reinforce the sense that a subject is so commonplace that it deserves no better than a cliché. Not conventional wisdom, I grant you, but edicts about proper writing can become clichés themselves, and writing guides are a dime a dozen.

Diction: The Mundane, the Exalted, the Fatuous

Diction—word choice, the particular vocabulary used—is also a part of design. Colloquial language will grate against, even mock, a scholarly argument; so will exalted language in the service of the mundane. It's like putting a Tutor gable on a hogan, or painting a hunting lodge flamingo pink. The language is out of character with the subject.

Still, for everything there is a time and place. A small dose of the vernacular can work like double washers on a machine bolt, allowing the parts to rotate without locking up. Some narratives need to move, and if everything is overtightened, the text freezes up. A selective colloquialism, either in wording or in structure, can keep you from assuming too much self-importance.

In "Los Angeles Against the Mountains," for example, John McPhee analyzes the attempts of the city to hold itself against natural forces that raise mountains, drive conflagrations, and slough off hillsides in the form of debris flows. Yet people nonetheless choose to plant themselves in harm's way. McPhee dismisses them as "dingbats in the line of fire." The colloquialism completely deflates any pretense of larger purpose they might offer for their choice. The commonsense judgment is the right one.[8]

The reverse problem is more prevalent for academic writing: knowing when, and when not, to adopt elevated language. Again, there is a case for both. An exalted word or allusion, where unexpected, can suddenly transform a mundane account into something richer. A character assumes a nobler role; an incident has echoes of a classical scene; the vernacular reveals an epistemological core. Such intentions, by way of example, lay behind my decision to describe in modestly elevated style a two-week pack trip in 1932 by high officials of the U.S. Forest Service. Forestry was then experiencing its version of the Dirty Thirties, with palls of smoke rather than blown dust, but the Forest Service was unclear about what, in fact, it might do. Not generally recognized as a philosophical society, this band of Forest Service officers trekked through the Northern Rockies and each night stopped for prolonged, quasi-formal discussions about the nature of the backcountry and what might or might not be done about it, all carefully recorded. "The conversations read like the imitation Platonic dialogues common during the Renaissance. But instead of Castiglione and Galileo, the authors had names like Headley, Show, Kelley, and Loveridge. During this curious expedition, no aspect of the troublesome backcountry management question went unexamined, and in the end the gathering ruled against Headley."[9]

The perhaps jarring allusion to Renaissance symposia was intended to transform the event from a bunch of good ol' boys swapping bear stories around a campfire into a debate about matters with serious consequences, ultimately grounded in a particular view of the world. The eventual outcome was something called the 10 A.M. policy, which guided federal fire practices for forty years and stirred up an ecological insurgency that we are still coping with. Not all reviewers agreed that the event warranted such attention, nor on the basis of rhetoric alone should they have. The passage works only if there is enough supporting evidence elsewhere or if the established context has built to a crescendo in which the heightened threats of nature prompt an equally heightened response from a professional bureaucracy. But whether readers agreed or not, the language forced them to consider the possibility.

In such ways, a modulated high style can signal that a subject otherwise thought beneath interest deserves serious consideration. Style and subject at first may seem out of sync, and the reader will either conclude (favorably) that the subject really does deserve an elevated standing or (unfavorably) that the work is an unconscious parody. The trick is to sustain the style, without stuttering or looking over your shoulder, long enough to convince the reader, and then allow the subject to impress itself. Still, the "meal," as Emerson put it, had better follow "in the firkin" quickly; for without real substance, stylistic claims to significance will soon scatter in the wind of rapidly skimmed pages.

Try to substitute diction for real data, an inflated prose for an genuine argument, or philo-babble for the inherent drama of an authentic narrative, and you will be quickly found out. To any discerning reader (assuming he or she stays with it), the effect is the opposite of what was intended. The writer looks foolish and pretentious, and the text bloated and distasteful, like a supersized order of fries still soggy with cooking oil. This is nonfiction's version of the prose incantation derided by fiction-writing guides. We live in a self-mocking or self-referential or at least postmodernist era, not a self-styled Augustan age; and instead of sounding like Edward Gibbon, the outcome may resemble faux Faulkner.

The rule remains: match subject and style. Using a Kenworth eighteen-wheeler to haul a bag of groceries or a NASCAR Ford to tow an exhibit of early Cubist collages to major museums is silly—but even amateur writers will recognize the absurdity in such travesties. Most failures occur in less obvious mismatches. A sad fact for serious writers to hold in mind is that the high style is inherently difficult to sustain, particularly in an age like ours, not given to epics. The other, unalterable fact is that getting the right word involves a correct pitch as well as a dictionary definition. Which is to say: it may be easier to elevate a more colloquial style through diction and voice than through exalted phrases and loftily complicated syntax.

Quotations

One of the obvious stylistic chasms between fiction and nonfiction involves dialogue. Novels and short stories revolve around scenes in which characters speak; and today's fashion is to have dialogue do much of the work that in the past might have rested on authorial narration. Unsurprisingly, this, too, has hardened into prescriptions; and more than anywhere else, this is the point where contemporary nonfiction, most splashily the New Journalism, echoes the styles of fiction.

The opportunities for dialogue-driven text are many, particularly where research pivots on interviews; and the temptation to tweak is equally strong. Within scholarship, some opportunities for extended quotation or even conversation do exist, as with transcripts. When nonfiction writers break the rules, it is often because they introduce dialogue into their text and tinker with the actual conversations to make them better fit the manuscript. The fictional imperative to rely on dialogue subverts the nonfictional injunction not to make stuff up. If the temptation is less in nonfictional genres other than memoir and narrative, it may be because the opportunities are rarer.

More commonly, you must handle quotations from written, not spoken, sources. The requisite skill lies in knowing how much to quote directly, how much to paraphrase, and how much of the source to include. In general, small quotations are better than block quotes, and smooth passages better than ones choppy with quoted snippets. Block quotes can shatter the flow of the manuscript and subvert the narrative "dream," the sense of being an observer at the events. Alluring as they seem to someone who has panned through thousands of documents and found only a few nuggets, the long quote is generally a mistake, if only because many readers will skip over it or because the particular point it intends to make gets lost in the verbiage.

Consider this sample from Catharine Parr Traill's book *The Backwoods of Canada* (1836), as Traill gives one of the clearest and most comprehensive accounts of landclearing fires by settlers.

> We had a glorious burning this summer after the ground was all logged up; that is, all the large timbers chopped into lengths, and drawn together in heaps with oxen. To effect this the more readily we called a logging-bee. We had a number of settlers attend, with yokes of oxen and men to assist us. After that was over, my husband, with the men-servants, set the heaps on fire; and a magnificent sight it was to see such a conflagration all round us. I was a little nervous at first on account of the nearness of some of the log-heaps to the house, but care is always taken to fire them with the wind blowing a direction away from the building. Accidents have sometimes happened, but they are of rarer occurrence than might be expected, when we consider the subtlety and destructiveness of the element employed on the occasion.
>
> If the weather be very dry, and a brisk wind blowing,

the work of destruction proceeds with astonishing rapidity; sometimes the fire will communicate with the forest and run over many hundreds of acres. This is not considered favourable for clearing, as it destroys the underbrush and light timbers, which are almost indispensable for ensuring a good burning. It is, however, a magnificent sight to see the blazing trees and watch the awful progress of the conflagration, as it hurries onward, consuming all before it, or leaving such scorching mementoes as have blasted the forest growth for years.

The passage goes on for pages, altogether a remarkable and nearly unique summary. In a documentary collection it would be accepted in a heartbeat, as is. In a larger narrative, it might cavitate the text, like a large sinkhole that suddenly collapses in a highway.[10]

How best to restate it? That will depend on context. The sample that follows emphasizes the fire component and Traill's attitude toward the burning, and so keeps in quotation those phrases and passages that most capture those features. (Another manuscript might well want to accent Traill's matter-of-fact stance toward pioneering or her plain-style prose.) The outcome remains a trifle bumpy, though it has eliminated the block quote that otherwise barred the trail of prose like a fallen fir.

They had a "glorious burning" that summer, after convening a logging-bee. The assembled neighbors chopped up the felled trees, and gathered the debris into heaps with oxen. Then Traill and the hired hands set the piles ablaze. The sight was "magnificent," a "conflagration all round us," though Catharine worried because of the nearness of the cabin. "But care is always taken to fire [the piles] with the wind blowing in a direction away from the building," and while accidents did happen, they were rarer than one might expect. Care extended as well to the surrounding woods, for the flames could bolt and overrun the countryside. Even so, such scenes too could mesmerize, as the conflagration made its "awful progress" onward.

With the revision referenced, a serious reader could indulge in Traill's own account if he or she so wished.

More typical is the situation in which the text incorporates a longish quote but one that is short of block-quote mass. For example, how Troy, New York, got its name has baffled many observers, beginning with the "Albany editor" mentioned in George Stewart's *Names on the Land*. "But in the retrospect of history," Stewart writes, "it is not at all surprising. The ground had been well prepared. Why Troy rather than Rome or Constantinople may be questioned. But at least, by virtue of the poets, Troy was known as widely as Rome itself. Like Sparta also it symbolized the masculine virtues."[11]

A perfectly acceptable passage. One might change it only if the house style, or the design of the manuscript overall, discouraged quotations of this length, or if the context of this particular passage argued for keeping most of the text in the author's voice. For example:

How Troy, New York, got its name has baffled many observers, the occasional "Albany editor" among them, as George Stewart notes. But the reasons are not surprising. "Why Troy rather than Rome or Constantinople may be questioned," but classicism was in the air, Troy

was as widely known "as Rome itself," and like Sparta it
suitably symbolized "the masculine virtues."

Citations

What is not arbitrary in nonfiction is the requirement to
identify the source of any quotation, or any passage being
paraphrased. This is nonnegotiable: such references are the
"science" behind the scholarship, in that someone else
should be able to verify every source—replicate the experiment, as it were. Understandably, those writers with some
sense of style, sentence tempo, or textual fluency may balk
at the thought of scattering citations throughout the manuscript like caltrops waiting to lame the reader. But there are
ways to read your text and cite it too. There are always alternatives.

The clumsiest is fast becoming the most common: the scientific citation in which the reference is inserted in the text
parenthetically, as in (Norton, 1982). In cases where the citation includes multiple sources, or where every sentence
has one or several citations, the outcome resembles computer code more than prose. While the implication is that
the text is building an edifice out of the hewn stones of previous research, the effect, for the reader, is a stone wall. A
slightly better version allots to each reference a number,
and then inscribes the number in parentheses rather than
the citation's name, rank, and serial number. Except as satire, this citation style has little place in serious nonfiction
with any literary sensibility, and typically it does not include
page numbers, which makes it all but worthless where books
are referenced.

Software makes irrelevant the difference in typesetting costs between footnotes and endnotes, but there are preferences among writers, editors, and readers, and today's druthers are for endnotes. That shifts the question to whether the superscripts for each should follow the sentence in which a quote or reference appears, or whether the sources can be grouped by paragraph. More preferences, more druthers. My own taste is for paragraph citation because it reduces textual clutter and involves less editorial fuss than the alternative taken by many trade books, which is to tag the source within the endnotes by page, paragraph or line, and phrase. This is an elegant solution, but one that will probably not be available to most scholarly or academic-trade manuscripts. As a matter of craft, such notes complement the index.

A few sample citation styles, as I would judge them:

The good: that is, citations that do not break the flow of the text. First, many quotes, a one-paragraph citation, from *Year of the Fires:*

> After a summer spent looking forward with dread, in autumn people looked back with nostalgia. Meyer Wolff recalled as indelible the delicious smell of fresh rain. Mrs. Swaine of Mullan remembered it as "a terrible ordeal, but I wouldn't have missed it for anything." Frances Eaton was "glad to leave this land of snowslides and forest" and confessed that "if ever I come back, it will be when I want to die more than I do now." Bill Greeley never forgot, for "the summer of 1910 brought home the hard realities of the job." Ideals and inspirational rhetoric plummeted to earth with "the cost in hardship and sweat, in danger and human lives. And I had to face

the bitter lessons of defeat. For the first time I understood in cold terms the size of the job cut out for us."
Elers Koch remembered, and worried that the collective
memory might fade if it were not properly recorded, as
he determined to do, not for publication but "primarily
as a record for the Forest Service, so that the story will
not be lost." Ed Pulaski remembered, and asked Percy
Stewart if he still had "bad dreams of forest fires." Will
Morris remembered other fiery dreams and how, during
the long ordeal, even in their sleep, they would "be fighting fire all night." But he also recalled fondly those last
days with the "faithful few" who had stayed with him on
the line and how, around the evening campfire, he had
a chance "to size [them] up." He recalled a young En-
glishman, a singer and poet, a veteran of the Boer War.
He recalled two Montenegrins, the best and most faithful workers he ever had. He recalled two southern boys,
"a different type" from the others, good workers, out for
adventure in the West, which he believed they got. He
recalled young Burke, a foreman, later a guard and then
a ranger, the "wag of the camp," who said of their first
cook that "he was so greasy that every morning he had
to roll in the ashes of the fire to keep from sliding down
the hill." He also recalled the rain and how they had let
it pour off their faces and wash away the grime and the
weariness and the fear and how they had bidden "affec-
tionate farewells," knowing that they would never see
one another again.[*]

[*]Ibid., 5; Mrs. Swaine, "Our Experience with the Forest
Fires, by Mrs. Swaine," in Elers Koch, *When the Mountains
Roared: Stories from the 1910 Fire* (U.S. Forest Service, Idaho

Panhandle Forests, n.d.), 37; Mrs. Frances Bogert Eaton, "'The Sun Rises in a Bank of Smoke and Sets in a Bank of Smoke': Letters from the 1910 Fire," *Idaho Yesterdays* (Fall 1995), 21; William B. Greeley, *Forests and Men* (Garden City, N.J.: Doubleday, 1951), 18; Koch, *When the Mountains Roared,* 1; Pulaski, quoted in Robert Percy Stewart, "'The Fire Was on All Sides of Us': A Ranger's Reminiscence," *Idaho Yesterdays* (Fall 1995), 25; Morris Letters, September 6, 1910, 124; and Morris, *Great Fires,* 7–8.

Second, with citation numbering removed and quotes identified by page and line in an endnote section, from David McCulloch's account of the building of the Panama Canal, *The Path between the Seas:*

It was not for him to court popularity. He wanted loyalty first, not to him but to the work, that above all. He abhorred waste and inefficiency and he was determined to weed out incompetents. Nor was there ever to be any doubt as to his own authority. "What the Colonel said he meant," a steam-shovel engineer remembered. "What he asked for he got. It didn't take us long to find that out." Requests or directives from his office were not to be regarded as subjects for discussion. When the head of the Commissary Department, a popular and influential figure, informed Goethals that he would resign if Goethals persisted in certain changes in the purchasing procedure, Goethals at once informed him that his resignation was accepted and refused to listen when he came to retract the threat. "It will help bring the outfit into line," Goethals noted privately. "I can stand it if they can." He put Lieutenant Wood in as a replacement. "I just put it up to him to make good," he wrote.

The citations were recorded in this way:

PAGE

535   "What the Colonel said he meant": Edgar Young, "The
         Colonel Passes," *New York Herald-Tribune,* February 5, 1928.

535   "It will help bring the outfit into line": Goethals to G. R.
         Goethals, May 1, 1907, Goethals Papers.

The bad: which may be visually obnoxious or unobtrusive
but which fails to identify the source in any meaningful way.
An otherwise interesting book, *Humboldt's Cosmos,* sloughs
off its scholarly obligations by noting under sources: "All
Humboldt quotations and details of his journey are taken
from his *Personal Narrative,* except as noted below," but
never gives the actual pages, and then under "below" lists
such useless references as "Emerson quotation: De Terre,"
or "Gould quotation: Gould," without giving either the
pages in which the quote appears or the source from which
it is taken, thus forcing the reader to scour the bibliography
to locate the original. Calling the work popular history may
argue for keeping note numbers out of the text, but does
not excuse lame documentation, which is, in truth, a mock-
ery of the process. Better to have avoided giving any scholarly apparatus at all.[12]

And the ugly: referencing that makes reading into the equivalent of driving a badly washboarded road.

> Remotely sensed data have been used to detect active
> fires (Roy *et al.* 1999; Ichoku *et al.* 2003); map fire ex-
> tents at local (Parsons 2003; Holden *et al.* 2005), regional
> (Eva and Lambin 1998a; Smith *et al.* 2002), and conti-

nental (Scholes *et al.* 1996) scales; estimate surface and crown fuel loading (Nelson *et al.* 1988; Means *et al.* 1999; Lefsky *et al.* 2002; Falkowski *et al.* 2005); assess active fire behavior (Kaufman *et al.* 1998; Woster *et al.* 2003; Smith and Wooster 2005; Dennison 2006; Dennison *et al.* 2006); examine post-fire vegetation response (Turner *et al.* 1994; White *et al.* 1996; Diaz-Delgado *et al.* 2003), and identify areas where natural recovery may prove to be problematic (Bobbe *et al.* 2001; Ruiz-Gallardo *et al.* 2004).[13]

Got all that?

You be the judge. But judge as a reader wanting both flow and fact, not as a writer seeking to avoid the hard work of citation or the even harder work of harnessing real style to skittish sources.

chapter 13

Character

In which humans' most enduring interest, themselves and other people, is discussed as a literary concern, and we see how character can be sharpened, refracted, massed, and diffused

Character and plot—people doing things and having things done to them—are the core of imaginative literature. Not all nonfiction pivots as singularly around character as fiction does; a nonfiction text may argue a thesis or analyze a new source of data. But few texts of any kind will claim much readership without a central character or a cast of surrogates. Otherwise they'll be conveying information without drama. And even when character is not the central focus, the craft through which character appears in a text can apply to other features which function as character equivalents. The same techniques can embolden settings, sharpen events, allow natural processes and inanimate objects to impart narrative momentum, and give dramatic presence to ideas and institutions.

What does a character do in a text? At the simplest level, readers can identify with them—characters literally personify the story or theme. Most readers want to read about people; a book that can introduce characters even if its primary topic is a place, a social institution, or a scientific concept will elicit more reader interest; and of course character may be the object of inquiry, not simply a narrative device. Introducing character, or anchoring the text through characters, helps to crystallize the drama. While character alone can rarely carry a text—writing still requires setting and plot, and must sit within the overall design—texts without character will rarely leap beyond the genre of a treatise. They will remain theses or arguments but will lack the drama or interest that can carry your voice to a broader audience.

For many scholars trained in social science, who view interpretive reality as grounded in the statistics of aggregate social action and who may regard any appeal to individual actors as suspect, an emphasis on character will be anathema, and a text organized around character profiles dubious. Highlighting characters is either decorative or diversionary, either an appeal to a prurient "human interest" or a device to avoid the real drivers of behavior. Yet one can hold a mirror to such blanket critiques: they are themselves ideological. The problem, if any exists, lies not in the literary techniques or characterization, but in the claims made about the role and significance of characters in the particular text at hand. If a character is wrongly portrayed, if a person's action is inflated beyond what the evidence supports, then the characterization needs rewriting. No text requires characters; if you simply distrust character, or human agency in general, write something else. (Besides, nothing lies like statistics, and experts in the "hard" sciences who dismiss writings in "softer" fields as anecdotal because they don't include enough numbers or the numbers don't add up have a pretty dismal success ratio. The close observers and thick describers can get it right, and those implacable numbers frequently turn out to be themselves anecdotal.) Skillful characterizations will not make a text right; neither will the banishment of characterization. And most readers will likely agree with Shakespeare that the fault lies not in the stars but in ourselves.

In a like manner, settings, events, institutions, and ideas can all be animated and granted some role through the same kinds of techniques that bring characters to life. The simplest way is to identify them directly with a character, perhaps the person who invented or championed them; but they can also stand alone, if they are portrayed with care—that is, if you do not attempt to anthropomorphize the inanimate. Instead, the craft lies in identifying some distinctive features (that telling detail, that revelatory scene) because they help to distinguish the subject, and in granting some agency and even imputing some moral sense, not because a bank or an army or a country or a river can choose, as a human being does, but because they are created by people or can prompt people to act. Even natural phenomena can become a catalyst: they can force action; they can cause people to choose, and by so doing, they can propel the moral drama of the text and can themselves become, in a curious yet undeniable way, part of that drama— which is to say, they act as a contributing character and assume some traits according to the responses they elicit. They do what, in another context, a character might do. Without making them a tangible persona, a skillful writer can grant them the literary role of one.

Depending on their purpose, characters can thus work in various ways in a manuscript. They may justify a passing reference, or a sketch, or a more robust profile; they may be developed once and then recalled without further elaboration, or they may be developed in sequence, with a different trait highlighted at each appearance; or they may command the entire manuscript with an outright biography. How to write each use depends, as always, on context: on setting, on sources, on purpose. The trick is to get the right particulars that make the abstract real and give heft to context without burying the personality in a sludge of specifics.

Begin with the case of a biography or history in which there is a passing reference to an individual, a reference that serves merely as a signpost along the narrative track. What kind of introduction does such a character need? It depends. To say, for example, that the protagonist "visited the society's next-ranking official" conveys a sense of impersonal bureaucracy, going through a soulless hierarchy of forms and offices. Giving the official a name and a title helps to ground the text and implies a social contact ("He next visited William Harris, the secretary of the society"). Or there might be a cavalcade of officials, each named and titled, and by listing them, one after another, you give the impression that they are all interchangeable and ineffective. Details help—that's a general rule. But the wrong details or too many details without an organizing conceit behind them only clutter the text, and the reader has to pick his way through the prose as he might negotiate a child's playroom with all the toys scattered about.

Sometimes the person is worth a sketch, or perhaps an in-text profile. If there is more than antiquarian gossip at stake, if the character will serve as a foil or will shepherd the drama, then a paragraph or two may be necessary, or perhaps a few pages—how much depends on how deeply the character adds to the overall action. Or if your strategy is to develop a central character through several scenes, the parts eventually coalescing into a full-bodied portrait, then furnish something more robust than a character reference. But what? Do we, as readers, need to know height, weight, hair color, age, residence? Or education, taste in art, years at a desk? Is this a job application, a curriculum vitae, or the character equivalent of a CAT scan? How does the person fit into your text at this moment? Does he advance the action, explain an institution, personify a setting, or enter the roster of dramatis personae? Ultimately we want to know how the character contributes to the theme or drama of the text. You need to supply those traits that assist, and scrap others unless they add a touch of color or an enlightening detail. In the case of scholarship, a character can serve to coalesce, as if they were bits of lint, many particles of information otherwise scattered; but even here the critical traits must bind the others.

Characters may appear in different ways to diverse ends. They may stand alone, as when a profile is developed into an essay. They may be part of central casting, one or several personalities around whom the story turns. They may function as secondary characters, or foils, against whom the main character may be tried or revealed. They may be introduced all at once, or serially. The proper choice is the technique that best suits the book's design. Having the action hinge on character is marvelous so long as the text argues that individual choice matters, or that a suitable character may serve as synecdoche for larger forces or events that are crystallized in that character's behavior.

What follows is a sampler of character roles—character as a pivot of action, character as a foil and catalyst, character as itself the focus of interest, and so on. But as with any good writing, other elements of style are present and deserve consideration, a reminder (one we cannot too often repeat) that gifted writing resides not in one trait or another but in how they come together.

Central Character, Introduced Piecemeal through the Larger Narrative

GENERAL JOSEPH JOFFRE
    in Barbara Tuchman, *The Guns of August*

A critical feature of Joffre's character, as Tuchman understands and presents it, is his imperturbability. His physical presence (a bit overstuffed) and his habits (he hated to have his routine interrupted) illustrate and foreshadow his central action in the tragic drama of the First World War, the Battle of the Marne. All the ingredients have been introduced, bit by bit: Joffre's rise amid the disintegration and decline of others, his implacable routine, the vortex of armies swirling east of Paris, the competing calls to rally, retreat, attack—all are present but dissolved in solution, as it were. What the portrait needs in order to precipitate that critical moment is a revealing detail or episode, the granitic core of personality amid the inchoate moment of choice. "Silent, astride a straw-bottomed chair facing Berthelot's wall map, Joffre considered the problem."

> Joffre now faced the greater decision: whether to carry out the planned retreat to the Seine or seize the opportunity—and the risk—and face the enemy now. The heat was overpowering. Joffre went outside and sat down in the shade of a weeping ash in the school playground. By nature an arbiter, he collected the opinions of others,

sorted them, weighed the personal coefficient of the speaker, adjusted the scale, and eventually announced his verdict. The decision was always his. If he succeeded his would be the glory; if it failed he would be held responsible. In the problem now before him the fate of France was at stake.[1]

He makes some inquiries, has to stiffen the resolve of commanders and allies, but the decision is made. "Gentlemen, we will fight on the Marne." The moment matters, as Tuchman notes, not because it determined the outcome of the war but because it meant the war would go on, and on. Joffre's decision was not a clarion call to advance but a resolve to stay, so the description of his choice, which he made amid oppressive heat, under a "weeping ash" in a school playground, emphasizes both the character behind the decision and its ironic banality ("straw-bottomed chair") when measured against the stakes involved ("the fate of France"). The details help to root the decision in the character of one man, and by the ordinariness of the setting strip it of any apotheosis. By the time he is called upon to decide, we know, thanks to Tuchman's careful preparation, how he will choose and why and what the consequences will be.

Secondary Character, or Foil: Take One

HARALD HÅRDRÅTA

in David Howarth, *1066: The Year of the Conquest*

In his account of the Norman invasion, David Howarth inserts a fascinating profile of Harald Hårdråta, the Norseman who invaded northern England just before William of

Normandy invaded its southern shore. Howarth introduces Harald with a succinct sketch.

> Although he lived when the peak of Viking enterprise was past, he was typical of the Vikings' unique poetic barbarity. He once said of himself, in verse, that he had eight accomplishments: he could shoe a horse, ride, swim, ski, shoot, throw javelins, play the harp, and compose poetry. Snorri adds to this that he was enormously tall and broad, had very large hands and feet and a very loud voice, fair hair and beard and a long moustache, and one eyebrow higher than the other.[2]

The cameo is sharp, common enough as a formula, and foreshadowing in its emphasis on Harald's sheer physical presence. But the real pieces of Harald's personality assemble not from accounts of his appearance but from his behavior. These Howarth relates in a style that falls somewhere between a c.v. and a bardic ode. The record of mayhem matters because Harald is what he does, and he does everything, so much so that Howarth concludes: "Nobody but a Norseman could have lived such a life in that era." That suits his role in *1066:* he exists to force action and thus reveal the character of Harold of England.[3]

A fictional writer of contemporary tastes would likely end the portrait there. Harald's deeds speak for themselves, the way dialogue alone can reveal a personality. But Howarth adds an authorial coda: he identifies Harald Hårdråta as a supreme example of a type, which suggests something of the violence abundant in that world, for Harald's "incessant battles were not mainly a means to political ends, or even a means of enriching himself. They were fought for the sheer delight of fighting."[4]

The word "berserk" has survived from the Norseman's language. A man who went berserk was seized by a battle-madness far beyond courage: he killed and killed, without mercy, reason or fear, and did not stop until there was nobody left to kill, or until he fell dead himself. Such berserkers were the heroes of the Norsemen. Norse poetry glories in the feats of men who went mad in battle, men who were called in the awkward composite words weapon-strong, steel-grim, sword-eager, war-happy, raven-feeders . . .

Harald, in one word, was berserk; the most celebrated, feared and admired berserker of that century.[5]

While luridly fascinating in its own right, and successful because Howarth does not merely bestow a label on Harald but heaps graphic details on the platter, the profile is critical to the book because Harald leads one of the two rival groups competing for England, the Norsemen and the Normans. King Harold of England fights and wins against Harald Hårdråta, a contest of physical courage. Against Duke William, however, he falters. There is, we are led to understand, some flaw, some weakness of conscience perhaps, that subtlely enfeebles him and makes the contest at Hastings a matter of character beyond a simple warrior's code. By first defeating Harald the Berserker, however, Harold shows that he can fight and lead men, which he does against the most ferocious campaigner of the day. We measure King Harold against the challenges overcome; and for that, Howarth had to give Harald Hårdråta a profile of such depth and gory ferocity that we can appreciate the magnitude of King Harold's triumph over him and the tragedy of Harold's subsequent failure at Hastings.

Secondary Character, or Foil: Take Two

A CAST OF PERSONALITIES

in Wallace Stegner, *Beyond the Hundredth Meridian*

Stegner's biography of Major John Wesley Powell is a veritable gallery of historical characters, some of whom knew Powell personally, some of whom didn't, but all of whom, through deed and insights, illuminate some aspect of Powell's character.

Henry Adams, Sam Adams, William Gilpin, Clarence King, Senator William Stewart, and a score of others—all are repeatedly compared and contrasted with Powell, and hence add brush strokes toward a fuller portrait. Henry Adams' background of privilege and education contrasts with Powell's frontier self-education and its tough virtues; Sam Adams' claim of first-descent through the Grand Canyon—the boast of a frontier blowhard—contrasts with Powell's attempts at a scientific expedition; the failed public-service career of Clarence King, "the best and brightest man of his generation," as John Hay called him, contrasts sharply with Powell's; "Big Bill" Stewart of Nevada, a powerful frontiersman-turned-politician, was "one to delight a caricaturist and depress a patriot," and his clash with Powell goes beyond personality into a political brouhaha over western settlement that will leave Powell fatally crippled.

By sketching Stewart as a powerful presence—"robust, aggressive, contentious, narrow, self-made, impatient of 'theorists,' irritated by abstract principles, a Nevada lawyer, miner, Indian-killer; a fixer, a getter-done, an indefatigable manipulator around the whiskey and cigars, a dragon whose cave was the smoke-filled room"—Stegner grants Powell's loss some measure of heroic tenacity. Theirs is a clash of wills, two champions of conflicting ideas. That Stewart is both formidable and oddly attractive in his impatient energies makes the contest engaging. It would be one thing for Powell to fail before Congress because he cannot run a bureaucracy; it is another for this one-armed veteran of the Civil War and the Grand Canyon to fall before the irresistible political personification of American westering itself.[6]

That is the brilliant side of the way Stegner uses foils in his portraiture. The dark side is that he uses this gallery selectively to justify Powell in his actions. There is always someone among the book's crowd who does something dumber, less noble, or more reckless. Does Powell rely on amateurish relatives? The Hayden survey uses political hacks. Does Powell exaggerate his journey down the Colorado, combining his two trips into one? Sam Adams either fabricated his out of whole cloth, or saw the scene only through sunstroked hallucination. Does Powell pick the wrong fight, and lose? Clarence King refused to fight, and then joined the opposition in a Gilded Age lust for wealth. Whatever flaw Stegner reveals in Powell, he softens its effect by resurrecting one of the many foils in the text.

Those who disagree with Stegner's judgment may fault his use of literary techniques, hinting that superior craft makes his suspect judgments both vivid and convincing, and intimating that Stegner's reliance on technique may be the ultimate cause of his flawed evaluations, that his deployment of literary methods undermines his use of evidence. But this observation simply ascribes to technique what is a disagreement over scholarship or a quarrel over interpretation. The real challenge may be critics' worry that particles of data will not by themselves counter Stegner's shaded portrait: the critic must, in the end, answer that portrait with another, which is equally compelling.

Stand-Alone Profile: A Biography in Miniature

"JAMES PIKE, AMERICAN"
    in Joan Didion, *The White Album*

There is a genre, endlessly fascinating, that consists of character profiles, in and of themselves, whether or not they come embedded in another text. They are, in effect, cameo biographies. Because they are brief, they cannot pretend to tally all the experiences of a life, and because they stand alone, they cannot rely on context to fill gaps, save for whatever common understanding the intended reader might be expected to bring. The profile stands between the character sketch within a text and a full-bore biography. The former must genuflect toward, and can draw from, a larger work; the latter must hold all within it. The profile should contain everything necessary, and cannot afford anything more.

Its nucleus is the telling trait: the character element, flawed or saintly, that best distills the whole person, and the revealing detail, symbol, gesture, or event that best expresses that trait. Like painting teacups, the technique requires a light touch that can't be too fussy or diverted by items that, while true, may deflect from the essence. A scholarly study might try to fill as much as possible—amassing all the pertinent and collaborating information it can—while a journalistic profile might try to strip out everything not absolutely essential. Still, only so much can get into either text, and almost certainly that selected pith cannot carry the characterization without authorial commentary, any more than DNA can by itself express an organism.

In introducing the Episcopal clergyman James Pike as an archetypal Westerner, a "great literary character," a latter-day Gatsby, Joan Didion both poses and answers a rhetorical

question, and does so by noting overtly the value of the revelatory detail.

> What was one to make of him. Five years after he fin-
> ished Grace [Cathedral], James Albert Pike left the Epis-
> copal Church altogether, detailing his pique in the pages
> of *Look,* and drove into the Jordanian desert in a white
> Ford Cortina rented from Avis. He went with his for-
> mer student and bride of nine months, Diane. Later she
> would say that they wanted to experience the wilder-
> ness as Jesus had. They equipped themselves for this
> mission with an Avis map and two bottles of Coca-Cola.
> The young Mrs. Pike got out alive. Five days after James
> Albert Pike's body was retrieved from a canyon near the
> Dead Sea a Solemn Requiem Mass was offered for him
> at the cathedral his own hubris had finished in San Fran-
> cisco. Outside on the Grace steps the cameras watched
> the Black Panthers demonstrating to free Bobby Seale.
> Inside the Grace nave Diane Kennedy Pike and her two
> predecessors, Jane Alvies Pike and Esther Yanovsky Pike,
> watched the cameras and one another.
>
> That was 1969. For some years afterward I could make
> nothing at all of this peculiar and strikingly "now" story,
> so vast and atavistic was my irritation with the kind of
> man my grandmother would have called "just a damn
> old fool," the kind of man who would go into the desert
> with the sappy Diane and two bottles of Coca-Cola, but I
> see now that Diane and the Coca-Cola are precisely the
> details which lift the narrative into apologue.[7]

And later, explaining what may be Pike's defining trait
as Didion sees it, a willingness to dismiss annoyances and
begin anew: "'Jim never cleaned up after himself,' a friend

notes, recalling his habit of opening a shirt and letting the cardboards lie where they fell, and this élan seems to have applied to more than his laundry." Didion parlays that incident into her promised apologue as she tracks the career, both careless and calculating, of a "man who moved through life believing that he was entitled to forget it and start over, to shed women when they became difficult and allegiances when they became tedious and simply *move on*." This was, she concludes, in language that reinforces her image of Pike as Westerner, a "moral frontiersmanship." She then enlarges on his value as a "Michelin to his time and place." He was "everywhere at the right time." This "sense that the world can be reinvented smells of the Sixties in this country, those years when no one at all seemed to have any memory or mooring, and in a way the Sixties were the years for which James Albert Pike was born."[8]

In brief compass, Didion moves from a telling detail, the dropped cardboard from new shirts, to the pith of Pike's nature, his penchant for moving on and ignoring the cleanup, to a disposition that might characterize a decade of national life. Didion makes no attempt to chronicle all the quirks or to knead in all the grit of a complex life; she aims only to profile it rather as a novelist might ("a great literary character") by locking her literary radar onto the essential target and letting her critical missiles fly.

Character Gallery

AMERICA'S DIPLOMATS AT THE TREATY OF GHENT
  in George Dangerfield, *The Era of Good Feelings*

The book, like the era it portrays, opens with the negotiations that led to the 1814 Treaty of Ghent, which ended the ill-conceived and ill-fought War of 1812. There were five American commissioners, three of whom really mattered, and each of the three comes in for an extensive profile. Albert Gallatin, John Quincy Adams, and Henry Clay—prominent politicians in their own right—here converge to subordinate their particular ideologies and personal idiosyncrasies to a common good that none of them, initially, believed truly possible. "All five peace commissioners were convinced that they were doomed to lock horns with their English opposites and then retire from the combat with nothing to show for their efforts. They were disagreed only over the length of time this encounter would consume." The conflict, in brief, was both personal and national.[9]

Here is a piece of that mosaic, part of the preliminaries that help to establish the presence of Henry Clay:

> Henry Clay carried with him into anything he did a captivating vitality; it was this that made him so much loved by his countrymen, though, for other reasons of a political nature, they did not altogether trust him. Living in an age, and coming from a background, that did not frown upon dissipation, he was not the man to deny himself its pleasures. He would sit up night after night, drinking and gambling—at loo or brag, at old sledge or all-fours. "Isn't it a pity," said a New England lady to Lucretia Clay, "that your husband gambles so much?" "Oh, I don't know," was the tranquil reply, straight from the heart of Kentucky, "he usually wins." . . . Once when Clay was Speaker of the House, a friend ventured to remonstrate with him after an all-night carousal. "How can you preside over the House today?" "Come and see," said Clay. On at least two occasions at Ghent (there were probably others) the laborious Adams, rising before

dawn to begin his day's work, heard a card party breaking up in Clay's chambers: and the careful New En-
glander makes a note of the time—3.45 and 4.30. To
Clay, who took the negotiations just as seriously as Adams did, these were very reasonable hours.[10]

Now, John Quincy Adams: "*A bull-dog among spaniels!* The
tribute is an unconscious one, but it is a tribute none the
less. If he could not fawn, he could fight. In the intensity of
his self-scourgings one can detect a certain pride."

He fought persistently, splenetically—sometimes ex-
pending his energies upon the meanest objects, sometimes putting them to the service of purely personal ambitions, but more often dedicating them to what he
believed to be the cause of justice and of virtue. For he
was, above all things, a moral man; it is, indeed, the clue
to his character. And though one hesitates to apply the
extinguishing substantive "puritan" to so complex a personality, there were certain aspects of Adams's character
which no other word seems to fit. He was a puritan in his
distrust of political expedients; a puritan in his hatred
of himself; a puritan in his belief—nowhere expressed
but everywhere apparent—that this hatred was evidence
of an innate superiority; a puritan in his anxious welcome of personal disaster and in his conviction that every great success must be followed by a compensatory
failure; a puritan in his individualism; and a puritan in
his virulence.[11]

Clay's vitality and gambler's verve and Adams' political
puritanism—the American delegation would need both in
its negotiations with its British counterparts, but the two

men would clash just as often. The various conflicts within and without crisscross the text like veins of quartz through granite. That, in turn, foreshadows the generally conciliatory and robust Era of Good Feelings that succeeds the war.

Though the Hotel de Pays Bas was "commodious," in Adams' words, it was "not easy to find a contractor who would accommodate himself to five separate and distinct humors." If his language is formal, and the book's structure almost neoclassical, that was the spirit of the age, and in the end, Dangerfield's text serves like the Hotel de Pays Bas in which he negotiates among his fractious characters a working thematic peace as effective as the military peace they achieved at Ghent.[12]

Character Developed by Quotations

BILLY BEANE

in Michael Lewis, *Moneyball*

The prescribed way to develop character is to let actions speak louder than words. Here, in Lewis' study of a major-league baseball team and its manager, we watch Billy Beane, high-school superstar, reveal his physical talents when, as a mere freshman, he pitches the final varsity game of the season: he "threw a shutout with ten strikeouts, and went two for four at the plate."

> In the first big game after Billy had come to the scouts' attention, Billy pitched a two-hitter, stole four bases, and hit three triples. Twenty-two years later the triples would remain a California schoolboy record, but it was the way he'd hit them that stuck in the mind. The ballpark that day had no fences; it was just an endless hot tundra in

the San Diego suburbs. After Billy hit the first triple over the heads of the opposing outfielders, the outfielders played him deeper. When he hit it over their heads the second time, the outfielders moved back again, and played him roughly where the parking lot would have been outside a big league stadium. Whereupon Billy hit it over their heads a third time. The crowd had actually laughed the last time he'd done it. That's how it was with Billy when he played anything, but especially when he played baseball: blink and you might miss something you'd never see again.[13]

Billy's undeniable skills are there for all to see. But he falters in the major leagues, not from physical liabilities but from mental ones. To convey the marvel of his promise and the mystery of his failure, Lewis turns to a roster of commentaries by those who know Beane. They carry the burden of interpretation, or, more properly, the difficulty of surmising subjective explanations.

Billy's failure was less interesting than the many attempts to explain it. His teammate and friend, Chris Pittaro, said, "Billy was as competitive and intense as anyone I ever played with. He never let his talent dictate. He fought himself too hard." Billy's high school coach, Sam Blalock, says that "he would have made it if he'd had the intangibles—if he would have had a better self-image. I think he would have been a big star in the big leagues. No. I *know*. He was amazing. If he'd wanted to, he could even have made it as a pitcher." The scouts who had been so high on Billy when he was seventeen years old still spoke of him in odd tones when he was twenty-five, as if he'd become exactly what they all said he would be and it was only by some piece of sorcery that he didn't have the numbers to prove it. Paul Weaver: "The guy had it all. But some guys just never figure it out. Whatever it is that allows you to perform day in, day out, and to make adjustments, he didn't have it. The game is that way." Roger Jongewaard: "He had the talent to be a superstar. A Mike Schmidt–type player. His problem was makeup. I thought Billy had makeup on his side. But he tried too hard. He tried to force it. He couldn't stay loose."[14]

Letting others comment is like shining multiple flashlights on a statue in the dark. The image deepens from two dimensions to three; its relief roughens; its texture takes on shadings. While an author could do this unaided, relying on snippets of quotation and incidents, having other people do it emphasizes the social nature of character. You as author don't have to force it. You can stay loose.

Character Surrogates: A Place or Natural Phenomenon as Functional Character

Anthropomorphizing is normally a quick ticket to critical obscurity, if not ridicule. Yet there is no reason that settings, buildings, natural forces—a mountain, a river, a storm, a locomotive, a skyscraper, an idea, an institution—might not serve as character surrogates, which is to say, might not represent or force action and hence choice among a text's cast of human characters. A place may become a presence, not merely an inert stage; an event may drive a plot, putting people in conflict with it or one another; an idea or discovery may not merely be a goal toward which people aspire but may assume unexpected proportions and kindle motivations that allow it to take on, as the saying goes, a life of its own. Nonhuman features function as covert literary actors. In using such character surrogates, you can enliven a text by not having to halt its flow in order to set a scene or explain some idea; they simply weave into the narrative. A setting becomes a presence, and an event a plot.

The literary task is easiest if the feature is the product at least partly of human construction, because it can then stand as a proxy for people and transmit the traits of its creator. A dam, a network of levees, an irrigated field, a national monument—all express the choices of their designers, as much as any other work of art. But even if the feature obeys little beyond its own logic, it can still do its work, serving as a foil or rival, delimiting the domain of human agency, and exposing the follies of hubris. The bad strategy is to make the characterization overt (a river named Fred, a tree called Wilma), and to lecture on why this object or place has "agency." The wise course is to let the feature reveal itself through its actions, or, more correctly, through the actions it prompts. The techniques involved are interchangeable with those for characterization overall.

By way of example, let Bernard DeVoto use contrasting landscapes to define the changing character of the American frontiersman. "Previously, the nation had had two symbols of solitude, the forest and the prairies; now it had a third, the mountains."

> This was the arid country, the land of little rain; the Americans had not known drouth. It was the dead country; they had known only fecundity. It was the open country; they had moved through the forests, past the oak opening, to the high prairie grass. It was the country of intense sun; they had always had shade to hide in. The wilderness they had crossed had been a passive wilder-

ness, its ferocity without passion and only loosed when
one blundered; but this was an aggressive wilderness, its
ferocity came out to meet you and the conditions of survival required a whole new technique.

The change in setting yielded a change in frontiersman.

The Long Hunter had slipped through forest shadows
or paddled his dugout up easy streams, but the mountain man must take to horse in a treeless country whose
rivers were far apart and altogether unnavigable. Before
this there had been no thirst; now the creek that dwin-
dled in the alkali or the little spring bubbling for a yard
or two where the sagebrush turned a brighter green was
what your life hung on. Before this one had had only to
look for game; now one might go for days without sight
of food, learn to live on rattlesnake or prairie dog, or
when those failed on the bulbs of desert plants, or when
they failed on the stewed gelatine of parfleche soles.
Moreover, in that earlier wilderness, a week's travel, or
two weeks' travel, would always bring you to where this
year's huts were going up, but in the new a white man's
face was three months' travel, or six months', or a year
away.

DeVoto concludes that "mountain craft was a technologi-
cal adaptation to these hazards," and of course so was the
mountain man.[15]
Let me try my own hand at this task with two samples
drawn from a study of fire in Canada. The first will introduce a landscape of fire, a task akin to introducing a character at the onset of a narrative. The second will "characterize" a historic fire, as one might a famous historical actor.

Between the Arctic and the Cordilleras, between the cold-dry climes of the tundra and the warm-dry and warm-wet of the grasslands and mountain woodlands, stretches the boreal forest, Canada's vastest woods. The belt narrows between James Bay and the Great Lakes, and nearly doubles toward the Rockies, but its sweep encompasses the bulk of continental Canada. Within its immense arc reside Canada's largest fires, its greatest fire problems, and its most distinctive fire regimes, the ones that best define Canada as a fire nation. Its boreal forest is to Canada what the arid Outback is to Australia. Over 90 percent of the country's big fires, which account for over 97 percent of its burned area, lie within the boreal belt. Without its burning boreal bush, Canada would be a middling firepower. With that flaming landscape, however, Canada becomes a global presence for Earthly fire ecology, fire science, and fire institutions. A red maple leaf may decorate its national flag, but a crimson crown fire swelling through its boreal conifers would be a more apt symbol of what makes Canada biotically majestic.[16]

The passage tries to capture the defining traits of the boreal forest as a fire forest: why it burns, how it burns, and how it sits within Canada—all the paradoxes of its existence. Because the passage belongs within a scholarly study, there is more detail than a journalistic profile would tolerate. But it sets up the fundamental conflict within the larger book, namely, the competition between the rhythms (and scale) of boreal burning and the cadences of human institutions.

Now move from a landscape to an event, a historically significant fire, profiled as one might portray a human actor:

There are big fires and great fires; benign fires and malignant fires; founding fires, defining fires, memorable fires; fires that announce eras, fires that symbolize eras, fires that end eras. The Miramichi fire of 1825—the Great Fire of New Brunswick—was all of the above. Canada had long abounded in giant fires, but not until the Miramichi had it spawned a monster, one capable of savaging whole settlements and worthy of written records by eye-witnesses. So, too, Europeans had from their earliest encounters experienced threatening fires, most from their own slovenly habits and ignorance, and they had chronicled a long litany of fiery portents, of Dark Days and the rumble of distant flames. But not until the autumn of 1825 did that seasonal roll call of slash fires and smoke palls suddenly reach a critical mass and explode with almost apocalyptic violence. The Miramichi fires did more than torch wild forests, rude farms, logging camps, and rough-hewn towns: they announced a new regimen of fire in Canada, and they inscribed, literally, a new set-piece of Canadiana. If the clearing fire was the celebratory bonfire of colonization, the conflagration was its evil twin, and the Miramichi fire, like a Dark Annunciation, first showed the face of that horror.[17]

We measure our heroes by the villains they fight, and an extended portrait of Miramichi, placing it among the rogues' gallery of historically villainous burns, helps to establish the character of the human response. The fire forces action; and done right, the fire becomes animated without being anthropomorphized.

chapter 14

Setting

In which the context that is often all is given a
tangible presence, and in which stages are not merely
set but settings do the stagings

All texts require context, but not all require a setting, as conventionally defined. A thesis might amble from one cache of evidence to another without regard for where, outside the mind, the action takes place, and the uninitiated might consider a setting as little more than literary wallpaper. But even wallpaper creates a mood, and there are times when setting may define or inform action, when it becomes a shaping presence. Like other elements of a text, it must share a project's design.

As with characters, setting can mean and do various things. It may be the principal subject, in a study of place such as Yellowstone or Pittsburgh. It may serve to define or evoke the temper of an occasion, as does the foreboding if slightly melodramatic "daybreak," with "the dawn overcast, the skies heavy and sullen," that opens Arthur Schlesinger Jr.'s prologue to *The Age of Jackson*. It may help to define the action, by provoking decisions or limiting what choices might be made, or by exhibiting their outcomes, as a landscape's scar tissue of roads, overturned sod, or renewed woods might show the nature of choices taken and help the reader to judge them. A hilly terrain can shape a battle; a broad floodplain can intensify the foreboding prospect of ruptured levees; a hillside stripped of soils can reveal the wretched legacy of poor landclearing. A setting may illustrate the character of a protagonist who has sculpted it or defiantly ignored it, be it a woods or a building or a religious order. The long-plowed clay earth of the Paris basin reveals one kind of society; the Selway Wilderness of Idaho, another. Particularly for geography and environmental history, the setting may itself be the theme of the manuscript, which orbits around the study of a place: Henry Ford's monster plant on the Rouge River, New Orleans lying vulnerable below its levees, the radiant summits of the Sierra Nevada.

In all of these instances, setting becomes a presence, a symbol, even an agent, not simply furniture casually selected and indifferently arranged without regard to the text overall. It adds context: it illuminates characters, themes, and events. A well-executed setting will enhance action and understanding; a poorly done one will inhibit it. Whether or not a setting forces a text's characters to choose, it certainly forces the author to do so.

The range of options is as broad as that for character, and the criteria are analogous. Tell as much as you need to, no more, no less. Get particulars, but get the right ones. Highlight the distinctive detail that reveals and that may morph into symbol or synecdoche.

The passing reference has its place. It may suffice to say that the event occurred in Philadelphia or Death Valley or in rush-hour traffic on I-35. The magnitude and value of elaboration can scale up from there. You might say that the conversation took place in a shabby Omaha hotel room, decades past its prime, suggesting that the event is likewise ignoble or, if ironic, possessed of moral magnificence unreflected by the surroundings. Thus in describing the assassinations of Abraham Lincoln, John Kennedy, and Martin Luther King Jr., you might elaborate on the mundane settings that contrast with the significance of the action, implicitly arguing the sordidness of the events, or the banality of their perpetrators, by denying them an exalted locale. The options are endless. The required authorial skills are interchangeable with those used to elicit characters: know what traits matter, know how to accent them, know how to shed the rest.

Take, as examples, two contrasting studies. One is a long profile of the geologist David Love and his native landscape, Wyoming, and the other, a dense sketch of Claude François Denecourt and the Forest of Fontainebleau. In each the person and the place assume one another's form, or character, if you will. In the first, the place imposes on the personality; in the second, the person sculpts the place in his own image.

In *Rising from the Plains,* John McPhee limns a harsh landscape, hostile to people, and toxic generally to life. Everything about Wyoming is hard and physical; its weather is brutal, its rocks too often poisonous with selenium, uranium, petroleum, sodium sulfates, a lithic pharmacy of geotoxicity. David Love, however, grew up on a pioneering ranch in its center, made its geology his special field of expertise, and is measured against it. "Geologists tend to have been strongly influenced by the rocks among which they grew up," McPhee intones blandly, noting that the Dutch excel in sediments, the Swiss in mountains, Californians in strange and complex assemblages, but that a "geologist who grew up in Wyoming would have something of everything above."

A geologist who grew up in Wyoming could not ignore economic geology, could not ignore vertebrate paleontology, could not ignore the narrative details in any chapter of time (every period in the history of the world was represented in Wyoming). Wyoming geology would above all tend to produce a generalist, with an eye that had seen a lot of rocks, and a four-dimensional gift for fitting them together and arriving at the substance of their story—a scenarist and lithographer of what geologists like to call the Big Picture.[1]

A Wyoming geologist would be someone with a lot of time in the field. He would have found a way to live with, yet transcend, that setting. He would look a lot like David Love, who slept a quarter of his life's nights outdoors in direct contact with a raw Wyoming and grew up with a yearning to understand how that country itself had grown up.

His was an isolated life in a harsh land. He and his siblings "were the only children in a thousand square miles, where children outnumbered the indigenous trees." The land's challenges were not only physical but intellectual, and ultimately moral, and against them David Love is tested. (The book opens with a sketch of his Vassar-educated mother arriving at the ranch, setting up the classic Western conflict between civilization and wilderness.) The tests mount, the adventures build, as McPhee and Love trek around the landscape, which Love knows as thoroughly as a suburbanite knows his backyard. David Love's character, like the Rockies, ultimately rises above the land's noxious touch and, by surmounting its challenges, above the plain stock of most people.[2]

By contrast, in *Landscape and Memory* Simon Schama portrays Claude Denecourt as an Enlightenment Pan, or Sylvanus, a modern gnome of the woods in a highly cultivated landscape, the Forest of Fontainebleau, not far from Paris. Eventually, Denecourt impresses his own personality onto the place. The two become inseparable. To know one is to know the other; to describe one, to describe the other. "So Claude François walked and walked and walked, winding his way through the densest and darkest areas, treading gingerly past the sleeping vipers, counting the much depleted population of deer and pig, laying down marks so that he could recognize his way back."

> Sometimes he thought he could even improve on what nature offered. One night, as he lay on a sandstone ledge, the crumbly soil gave under him and he fell into a small cavern. Crawling along a narrow natural tunnel, he emerged into another space. The experience was at once frightening and, in a not disagreeable way, exciting. But would it not be more enthralling if the little hollows could be made more cavernous, in the proper Salvator Rosa manner? What would be wrong with taking up nature's suggestions and supplying, here and there, a little picturesque improvement? So Denecourt, with a friend, Bournet, who had joined him, took his pick and chisel and made crevices into caves and caves into splendid "grottoes" and caverns, wetting the walls to encourage moss and mushrooms, letting the perfectly sour smell of earth and leafmold fill the dank interior.[3]

This is a biography of an artist in the making, one working with the natural features of Fontainebleau. Denecourt names; he shapes; he smoothes and roughens; and he plots pathways through the woods with painted blue arrows.

> The blue arrows were the syntax of Denecourt's grammar of woodland walks: what gave it direction and coherence. He would go out at night with a covered lamp, and a pot of blue paint beneath his coat, and apply them

to the precise places where he anticipated his walk-
ers would need direction. He was inventing the trail. It
was simple enough. But no one had ever done it before.[4]

Art invites an art critic, and Schama's account is one in
which an artist discovers his theme, perfects his technique
and medium, and creates a masterpiece. With Love's labors
in Wyoming, the land is immutably there, its lithic material-
ity to be understood and occasionally moved around, such
that McPhee begins with the geology, a hard language of
science, sentences as direct as a rock hammer, and lets the
land's unyielding character confront the man. With Fontainebleau, the woods are malleable, the clay and marble of
a sculptor's studio, and Schama's rendering is the story of a
man, textured with allusions to classical Arcadia. The language is more allusive, wandering through the picturesque,
adorned with the garb of civilization. The woods do not exist in and of themselves: they become what art makes them.
The relevant details are not those of Eocene strata and over-
thrust zones, but those of the particles of a culture drawn
out and dug into soil that turns land into landscape.

What each account shares is a reconciliation between
person and place. The setting becomes the story.

Landscape as Setting the Circumstances for Character

WESTERN NEW SOUTH WALES
  in Jill Ker Conway, *The Road from Coorain*

The book is a memoir, and Conway opens with a panorama
of the place where she was raised, the unforgiving near-
Outback of Australia, the sometime-grasslands of the New
South Wales western plains.

The landscape is flat, sunburnt, barely more than desert, and to the uninitiated, a monotony. Yet against this panorama of crushing plainness, there are many nuances and details, easily overlooked, that define the character of life on the land. To see them you need an artist's eye and a delicacy of senses, a vision very different from that of the region's dominant ethos, a grim stoicism. The plant life mirrors human society, rooted in hard will and only rarely flourishing ("in a good season"), but with patches of color and delicacy, like those odd characters who somehow transcend the circumstances of their birth.

Too many seasons were not good, however, and the gross disposition of this geography and its human history cultivated a peculiar "bush ethos,"

> which grew up from making a virtue out of loneliness and hardship built on the stoic virtues of convict Australia. Settled life and domesticity were soft and demoralizing. A "real man" despised comfort and scorned the expression of emotion. The important things in life were hard work, self-sufficiency, physical endurance, and loyalty to one's male friends, one's "mates." Knowledge about nature, the care of animals, practical mechanics was respected, but speculation and the world of ideas were signs of softness and impracticality. Religion and belief in a benevolent deity were foolish because daily life demonstrated beyond doubt that the universe was hostile. The weather, the fates, the bank that held the mortgage, bushfires—disaster in some form—would get a man in the end. When disaster struck, what mattered was unflinching courage and the refusal to consider despair.
>
> Very few women could stand the isolation.[5]

After several pages of detailed observation, in which the immense weight of the setting impresses itself onto the imagination, this conclusion seems exactly right. It matters, though, that the natural setting, not the bush ethos, begins the text, for the latter grows out of the former. The only alternative to those who live here is to accept that ethos, or to move. The wives and children of prosperous settlers do move, relocating to a rural town, although their continued prosperity still depends on the brutal whimsy of the environment. The ambitious, the artistic, those who wished for something more, have to keep going, which is what Jill Ker Conway does. The power of the road *from* Coorain, however, derives from the tenacity of its origins. That opening scene sets her memoir on the path that follows.

A Landscape Setting That Foreshadows Events To Come

MANN GULCH

   in Norman Maclean, *Young Men and Fire*

Norman Maclean introduces Mann Gulch, the scene of the blowup fire that constitutes the book's central event, with a quote from the official post-fire *Report of the Board of Review:* "The general area is steep and jagged on the Meriwether side and is said to be one of the roughest areas east of the Continent Divide." The observation is bland to the point of obscurity, and he contrasts it with one that better suits the story to follow. "'From the singular appearance of this place I called it the gates of the rocky mountains,' Captain Lewis said in his journals. Its singular appearance makes it a fitting backdrop for early and everlasting drama in which nature plays the leading role."

Far, far ahead are the mountains black with the haze that makes mountains look from the plains as if they were clouds of smoke from a great forest fire. As they and you come closer, the haze of the mountains breaks apart and reluctantly allows the yellow plains a final appearance. This is literally the way it was in Mann Gulch before the fire burned it out in a matter of minutes. It was the place in the Gates where the struggle between mountains and plains came face to face—below Mann Gulch belongs to the plains, upriver to the mountains and timber. Mann Gulch itself where the grave markers are was yellow with tall grass. The differences are not only scenic—there are differences between the behavior of grass and timber fires, and the differences can be tragic if firefighters don't know them.[6]

Maclean's band of smokejumpers are, unbeknownst to them but foreshadowed in the very character of Mann Gulch, "on their way to a blowup, a catastrophic collision of fire, clouds, and winds. With almost dramatic fitness, the collision was to occur where vast geologic confrontations had occurred millions and millions of years ago."[7]

Another aesthetic might fret over Maclean's extensive exegesis of his own description. Wouldn't it be better to describe the place in such a way that the meaning is inherent in the text? This would foreshadow the events, would help to set up the expectation that another catastrophe was imminent, would help to build up a static charge of suspense. But Maclean has already announced what will happen. In this geologic crucible, a miniature world, a crew will be born, live briefly, and die. What he wants to prepare us for is his quest after the meaning of what occurred. The place has to embody something more than a prelude to action. So he ends his description by moving those physical features into a moral universe, and this technique makes a natural blowup into a human catastrophe. "Do not be deceived, though, by the scenic beauty of the Gates of the Mountains into believing that the confrontations and terrors of nature are obsolescences frozen in stone, like the battles of satyrs in Greek bas-relief, remnants of mythology and witnessed if ever by dinosaurs and now only by seismographs." It is easy to assume, Maclean warns, that "as the result of modern science 'we have conquered nature.'" Instead, "we should be prepared for the possibility, even if we are going to accompany modern firefighters into Mann Gulch, that the terror of the universe has not yet fossilized and the universe has not run out of blowups." The universe is "composed of catastrophes and missing parts," and around the Gates of the Mountains "catastrophes everywhere enfold us as they do the river."[8]

Maclean's rendering of Mann Gulch sets not merely the action of a fire but the conditions of our understanding of what that fire might mean. The meditation that, by some aesthetic standards, might seem to mar the text with authorial intrusion, that encrusts bare description with commentary when the description itself might convey that meaning, is in fact the point of the text. It is Maclean's mind, not Mann Gulch, that is being described.

Built Environment as Embodying the Personality of Its Builder

SAN LORENZO DE ESCORIAL
  in Garrett Mattingly, *The Armada*

The action of Garrett Mattingly's account of the Spanish Armada hinges on the character of a man whose temporal power reached outward over vast lands but whose temperament drove him inward to ever smaller realms. "Nobody since the beginning of history had ever ruled so much of the earth's surface as Philip II of Spain. Nobody had ever owned so many titles of kingdoms, dukedoms, counties, principalities and lordships of all sorts. And nobody, surely, had ever had so many papers to read." Helpfully, Philip fashioned an ideal expression of his ambition, his power, his clerical zeal to read every dispatch, and his fatal instinct toward privacy: this was the construction of San Lorenzo de Escorial, which Mattingly accepts as "a symbol and a revelation." For Philip himself conceived the "monastery-palace," selected its site, fussed over its twenty-year construction, made its "main outlines" and many of its details "intimately his." Immediately, "Philip had begun to live inside his dream. The vast stone pile which he had drawn about him like a garment spoke of his peculiar self as no other building in Europe had ever echoed the spirit of a single man."[9]

Steadily, Mattingly's account advances inward, beginning with the geographic setting at the (kneeling) "knees" of the Guadarramas, and ending, stoned circle within circle, with the cell-like cubicle and secret passageways claimed by Philip, an echo of his thirst for privacy. The placing of the Escorial takes two forms, one which emphasizes its public stature and the other its private nooks. The first: "Philip's San Lorenzo is shut away at the center of the massive walled monastery like the innermost citadel of a fortress, like a sacred standard in the middle of a phalanx. St. Peter's stands for the spiritual counteroffensive of Rome, the confident, magniloquent advertisement of a catholic faith. The church of San Lorenzo stands for the embattled defense of orthodoxy by the temporal sword."[10]

That defines one contrast. The second description, moving farther into the interior corridors themselves, speaks to Philip's mind as it engaged the outside world.

> That the great monastery actually seemed to Philip a defiance and a threat to the heretics of Europe which those wicked revolutionaries would risk anything to spoil is more than a fantasy. He often said so, attributing every accident or delay to the machinations of heretic spies, and a building thought of in those terms could hardly fail to resemble a fortress. That the church at the center should be at the same time a tomb where, according to plans which affected the whole complex structure, masses in overpowering numbers were to be said for the soul of Philip and his relatives tells us less of the king's spiritual views than it does of his sense of the unique position which he and his family occupied in Christendom—just as the site he selected is eloquent of his elevation above even the greatest of his subjects. But the Escurial reveals more than Philip's public images of his public self. At the secret heart of the great building, right next to the monastery church, a meager suite of rooms is hidden. The most important pieces are a sort of study or workroom decently lighted but somehow meanly proportioned, and off it an alcove bedroom which has a shuttered little window opening into the church near the high altar. Monastery, palace and tomb prove only so many masks concealing a retreat, a refuge, almost a hiding place.[11]

It was amid such circumstances that Philip II conceived and directed the scheme that became the Armada. That project, its strength, its liabilities, its compound of geopolitical boldness and personal isolation—all are as much an expression of Philip as San Lorenzo de Escorial.

Mattingly's careful setting is not a dumb place where Philip II struts but a revelation of his character, and a foreshadowing of the immense events to come, the Armada as Escorial at sea. What makes the account particularly effective is that Mattingly does not simply declaim this symbolism but takes us through its nested, nautiline chambers and its construction by Philip II. Setting, symbol, and character all converge.

A Setting Very Well Known, or Known Widely but Incorrectly for Purposes of the Text

APPOMATTOX COURTHOUSE
in Bruce Catton, *This Hallowed Ground*

Few scenes are more recognizable to Americans than the meeting at Appomattox Courthouse between Ulysses S. Grant and Robert E. Lee, the commanding generals, respectively, of the Army of the Potomac and the Army of Northern Virginia, to sign the surrender agreement that effectively ended the American Civil War. The scene is a setting, and a problem, not because it must be hewn out of raw archives but precisely because it is so well known as to be a historical celebrity or a cliché. How to handle such material?

You might try to recapture that ineffable moment by building narrative suspense or by erecting a scaffolding out of obscure details that will likewise surprise. But any such approach must pretend that the reader doesn't know what happens or that the interest in the scene is other than the two giant personalities who must confront each other face to face. Bruce Catton simply admits the scene's status up front: not only the circumstances of 1865 but also the ones a century later by which it must be recorded. "Grant and Lee sat at two separate tables, the central figures in one of the greatest tableaus of American history."

> It was a great tableau not merely because of what these two men did but also because of what they were. No two Americans could have been in greater contrast. (Again, the staging was perfect.) Lee was legend incarnate—tall, gray, one of the handsomest and most imposing men who ever lived, dressed today in his best uniform, with a sword belted at his waist. Grant was—well, he was U. S. Grant, rather scrubby and undersized, wearing his working clothes, with mud-splattered boots and trousers and a private's rumpled blue coat with his lieutenant general's stars tacked to the shoulders. He wore no sword. The men who were with them noticed the contrast and remembered it. Grant himself seems to have felt it; years afterward, when he wrote his memoirs, he mentioned it and went to some lengths to explain why he did not go to this meeting togged out in dress uniform. (In effect, his explanation was that he was just too busy.)
>
> Yet the contrast went far beyond the matter of personal appearance. Two separate versions of America met in this room each perfectly embodied by its chosen representative.[12]

Catton then proceeds with a classic character profile that segues into symbolism but never loses the touch for detail.

His retelling of the event works, though, in good part because he accepts the power and prevalence of the existing image. He calls it what it is: "a great tableau." He plays with its inherent drama ("the staging was perfect"). He down-plays the contrast between the characters, focusing on their dress and depicting the vernacular Grant with vernacular expressions ("well, he was U. S. Grant"), a technique all the more effective because the book relates the war from a Northern perspective that might argue for Grant's apotheo-sis. The paragraph works to set up Catton's own elaboration of meanings, not by hype and triumphalism but by under-statement and by a confession that the exalted moment can speak, in its setting, for itself, and by accepting the place of the customary literary rendering in the common imagi-nation.

But Catton goes further. He embeds the surrender at Appomattox Courthouse within a larger subchapter that in-cludes the assassination of Abraham Lincoln. This prevents one celebrity set-piece from hijacking the larger narrative. He can let it speak for what it is, but pairing it with an al-most equally powerful story ensures that the opportunity it offers for rhetorical flourish does not overwhelm the whole text. It is one aftershock among many. Catton can play the setting without having it play him.

Not a bad way to cope with celebrity or to convert a cli-chéd scene into a revealing climax.

chapter 15

Point of View

In which we consider the way how we see affects what we see, and whether "we" should be "I" or a no one who is everyone

Point of view describes how you as author position yourself relative to characters, settings, and events. It says who is seeing the action, and from where. Since it affects how the text is interpreted and regarded, point of view overlaps with both voice and vision. But the latter encompass the former. Point of view places the reader to see and hear, or positions an in-text narrator to show and tell.

What vantage point you choose depends on your purpose. You can hover above the whole, presenting a quasi-objective vista over not only what happens but why and what it means. Or you can allow characters to tell the story in parts, each from his or her perspective, such that authorial control appears diffused or refracted—although this impression is a mirage, for your authorial self still shapes all, including the choice of what characters will speak and when, and what incidents will be highlighted and how. Or you can create a persona, a narrator within the text who tells the story and can do so with a perspective and voice different from the ones you normally use. (Journalistic accounts are especially fond of this technique, which is also a staple of biography, where the text revolves around a character who may tell much of his or her own story.)

The same considerations apply to character equivalents. Since point of view describes how events and people are seen or felt, it is possible to use natural settings or processes. Yosemite Valley or the Mississippi Flood of 1927 can't speak, of course, but events can be ordered around them such that they act as an organizing perspective: the narration appears as they might have seen it. While woods, mountains, and floods can't have voice, they can have focus, and can help to shift point of view in useful ways.

Once you appreciate the larger issue, the options are surprisingly rich, although generally restricted to outright narratives. (It's hard to imagine multiple points of view in a thesis about Euclid's fifth postulate, for example. Such attempts do happen, typically in an effort to make rigorous material "accessible" and reader-friendly, but all too often they simply sound whimsical and patronizing.)

The choices for nonfiction would seem to be two. You can write from the vantage point of an omniscient author who knows all there is to know and conveys that knowledge from a God-like vantage point. Or you can write from a first-person perspective, telling the story (often your own) in your particular words from an admittedly restricted view. The first is typical of big-screen histories and scientific syntheses; the second, of memoir and journalistic texts based on travels, incidents, and interviews in which the author is a participant.

The truth is that the choices are several, although not as robust as those available for fiction. Why? In fiction, the author knows what the characters feel and think and see, and can play with that material. The writer can tell the story entirely from the perspective of one character, or can employ a suite of characters, each of whom sees his or her own fraction of the whole and can narrate in the first person. In nonfiction (apart from memoir), the author can work only with the evidence available. Sources such as letters, diaries, and autobiography allow for a personal voice, expressed through a character's own words, but it must be placed within a larger frame set by the author. The use of third-person narration is, in fact, part of what conveys to the reader that the text is authentic, and not dependent on any individual's particular vantage point.

If there would seem to be no other choice, that's because the omniscient narrator is typically part of the genre. It seems necessary because it is common. In practice, several possibilities exist, and in recent years recognition that every text must contain an authorial point of view has encouraged nonfiction writers to state in some kind of preface the basis for their own perspectives. As with fiction, there is ample opportunity for you as author to differ from an in-text narrator. A witness may be unreliable, or a character or a source may be at variance with the general evidence. A distance exists between you as author and those characters you may use within the text to recount parts of the narrative, and this can apply even to a persona you insert. In this distance resides much of the irony endemic to modern literature.

Generally, the first-person narrator doesn't stray far from memoir or autobiography, or from the documented quotes of a character within the text. If the action occurs recently, and to the author, then the first-person voice may be the right one. The author not only experiences the action but understands its significance. This might be the case in a travel book or in a quest of some sort, be it to understand

a scientific project, to uncover the hidden life of some remote relative, or to visit an iconic place. In such cases the
text becomes an original document in itself, a record of its
narrator, for which a first-person voice would be appropri-
ate and perhaps mandatory, or at least without usable alternatives.

It can seem weird, for example, to speak of yourself in
the third person, although Xenophon and Caesar got away
with it in their war commentaries. But it becomes positively
creepy when Henry Adams uses it in his quirky autobiography *The Education of Henry Adams.* "He fell behind his
brothers two or three inches in height, and proportionally
in bone and weight. His character and processes of mind
seemed to share in this fining-down process of scale. He was
not good in a fight, and his nerves were more delicate than
boys' nerves ought to be. He exaggerated these weaknesses
as he grew older." Or, "Henry Adams escaped but he never
tried to be useful again." A little bit of this goes a long way,
but Adams made it go 505 pages, which may indeed reflect,
as he insisted, a failure of education.[1]

A second-person perspective, as William Germano ob-
serves, can sound like something out of the *Twilight Zone.*
"You are researching the cost of housing in Hong Kong
when you discover a disturbing fact about drywall construction." Yet an occasional appeal to the second person can
break up the tempo and tone of a text. For example, consider this passage from Bernard DeVoto about John Charles
Fremont's posturing during the Bear Flag rebellion: "However you care to interpret what followed, you can get supporting evidence at the source. Fremont had come back to
California to initiate a movement which should seize it for
the flag—whether as an act of war against Mexico or as a
safeguard against Great Britain did not matter to him and

should not matter to us." Try to write this from a traditional third-person omniscient viewpoint: "It is possible to interpret what followed many ways, and each way offers supporting evidence." Or worse: "Historians interpret the primary sources differently and draw various conclusions." As a method for discussing historiography, fine. As a means to advance a narrative, lethally dull and distracting. Instead, turn to the second-person voice to make a text more colloquial. The device is especially common for instruction manuals, full of imperatives and over-your-shoulder advice ("hammer the tack gently into place," "you should now see the main outlines"). You might well imagine it used in a text about how to write.[2]

The use of the first-person plural, however, may feel less eerie than arcane. The editorial "we" is not much in fashion these days of niche markets, marginal cultural consensus, and the substitution of personal attitude for public opinion. Intellectual fashion dictates that no writer can claim concord with others, certainly not if gender, race, ethnicity, or class differ. Still, some authors such as Alfred Crosby can manage the trick without offense, perhaps because they refract their perspective through nature or they invite the reader to join the writer in what almost seems a conversation. Note how deftly it can manage otherwise ponderous topics.

What date shall we pick for completion of the Old World Neolithic Revolution in the lands of its origin? Suppose we have it terminate a neat 5,000 years ago with domestication of the horse—an arbitrary choice, perhaps, but a good approximation. Between that era and time of development of the societies that sent Columbus and other voyagers across the oceans, roughly 4,000 years passed, during which little of importance happened, relative to what had gone before.

Let us apply the technique of time-lapse photography to the four millennia following completion of the Old World Neolithic, exposing a frame only every half century or so. When we then view our film at normal speed, we are struck with the uneventfulness of this long period.[3]

Far less happy is the outcome when you avoid the first-person plural by appealing to third-person surrogates. To say, for instance, "the historian" or "anthropologists today" is to appeal merely to the putative authority of an intellectual guild. The result can be both false and ugly. Use "we." Or "I." Or find another way to restate the sentence (there are, as Mr. Spock says, always . . .). Using phrases like these is a narrative cliché, and an unnatural act that comes from long practice under such stern instructors as a dissertation committee, part of an initiation ritual into the academic fraternity.

Point of view may be a concept more readily illustrated than defined. The sampling below suggests how even an omniscient narrator may become multiple and may morph into something of a ventriloquist, throwing his voice through characters in the text.

How Authorial Point of View Differs from That of Characters

"THE MANY DEATHS OF GENERAL WOLFE"
in Simon Schama, *Dead Certainties*

Employing points of view other than the omniscient narrator's is not the same as using a variety of characters, each of whom narrates selected events through his or her own point of view. Simon Schama tells the story of General James Wolfe's death four times: once through the perspective of a private soldier, once through Wolfe, once as Benjamin West did in his masterful painting, and once as Francis Parkman did in the climax to his historical epic about the contesting North American empires of France and England. Each interprets the story through the prism of his own experience. The maladies of each viewer are painted or written into the text in a series of brilliant portraits.

Schama makes the point clearly: an absolute perspective is impossible. But revealing the manifold origins of these perspectives through the life of their viewer is not the same as having the viewer tell the story. In this way, West's painting gets analyzed for its complex rearrangements (ultimately a historical "fiction"), while Parkman's bizarre and brooding neuroses, weirdly similar to Wolfe's, inform his tableau, and make the lives of both men their greatest work of art. In each sketch, however, the narrator is unquestionably Simon Schama, describing how each man came to his view, not each man speaking more or less for himself. None tells the story: Schama does that by overtly interpreting their work through their lives.

The exception is the opening account, in which a British soldier describes the evening ascent of the cliffs below Quebec City and draws his own personal portrait of the general, who appears quite different from the "Roman" he was later made out to be. Revealingly, this sketch is fiction, which is where experiments in point of view tend to go. For the others, Schama was unable (or unwilling) to surrender his authorial standing. He would explain how the others came to their view, but he would not let *them* so explain. The exercise may thus illustrate characterization as point of view.

An In-Text Narrator Holding Together Several Narrations

JAMES CLYMAN

in Bernard DeVoto, *The Year of Decision: 1846*

In distilling America's "continental mind," as he calls it, De-Voto weaves multiple strands of a pivotal year, 1846, into a grand tapestry, using a technique similar to that of thriller novelists. The threads are many, fierce, and epic. There is the folk migration west culminating in the tragedy of the Donner Party, the many battles and personalities of the Mexican War, the Mormon hegira to the Great Salt Lake while contributing a battalion to the war, the *opéra bouffe* revolution of the Bear Flag Republic, the fetid politics of the national capital—all orchestrated by an implicit sense of "destiny" that keeps the general movement westward under the banner of DeVoto's narrative arc.

But something in the text, some character or plot element, is needed to keep them all on track; and DeVoto moreover insists that his "purpose" is "literary," namely, to realize that frontier era as "personal experience." These two ambitions require that someone in the text act as guide, cipher, commentator—in brief, as a surrogate author. DeVoto provides such a person in James Clyman, a former mountain man whose career distills the preceding drama in the West and who now finds himself consistently close to the action. When he first appears, "encamped in the mountain chaos of northern California," he notes in his journal that "you don't know nothing certain unless you see it yourself." Clyman serves as that on-site witness. From time to time, he allows DeVoto to recalibrate his oft-raucous authorial voice by having someone on the scene speak for him.[4]

> He [Clyman] is there with Lansford Hastings, trekking
> east across the Great Basin. Some of the party wanted to

keep to the safe, familiar way. But Hastings was hurrying to change the destiny of nations: the empire-builder felt that the Conquest of California might hinge on his choice of a route. In his book he had said that the straight line from the Humboldt to Great Salt Lake and thence to Fort Bridger was the best, easiest, and quickest California trail. When he commended this trail to the public he had never seen it. In fact, there was no trail in any proper sense and it seemed a good idea, since he was going to recommend it to this year's emigrants, to see what it looked like. He won. The party moved onto the Salt Desert, . . . Jim making prophetic notes on the difficulty of this country.

The contrast with Hastings sharpens. "If the young man, stuffed with vision, ignorance, and the will to lie for empire's sake has had any romantic appeal so far, he now loses it."

Jim Clyman found him less than appealing. Jim had just traveled with him the route he intended to recommend to the emigrants. To Jim's intelligence—undeluded, far greater than Hastings', and weathered by a lifetime of pioneering—it was an extremely dangerous route. The mountain man's eyes, faded by years of scanning horizons under desert sun, must have hardened. He also had a duty to the emigration and with his handful of companions he started out to meet it.

Clyman serves as guide, as foil, and as prism for DeVoto's authorial presence, all personalized ("Jim") in a way DeVoto says he intended the book to do.[5]

Author as In-Text Persona

JOHN MCPHEE

Assembling California

Putting yourself as author into a text is a delicate affair. The technique works best when the project describes a quest or discovery and when the author is not the prime suspect— when the authorial persona can act as a prompt or foil in ways an omniscient narrator cannot. The strategy is standard fare for journalists, who often so insert themselves, fashioning a persona that can engage the subject while keeping at least a sliver of distance from themselves as the author.

In *Assembling California,* John McPhee uses his implied presence to talk to his protagonist, Eldredge Moores, and to others (and not to himself). Through scores of scenes McPhee relies on his in-text presence to force questions, to mine the critical ore of Moores' personality, or, more accurately, to let Moores' own comments and behavior reveal his character.

It was in Macedonia that I asked Moores how he felt about being in a profession that had identified the olivine that people would be ripping the mountainsides to take away, and he said, "Schizophrenic. I grew up in a mining family. . . . Now I'm a member of the Sierra Club."[6]

Leafing through the book, Moores picks up the information that the foundation and first story of Rhine House are limestone. He goes outside and squints at the house through his ten-power Hastings Triplet. "Jesus

Christ!" he says. For Moores, this is new ground. He has never before seen limestone that came out of a volcano. "It's poorly welded volcanic ash with lots of big vesicles, pumice lapilli," he goes on. "It's friable volcanic ash! A welded tuff! An ignimbrite!"[7]

The exchange is rich with McPhee's wry wit, but not with McPhee as an in-text character. The story is not about him. Elsewhere this exchange takes place:

> "To see through the topography and see how the rocks lie in three dimensions beneath the topography is the hardest thing to get across to a student." After a mile of silence, he added cryptically, "Left-handed people do it better."
>
> I said nothing for while, and then asked him, "Are you left-handed?"
>
> He said, "I'm ambidextrous."
>
> At it happens, I am left-handed, but I kept it to my-self.[8]

Exactly. (And as it happens, he also keeps to his authorial self.) It's a matter of taste, of course, though some tastes seem to offend uniformly across history and continents.

Consider this alternative from *Let the Sea Make a Noise* in which the author, evidently deluded into thinking that the act of writing is what really interests the reader, presents a self-referential passage in the apparent belief that historical narrative should emulate a Donald Barthelme short story. *"WordPerfect 5.0 'Grabber.' First Draft:* Japanese peasants, like those anywhere else, were accustomed to capricious taxation by the agents of castle or town . . ." A little peculiar but not off-putting; not yet. But wait another couple of pages for the author to insert a meditation on the act of his own writing.

> Not bad. Enough blood and drama to serve as a "grabber," and enough cultural and geopolitical conflict to hint at the themes of the book. Of course, I'll have to do a flashback to the Spanish arrival in the North Pacific . . . and say something about technology. The Shogun's main motive for *sakoku,* after all, was to prevent his domestic rivals for power from getting their hands on European ships and guns. So the story begins with Japan purposely spurning Western technology, and it ends today with Western nations fretting over the invasion of Japanese technology. Nice symmetry, professor. Thanks to *sakoku* the North Pacific becomes a "white man's lake," but now, only 140 years after Japan's reemergence, the white man's day appears to be over in the Pacific.
>
> Or is this too lugubrious an opening scene? May put off some readers. And there's no personal element, just nameless peasants and abstract geopolitics. I've got to personalize the saga from the get-go and advertise its humor as well as its drama. Alaska, maybe. The business about "Soapy" and Harriman's railroad reveries. So let's hit F7 to exit. Save document. Call it "Nagasaki" . . . whoops! Whoever said it's easy to use a portable computer on an airplane? Exit Word Perfect? No. Open new document, and . . .
>
> *Alaska "Grabber." First Draft:* These days the luxury cruises . . .[9]

It's the kind of passage that gives postmodernism a really bad name. The discussion reveals exactly the internal winnowing of ideas and expression that good writing requires. But good writing would not likely insert that interior debate directly into a text through so blatant an authorial intrusion: the author would remain in the subject without becoming the subject. There are far better ways to establish one's voice or to create a presence or to illustrate the perils of single-chronicle narratives. Let the sea make its own noise. Let your text speak for you.

chapter 16

Showing and Telling

Wherein we consider the difference between
narrating and analyzing, and how showing and
telling become bonded like runners in a three-
legged race, either to help or to hinder

Nonfiction needs both to show and to tell. Authorial discrimination and judgment are what distinguish a literary text from raw documents and data. The gathering and culling of sources is one task; it's a service most readers have neither the time nor the patience to undertake. But an informed reporting of what those sources say and how they might be understood makes up the rest of an authorial economy. The deployment of voice and judgment together constitutes much of the value-added in a text. The need to use both is clear. It's the doing of it that causes stumbles. This is where understanding when and how to show or tell or both comes into play.

The usual means is to stock the shelves with examples, which moves the text from simple assertion to documented demonstration. The particulars (those telling details again) make the prose vivid and the argument or story compelling. Many of the passages chosen earlier to illustrate parallelism and transitioning use such rhetorical devices precisely for the purpose of bulking up the prose with muscular examples. Sloppy writing might leave those illustrations as annoying flab.

Watch, for example, how Mark Fiege describes the work-
ings of an irrigated Idaho landscape as a "hybrid landscape,"
in which "clear distinctions between technology and natural systems dissolved," and nowhere more evidently than in
hydraulic technology, "in the dams, reservoirs, canals, and
ditches that provided the basis for irrigated agriculture."
The analogy to plumbing, he notes, is false. This was true
for dams, which became absorbed into the river system.
And it was true for other hydraulic structures:

> Canals and ditches similarly reflected a blurring of tech-
> nological aims and natural processes. Made from the
> very ground from which irrigators excavated them,
> made of permeable soil and rock, canals and ditches lost
> water to aquifers. They also attracted plants, and thus
> insects, birds, and rodents that in turn threatened to
> destroy the canals themselves. Drainage ditches, largely
> a technological response to seepage from canals, also
> drew wild flora and fauna.[1]

Here is an excellent example of telling, rich with examples
and empirical details, as clear in its aims as a well-engineered
canal.

Yet the false distinction it criticizes between natural and
artificial can equally characterize the distinction between
saying what is happening and having that argument made
manifest in the action described in the text. Contrast Fiege's
exposition above, as crisp as a tightly organized lecture, with
John Barry's description of the rupturing of levees during
the 1927 Mississippi flood, in which the artificial distinction
between built and natural, or water and land, dissolves.

> The river had leaned against the levees for weeks now,
> in many places for months, saturating them, pressing

against them. Seepage was seen the entire length of the system. Dozens of tributaries, small and large, east and west—the Tennessee, the Cumberland, the Yazoo, the Ohio in the east; the Arkansas, the White, the St. Francis, the Canadian, the Missouri in the west; and a hundred others—had burst onto the land. Water was spouting out of the containment system as if through holes punched in a hose. The river was still swelling, threatening to burst open the containment system entirely. The private and state levees on tributaries had already been overwhelmed. Only the U.S. government–standard levees still held. But the Mississippi was only now receiving the great runoff from the lower valley, and the great flood from its tributaries.[2]

Each passage does what the author intends, but note the difference in their effects. In *Irrigated Eden,* Mark Fiege assumes for himself the role of central agent: he is the one who channels the water to make his point. It's as though he is irrigating the text, and in so doing he demonstrates the complexity of the transported water on the land. In *Rising Tide,* John Barry submerges his presence to let the Mississippi become the active agent. Our point of view becomes that of the river. In both instances the text remains the construction of the author, and in both the author remains omniscient. But by shifting the ostensible point of view, by refracting it through the river, Barry allows the Mississippi to become the driver of plot.

There is another way in which prose needs to balance showing and telling, and it is among the hardest of skills, a breaking point for many nonfiction writers: you have to both narrate and comment, that is, to express both action and analysis in the same text. Either you tell a story (or develop a thesis) or you analyze a topic, but not both together. Those tasks require different styles, or, if you will, different points of view, in that you cannot maintain the perspective of a narrator while you interrupt the story to explain what is behind it. Sporting events, parades, and political conventions typically have two commentators, one for the play-by-play and another for color. Essentially the same roles are required in extended nonfiction.

The ideal would be a text that does both: it would, by showing, tell, or by clever telling, show. The ideal nonfiction text should, as Archibald MacLeish says of poems, "not mean but be"; or like Robert Frost's "piece of ice on a hot stove," it should "ride on its own melt." It should reveal its meaning by its voice and vision. That is what segregates literary nonfiction from a lecture. The reality, however, is that writers tend to orient their texts toward one polarity or the other, or flicker in and out of each as needed. They tell (argue, explain, develop a thesis) and insert examples, perhaps in the form of stories or anecdotes. Or they show (narrate, unfold a story), and attach particles of information to the story like barnacles to a ship; and the more barnacles accrued, the slower the progress. You analyze or you narrate. You use data to create a story, or you tell stories about your data. If you include both, you must in some way break up the text to do it.

The breaks may be structural: the text halts while a story or analysis is inserted. Or they may occur through a change in point of view: a character, perhaps an authorial persona, comes onstage to serve as explicator. Or the author may change voice, indicating a new point of view, doing what a persona would but without having to create an avatar within the text. Masters make these transitions seamlessly, the play-by-play and color commentary so perfectly syncopated the reader hardly knows a story has halted or a thesis has acquired an illustrative anecdote.

But for most of us, juggling those two perspectives is among the most elemental unexamined aspects of writing sustained nonfiction. Each perspective suffers the vice of its virtue. Too much straight talking and your readers may not understand your point; too much talking about, and they may not understand what the fuss is over. Too much commentary can frustrate a reader—all chewing, and not enough to chew on, a kind of bubblegum text. Likewise, unvarnished narration can leave a reader, especially one not versed in the topic, uncertain as to what really matters and what does not. Just which amid all these words is a telling detail and which is decoration? What, finally, is the point?

The ideal is, as always, a message wrapped in the proper medium. It is a text in which all the parts knot together, in which the meaning is inextricable from design, perspective from plot, vision from voice. This, after all, is the premise behind nonfiction writing as art. Great writers manage the job variously: some with voice, some with sidebars or even whole chapters of commentary, some simply in their choice of verbs and adjectives. Such devices can be employed at all levels, from sentences to vast manuscripts, with judgments exalted, wry, or just weary, and they can be used openly or embedded covertly within the general text. Commentary can be integrated in various ways—by the author declaiming or by characters acting as foils or by setting or by the plot, in which deeds speak more loudly than words. But the process works best when it avoids tearing the fabric of the imagined world the text has created.

The techniques are many. Here are some.

Text Designed to Integrate Sections of Narration with Sections of Analysis

GERMANY'S DECLARATION OF WAR AGAINST RUSSIA
  in Barbara Tuchman, *The Guns of August*

Tuchman comes close to having it all: a set-piece scene full of dialogue, a commentary upon it, and a running analysis of what it means.

> At seven o'clock in St. Petersburg, at the same hour when the Germans entered Luxembourg, Ambassador Pourtalès, his watery blue eyes red-rimmed, his white goatee quivering, presented Germany's declaration of war with shaking hand to Sazonov, the Russian Foreign Minister.
>
> "The curses of the nations will be upon you!" Sazonov exclaimed.
>
> "We are defending our honor," the German ambassador replied.
>
> "Your honor was not involved. But there is divine justice."
>
> "That's true," and muttering, "a divine justice, a divine justice," Pourtalès staggered to the window, leaned against it, and burst into tears. "So this is the end of my mission," he said when he could speak. Sazonov patted him on the shoulder, they embraced, and Pourtalès stumbled to the door, which he could hardly open with a trembling hand, and went out, murmuring, "Goodbye, goodbye."
>
> This affecting scene comes down to us as recorded by Sazonov with artistic additions by the French ambassador Paléologue, presumably from what Sazonov told him. Pourtalès reported only that he asked three times

for a reply to the ultimatum and after Sazonov answered negatively three times, "I handed over the note as instructed."

Why did it have to be handed over at all? Admiral von Tirpitz, the Naval Minister, had plaintively asked the night before when the declaration of war was being drafted. Speaking, he says, "more from instinct than from reason," he wanted to know why, if Germany did not plan to invade Russia, was it necessary to declare war and assume the odium of the attacking party? His question was particularly pertinent because Germany's object was to saddle Russia with war guilt in order to convince the German people that they were fighting in self-defense and especially in order to keep Italy tied to her engagements under the Triple Alliance.[3]

The commentary is never intrusive, appearing only to order the quotations, which carry most of the weight. The author acts as a kind of stage manager to ensure that the historical actors know their places, remember their lines, and have the correct props at the proper time.

Text Told by Examples

ON MAJOR JOHN WESLEY POWELL (AGAIN)
in Wallace Stegner, *Beyond the Hundredth Meridian*

The sequence of events, suitably arranged, can itself furnish authorial commentary. In the passage that follows, Wallace Stegner first sets up one series of events, the rise of John Wesley Powell in the Union army. Then, with a brief observation (expressed in a wonderful metaphor), he lets events unfold. Of course he has selected the particulars, their timing and tempo, and through them he silently but impressively channels his comments. First, the chronicle:

> [Powell was] not the kind to remain still, even in the army. He entered on April 14 as a private. By June he was a second lieutenant, by November a captain and something of an expert on fortifications, solidly enough established on Grant's staff at Cape Girardeau to ask as a personal favor a few days' leave to go to Detroit and marry his cousin Emma Dean. On April 5, 1862, he came out of the smoke and roar of Shiloh, mounted on General Wallace's horse and with his right arm smashed by a Minie ball. They removed his arm above the elbow in Savannah three days later.
>
> Losing one's right arm is a misfortune; to some it would be a disaster, to others an excuse. It affected Wes Powell's life about as much as a stone fallen into a swift stream affects the course of the river. With a velocity like his, he simply foamed over it. He did not even resign from the army, but returned after a leave and a stretch of recruiting duty, and served as an artillery officer with Grant, Sherman, and Thomas.

Powell resigned on January 2, 1865. He "came out of the war with a painful, twice-operated-upon stump, and weighing barely 110 pounds with a full beard."[4]

Stegner needn't say Powell was good: Powell's rapid ascent through the ranks speaks for itself. Nor need he elaborate on Powell's resolution; again, events say that for him. The cascade of duties and battles expresses perfectly the "foaming" career of Wes Powell. Still, those events speak only because Stegner has arranged them to do so, and has made them vivid through his narrative rhythm and the use of surprising details ("Minie ball," "with a full beard"). The old writing adage, "Trust your reader," here finds its scholarly corollary, "Trust your material."

Text Interrupted by Blatant Authorial Commentary

JOHN CHARLES FREMONT AS CONQUEROR
in Bernard DeVoto, *The Year of Decision: 1846*

The text stops while DeVoto explains (or, more properly, pronounces upon) Fremont's actions in California's Bear Flag Revolt. Whether you find this acceptable or not depends on how fully you agree with DeVoto's prior depiction of Fremont's political histrionics—namely, as those of a hammy actor in a drama of his own construction.

> A recognition stirs, different from Walpole's instruction in Cooper. This column of bearded horsemen with white teeth parading the streets of Monterey, this carefully spaced display of the Conqueror riding alone on a cheap errand while the audience cheers, this arrangement, this camera angle—it is labeled. The dramaturgy of Captain Fremont had changed its medium. The Conquest had got into the movies, where it was to stay.[5]

And after his role is denied by Commodore John D. Sloat: "This was embarrassing. The Conquest remained illegitimate and the Conqueror's status was that of a thug. The sense of grievance burst into flame and Fremont would presently write to Senator Benton [his father-in-law] an account of these events that lay somewhere between falsehood and hallucination." He then had "the sick thought that this might be the best time to go home."

But a different commodore arrived, to whom Sloat joy-
fully turned over command and responsibility. This is a
d'Artagnan part, played by Robert Field Stockton, an
energetic, imaginative personage cast as a sea dog. Commodore Stockton needed only to survey the situation
in order to understand the cinematic requirements. He
supplied them. He commissioned Fremont (it is a little
hard to see by what authority) as a major in the army,
made Gillespie a captain, and mustered in Fremont's
irregulars as the Navy Battalion of Mounted Riflemen.
That is, in strict accuracy, as the Horse Marines. He furi-
ously prepared to conquer the rest of California and, be
sure, he issued a proclamation.[6]

Text Interrupted by Muted Authorial Commentary

FIRST: ON THE SUCCESS OF EUROPEANS AND THEIR ALLIED
  BIOTA

as explained by Alfred Crosby in *Ecological Imperialism*

This example is less in-your-face, posed as a question rather
than a declaration, and answered by deflecting through a
tangle of exotic details. Here Alfred Crosby breaks his telling of the paradoxical story of how European peoples and
biota flourish, often more robustly, outside Europe. It helps,
perhaps, that he is speaking not about a person but about a
historical process populated by kiwis and dandelions, an approach that deflects the commentary away from what might
degenerate into an ad hominem rant.

The resolution of the paradox is simple to state, though
difficult to explain. North America, southern South

America, Australia, and New Zealand are far from Europe in distance but have climates similar to hers, and European flora and fauna, including human beings, can thrive in these regions if the competition is not too fierce. In general, the competition has been mild. On the pampa, Iberian horses and cattle have driven back the guanaco and rhea. In North America, speakers of Indo-European languages have overwhelmed speakers of Algonkin and Muskhogean and other Amerindian languages; in the antipodes, the dandelions and house cats of the Old World have marched forward, and kangaroo grass and kiwis have retreated. Why? Perhaps European humans have triumphed because of their superiority in arms, organization, and fanaticism, but what in heaven's name is the reason that the sun never sets on the empire of the dandelion? Perhaps the success of European imperialism has a biological, an ecological, component.[7]

SECOND: INTERRUPTING A LITANY OF ASPIRING NATURAL-ISTS TO COMMENT ON ONE OF PARTICULAR PERTINENCE in William Goetzmann, *New Lands, New Men*

Pause at Mark Catesby, for it was he who best dramatized the work of the naturalist and the abundance of America. A friend and neighbor of John Ray, who was struggling mightily to bring the new science to bear on the chaos of classically oriented natural history, Catesby first sailed to America in 1712 with his sister on her honeymoon. She had married a man named Cocke who lived in Virginia. Through him, Catesby met William Byrd II and other colonial patrons, and he spent seven years botanizing in the tidewater region and deep into Virginia's mountains. He also went to Bermuda and Jamaica. By 1719 he was back in England with boxes of American plants, one of which he presented to Samuel Dale, a powerful figure in the naturalists' world. Catesby's gift bore fruit. By the end of 1720, he was commissioned by the Royal Society to go to America "to Observe the Rarities of that Country for the uses and purposes of the Society."[8]

This a scholar's sketch, as stuffed with details as Catesby's field bag with specimens. But it siphons the larger narrative flow into a single spigot, makes the abstract particular, and enriches our sense of what it took to become a traveling naturalist. Having established Catesby's bona fides, Goetzmann returns to the sweep of naturalist treks across a not-yet-Enlightened America.

Description and Commentary Interwoven

ON HOWARD HUGHES

in Joan Didion, "7000 Romaine, Los Angeles 38"

In a classic profile Joan Didion slides seamlessly between factual assets and their appraisal, the two aspects intertwined like a vine and trellis. First, as a voice running alongside the facts:

"It must be part of some larger mission."

The phrase was exactly right. Anyone who skims the financial press knows that Hughes never has business "transactions," or "negotiations"; he has "missions." His central mission, as *Fortune* once put it in a series of love letters, has always been "to preserve his power as the proprietor of the largest pool of industrial wealth still under the absolute control of a single individual." Nor does Hughes have business "associates"; he has only "adversaries." When the adversaries "appear to be" threatening his absolute control, Hughes "might or might not" take action. It is such phrases as "appear to be" and "might or might not," peculiar to business reportage involving Hughes, that suggested the special mood of a Hughes mission. And here is what the action might or might not be: Hughes might warn, at the critical moment, "You're holding a gun to my head." If there is one thing Hughes dislikes, it is a gun to his head (generally this means a request for an appearance, or a discussion of policy), and at least one president of T.W.A., a company which, as Hughes ran it, bore an operational similarity only to the government of Honduras, departed on this note.

The stories are endless, infinitely familiar, traded by the faithful like baseball cards, fondled until they fray around the edges and blur into the apocryphal.

Hughes, Didion tells us through a source, fancies Las Vegas "because he likes to be able to find a restaurant open in case he wants a sandwich."[9]

And later, as a direct commentary: "Why do we like those stories so? Why do we tell them over and over? Why have we made a folk hero of a man who is the antithesis of all our official heroes, a haunted millionaire out of the West, trailing a legend of desperation and power and white sneakers? But then we have always done that." The point of the piece is to highlight America's folk passion for "absolute personal freedom, mobility, privacy"—"the desire to be able to find a restaurant open in case you want a sandwich, to be a free agent, live by one's own rules."[10]

We might borrow that final phrase for our own purposes. However much we might fantasize, Hughes-like, about living entirely by our own rules of writing, the likely outcome would resemble Hughes's own: the text as recluse. A text needs to be read, and most readers will want to be both told what is happening and told what it means, and they will demand sufficient information for them to understand what is happening and why.

Not all nonfiction has a narrative design that can show and tell seamlessly; most must do bits of both in syncopation. Moreover, readers almost always welcome background information, which keeps them from stumbling over the story, and they savor commentary, which makes the text more conversational. The greatest art achieves that effect without seeming to. But whether or not art rises to the task, craft must.

chapter 17

Editing II

*In which we return to the bottomless pit of revisions,
this time not in theory but in practice*

Begin simply with the ritual rewrite of a long passage into a
punchier and more succinct one.

The following text is intended to introduce a subchapter
on the history of forest fires in British Columbia with a target length of 9,000–10,000 words. This is an already twice-
revised draft in which the raw material has been assimilated
into serviceable prose.

> Mountains were not a fringe, nor forests an afterthought
> for British Columbia: the province had little else. The
> Cordillera bordered the boreal plain on the northeast,
> and, spectacularly, the Pacific on the southwest. Between
> them lay mountains, rumpled plateaus, and woods—
> pines, spruces, firs, Douglas firs, cedars, hemlocks; Rocky
> Mountain forests, boreal forests, temperate rainforests.
> In Queen Charlotte Islands was a sodden, west-coast
> echo of Cape Breton. In interior valleys, behind rain-
> shadowing ranges, amid a patchy semi-aridity, bunch-
> grass and shrubs sprouted. But the geography of British

Columbia was one of mountains and forests, wet to the west, dry to the east.

That determined the pattern of its fires, while peculiarities of its political economy determined the pattern of its fire institutions. Economics pushed it into commodities; politics, into corporatism. Timber quickly replaced furs and minerals as the basis for provincial wealth based on exports. There was little competition from agriculture. Logging created the slash that fueled settlement fires; loggers, not settlers, replaced the first wave of land-clearing loggers. Most distinctive, and determinative, was British Columbia's system of land tenure. Unlike the interior provinces sculpted out of Rupert's Land, the federal presence was minor in terms of land tenancy, and the 1930 transfer act extinguished most of that. Still, the Railways Belt was important as a model and catalyst. What the Railways Commission did elsewhere, the DFB did here. Unlike the eastern provinces, the land remained almost wholly Crown; a scant 4 percent of British Columbia's land base was private. Fire policies and programs evolved not, as elsewhere, in competition with other economic or social sectors but in close collaboration with the one factor that decided everything else: a timber industry fostered on public land.

What is wrong with this passage? Nothing substantive. It could be crisped up and spiced, as with any writing. But there are no flagrant violations of what passes for conventionally good prose. The issue is context. These paragraphs will not be standing on their own. In this instance, British Columbia must reside alongside a score of similar provin-

cial surveys in what threatens to become a sprawling confederation, which makes this particular passage too long,
too dense, and too complicated.

The first response is to cut. Those named forests, which
in another context might be welcomed as grounding the
text in details, can go. So can some historical particulars.
Two rounds of diligent plucking and pruning yield this se-
quel:

> Mountains were not a fringe, nor forests an afterthought
> for British Columbia: the province had little else. The
> Cordillera bordered the boreal plain on the northeast,
> and, spectacularly, the Pacific on the southwest. Between
> them lay mountains, rumpled plateaus, and woods, wet
> in the west and drier inland and to the east. While this
> coarse geography set the pattern of its fires, peculiari-
> ties of its political economy determined the pattern of
> its fire institutions. Economics pushed it into commodi-
> ties; politics, into corporatism. Timber quickly replaced
> furs and minerals. Logging created the slash that fueled
> settlement fires; more loggers, not settlers, replaced the
> first wave of land clearing. Especially, there was British
> Columbia's system of land tenure, almost wholly Crown
> and wholly provincial. Private land was a scant 4 percent
> of the total, and Dominion holdings were limited to the
> Railway Belt, which was ceded to the province in 1930.
> Fire policies and programs evolved not, as elsewhere, in
> competition with other economic or social sectors but in
> close collaboration with the one factor that decided ev-
> erything else: a timber industry fostered on public land.

This rewriting reduces the passage from 283 words to 181,
a reduction of 36 percent, which should, by normal expec-

tations, be counted as a triumph. The effect is achieved by compression: words removed, key ideas retained, the whole boiled down to a hard lump. But the outcome is dense and thematically opaque. It is awkward to extract and recall the critical points. They are all crammed into a common bucket, like clumps of blueberries.

This situation calls for another rewriting, this time not by compression but by reconfiguration and as sparely as possible.

> British Columbia was the oddity: a late, far-west colony confederated by rails; all mountainous, virtually all wooded, almost wholly Crown land. Private holdings were a scant 4 percent of the total, roughly proportional to the Railway Belt, which the Dominion ceded to the province in 1930. Its spirit was corporatist in political economy and conservationist in its ideals. Above all, it was a colossal timber mill.

No problem here with too much detail: the passage is a concise prelude to the dominant themes that will follow. We are down to 65 words, a 78 percent reduction from the original. Though it isn't quite Hemingwayesque, we are getting closer. The passage lays out the themes and nothing else.

Yet the passage doesn't work, again because of its larger context and because design demands some consistency between comparable parts. Here, the other provincial histories would have to emulate this one; or, if this one is written toward the end of the project, it will have to be brought into closer alignment with the others. The version is simply too spare, too elided, too peculiar. The exercise is useful because it forces us to identify the most basic motifs. Now we have to restore some flesh to that emaciated body.

British Columbia was an oddity: a far-west colony con-
federated to the rest by rails. It was all mountainous, virtually all wooded, almost wholly Crown land. A coarse
geography of rainfall divided its ranges and rumpled
plateaus into wet west and drier east; that set the pattern
of its fires. A peculiar political economy set the pattern
of its fire institutions. Timber replaced furs and minerals; logging created the slash that fueled settlement fires
elsewhere; and more loggers, not settlers, replaced the
first wave of land clearing. Fire programs evolved not,
as elsewhere, in competition with farming or fur trap-
ping but in close collaboration with the one factor that
decided everything else: a timber industry fostered on
public land. B.C. became a colossal timber mill.

Like western Canada overall, economics pushed the
province into commodities, politics into corporatism,
and timing into conservationist ideals. What made it distinctive was how these kneaded into the peculiarities of
its land ownership. Private holdings were scant (4 percent). The Dominion oversaw the Railway Belt from
1871 to 1930, a useful inspiration but not the basis for
permanent bureaus. From nearly the origins of its timber industry, the province recognized it needed fire protection and knew it had to do the job on its own.

This is good enough to include with the final manuscript
(207 words, a 27 percent reduction from the original). Both
the passage and the whole will undergo more revisions before they get into print, but the mix seems more or less
right.

The issue is not simply finding those overlush adjectives
or the occasional rogue adverb to cull out. The problem
is sense, and sense that depends on the passage's setting

within the whole. The last revision considerably expands the text from the prior draft, but it does so by appealing to contrasts between British Columbia and other provinces in order to sharpen meaning. This both gives the reader a bit of breathing room and positions the passage better within the whole. Note that the added details characterize not the province's geographic landscape but its political one. This is the equivalent of shunning character descriptions that rely only on physical traits ("six feet two inches," "200 pounds") and appealing instead to moral traits ("mean-spirited," "vindictive"). There is enough of the physical setting to accommodate the explanation, soon to follow, about how and why British Columbia evolved a double set of fire strategies. There is not so much that it deflects the thrust of the passage away from its political setting within confederation. That's what matters most. It is what an introduction must achieve, and what competent editors should make possible.

Now attend to the common question of how to convert textual source material into working text. For the exercise, let's rewrite the following passage from Alexander von Humboldt's *Personal Narrative of a Voyage to the Equinoctial Regions of the New Continent*. The occasion is the onset of Humboldt's five-year trek to the New World; the moment, June 1799; the location, the Canary Islands.

> On the morning of the 19th of June we caught sight of the point of Naga, but the Pico de Teide remained invisible. Land stood out vaguely because a thick fog effaced the details. As we approached the natural bay of Santa Cruz we watched the mist, driven by wind, draw near. The sea was very rough, as it usually is in this place. After

much sounding we anchored. The fog was so thick that visibility was limited to a few cables' length. Just as we were about to fire the customary salute the fog suddenly dissipated and the Pico de Teide appeared in a clearing above the clouds, illuminated by the first rays of sun, which had not reached us yet. We rushed to the bow of the corvette so as not to miss this marvelous spectacle, but at that very same moment we saw four English warships hove to near our stern, not far out in the open sea. We had passed them closely by in the thick fog that had prevented us from seeing the peak, and had thus been saved from the danger of being sent back to Europe. It would have been distressing for naturalists to have seen the Tenerife coasts from far off and not to have been able to land on soil crushed by volcanoes. We quickly weighed anchor and the *Pizarro* approached the fort as closely as possible to be under its protection. Here, two years before in an attempted landing, Admiral Nelson lost his arm to a cannon-ball. The English ships left the bay; a few days earlier they had chased the packet-boat *Alcudia,* which had left La Coruña just before we did. It had been forced into Las Palmas harbour, and several passengers were captured while being transferred to Santa Cruz in a launch.[1]

The passage includes several themes, each of which might be developed, or the whole rewritten to merge more smoothly with the general. What gets emphasized depends on context. If the larger theme is Great Moments in Exploration, a revision might look like this:

As they approached the Canaries, the historic port of departure for Spanish voyagers to the Americas, a rough sea slowed them, while thick fog, to Humboldt's intense frustration, blocked the classic view of the Pico de Teide. "It would have been distressing," he lamented, "for naturalists to have seen the Tenerife coasts from far off and not to have been able to land on soil crushed by volcanoes." Then the fog suddenly lifted.

"We rushed to the bow of the corvette," he exulted, "so as not to miss this marvelous spectacle." It was one of the sublime scenes of European discovery. Teide had long stood as a sentinel in Europe's maritime encounter with a wider world. Toward its towering peak Christopher Columbus and Ferdinand Magellan, and almost all other captains of the Great Voyages, had piloted, and from beneath its shadow they had then sailed Beyond.

But in Humboldt's hands it was to be recast as a stele of naturalist science. His ascent established a rite of passage for adventuring naturalists, the place where they field-tested themselves and their ideas. His reconnaissance of Teide became the measure for a century of Grand Reconnaissances throughout the American West, the Australian Outback, the Eurasian deserts, and the search for Africa's Mountains of the Moon. When he drew a map of the world's mountains, with those of the Americas to the left and those of Asia to the right, he placed Tenerife exactly in the center, for it was the index to which all others would refer.

But suppose, instead, that Humboldt's improbable trek is the point of the text. The rewriting might emphasize the fact that the journey had been difficult to launch at all.

Getting to the New World while the old one was aflame with the Napoleonic Wars was a tricky affair. Even to reach the Canaries, Spanish possessions since the fifteenth century and the classic point of departure for voyages to the New World, the *Pizarro* had to dodge a blockade outside La Coruña by the British Navy (only a few days earlier the packet-boat *Alcudia* had been chased into the harbor at Santa Cruz and some passengers intercepted). It was a sensitive site for the British, for here Admiral Nelson had lost an arm while storming the shore batteries. Now the customary rough seas met a thick fog. Humboldt's frustration mounted. It was unconscionable that he might sail within sight of Teide and not set foot on its soil.

Yet the fog was a blessing. As it abruptly lifted, and Teide sparkled in the sun, a convoy of British ships "hove to near their stern." The *Pizarro* hurriedly raised anchor and sought the protection of the fort. Humboldt's good fortune held: another test had passed. The daring trek to Madrid, the improbable appeal to Charles IV, the passage to the New World—truly it seemed that he was the incarnation of a second Columbus. Now he had reached the Canaries. Teide beamed, radiant above the clouds. On its beckoning slopes, the young Alexander commenced his career as an exploring naturalist.

Now rewrite from the perspective of the Canary Islands within the context of Europe's grand rhythms of exploration.

Europe had discovered, forgotten, and rediscovered the Canary Islands more than once. The Ancients knew them by several names, though the "Fortunate Isles" got fixed in Ptolemy's *Geographia* and in Pliny the Elder's *Natural History*. In the fourteenth century, recovered texts met rediscovered lands as Catalan merchants and Majorcan missionaries made landfall. Slavers followed traders; and conquistadors, proselytizers. Providentially astride the trade winds, the Canaries moved from European outlier to point of departure for European imperialism. It was the last port of call for the Great Voyages under Spanish auspices; here goods, plants, animals, and peoples passed out and back. Even in the mid-seventeenth century, the Spanish monarch declared the islands his greatest possession for they were the portal to empire.

But as empire sagged and as exploration gave way to routine trade, the Canaries receded to the margins. Other islands rose to prominence; other themes commanded the interest of intellectuals. Then the Enlightenment bonded with a Second Great Age of Discovery, and the Canaries became notable again, this time for exploring naturalists. There was a new global rivalry, now between Britain and France. There were new explorers, the old missionary impulse having secularized in naturalists such as Joseph Banks and Linnaeus' Apostles. But the role of Columbus-equivalent fell to Alexander von Humboldt, hailed as the scientific discoverer of the New World. A Second Great Age of Discovery was underway. This one, again, sailed from or referred to the Canaries.

Humboldt's account of Teide captured it all. "Just as we were about to fire the customary salute the fog suddenly dissipated and the Pico de Teide appeared in a clearing above the clouds, illuminated by the first rays of sun, which had not reached us yet. We rushed to the bow of the corvette so as not to miss this marvelous spectacle." It was a sublime moment, doubled by Humboldt's account of his subsequent ascent of Teide; together they became the standard for a generation of far-venturing naturalists. Charles Darwin spoke for them all when he lamented that he could not land on Tenerife but had to be content, while sailing past it, with reciting Humboldt's description from memory.

That contrast between fog and sun was a perfect tableau of the Enlightenment and its explorations. Out of the fog loomed the British warships that symbolized the geopolitical rivalry that sparked the new era; above the fog rose Teide, a naturalist's stele illuminated by the sun of Reason; through its dissipating shrouds dashed the *Pizzaro*, lifting the Canaries from geographic obscurantism and reconnecting them to another era of significance.

Note that all the revisions require an understanding that goes beyond the content of the text itself. In the third, Humboldt's account is distilled into two quoted sentences, with the rest paraphrased or interpreted within a broader context. Rewriting is a matter not of shuffling words but of shaping meaning. Other revisions are equally and easily possible; they might focus on Humboldt's biography, on Enlightenment science, on volcanic islands. Each would restructure the writing of a marvelously rich block quote.

Technical information often gets treated as either clunky or cute. Either it staggers from data point to data point, with no more internal order than a fistful of nails, or it slithers into coy allusions, authorial asides, and flighty analogies that further the text but not the reader's understanding. Sometimes the data, presented baldly, are the point—and the more directly they're laid out, the better. But those details may also obstruct other purposes such as narrative. In that case, you'll have to unclog the blockage.

Consider, for example, this lengthy passage from a technically dense text by Ellis Miner and Randii Wessen on Voyager 2's encounter with the planet Neptune. If the sample passage is a bit lengthy, even with elisions, that's because we need enough text to show how to transform data-heavy prose into a crisper narrative. (Note: the material elided is similar to that included in full for the first paragraph.)

> The actual encounter period began with the Observatory Phase (OB), extending from June 5, 1989, through August 6, 1989. OB was divided into three CCS computer loads: B901, B902, and B903. Although Voyager imaging of Neptune exceeded Earth-based resolution as early as May 1988, OB offered the first opportunity for nearly continuous observation of the planet and its system. The beginning of the command sequence saw the start of the first VPZOOM observation (V = Visual, P = Planet, ZOOM = Approach movie). Each VPZOOM observation consisted of five-color narrow-angle (NA) camera imaging of the planet every 72° of longitude (i.e., five times each rotation period). These imaging frames would be combined to make an approach movie to look for atmospheric features that moved across the face of Neptune. Five such movies done in OB were spaced in such a way that resolution had improved by a factor of 1.4 ($= \sqrt{2}$) in each successive series. These movies were designed to look for cloud features that might be followed as the planet rotated to determine prevailing wind speed at various latitudes.
>
> The start of OB also saw the initiation of the Ultraviolet Spectrometer (UVS) scans of the Neptune system to search for ultraviolet emissions from Neptune's atmosphere and from the space between Neptune and its satellites. These were designed to detect hydrogen and

other gases escaping from the planet or its satellites. The chemical composition of those gases provided clues about the chemical composition of Neptune's atmosphere or the surfaces of its satellites.

Voyager 2 continued its search for evidence that radio signals were being generated by solar wind interaction with Neptune's magnetic field. To accomplish this, quick bursts of high-rate Planetary Radio Astronomy (PRA) and Plasma Wave Subsystem (PWS) data were recorded once a day throughout the Observatory Phase. . . .

The Sun and other stars to be used in Near Encounter observations were measured twice by PPS and UVS during OB (B902) as a calibration of the star brightnesses. . . . The IRIS Flash-Off Heater (FOH) was turned off and the IRIS instrument was turned on in B902 to allow time for cool-down of the instrument for critical Far Encounter and Near Encounter observations. . . .

Periodic calibrations of the fields and particles instruments continued, including an abbreviated version of the roll and yaw maneuvering to calibrate MAG. RSS also performed "occultation-like" tests in B902 to exercise both the spacecraft radio system and the ground systems and personnel in preparation for the Neptune occultation experiment. . . .

As Voyager 2 raced toward Neptune, images were continuously shuttered on either side of the planet to look for ring material and new satellites. As previously discussed, the Navigation Team was counting on these searches to discover at least one new satellite to guide Voyager 2 more accurately to its aim-point. In early July, during B902, it happened: the first new satellite was discovered. It was called 1989N1, was irregularly shaped, and had a radius of about 200 km. The Voyager Project began determining the orbit for the new satellite and then started calculating scan platform coordinates for the retargetable OPNAV frames. With more than a month before Neptune's closest approach, 1989N1 had indeed been found early enough for it to be used to navigate Voyager to its desired aim-point.

When it rains it pours. Throughout July more and more satellites were discovered.[2]

What's wrong with this passage? Nothing, inherently. It may appear drab and dry, but it is accurate, complete, and detailed. It condenses a great deal of material that's far more technical than its own presentation. It is, in fact, a first-order popularization that carries information to a wider readership than the original reports could ever hope to do. The passage becomes problematic only if you want a text that emphasizes narrative or that seeks to appeal to a still-wider general audience for which the encounter, not its data, holds primary interest.[3]

To make the text into a stronger story, remove the clutter of acronyms, shorten the explanatory and descriptive passages, replace the passive voice with an active one, and vary (and quicken) the sentence cadences. It will often help if you introduce some parallelism in order to allow the prose to pick up its tempo, thus speeding the reader along much as Voyager 2 accelerates toward its encounter with Neptune.

On June 5, 1989, more than 3.5 years after leaving Uranus, Voyager 2 entered its two-month-long observatory phase.

It received three sets of new commands. Following their instructions, it directed its narrow-angle camera

into a long sequence of images—five to each planetary rotation—that would make a movie of Neptunian
weather. It scanned for ultraviolet emissions that might
identify atmospheric chemistry. It searched for radio signals birthed where Neptune's magnetic field met the solar wind and for high-frequency radio waves that could
measure more accurately the opaque planet's rate of rotation. It measured the brightness of the Sun and of selected stars whose position could help the craft navigate
through near-encounter events. It readied its infrared
instruments by turning their flash-heater on and then
off. It continued, as it had throughout its long trek
across interplanetary space, to sample fields and particles, from time to time recalibrating its instruments by
rolls and yaws that allowed researchers to account for
the influence of the spacecraft itself. It commenced a
series of occultation experiments, in which it would send
radio waves to Earth through the planet's atmosphere.
And it searched for rings and satellites.

Its cameras imaged each side of Neptune, and in early
July, Voyager 2 found its first new satellite, 1989N1. The
discovery gave the navigation team what it most sought:
a new coordinate by which to guide Voyager through
near-encounter maneuvers. Others soon followed; by
the end of the month, Voyager had discovered four new
moons.

Is this better? It is, if the purpose is to speed the reader
along a narrative trajectory whose point is the encounter as
an event, not as a body of collected data. The string of
declarative sentences that recounts Voyager's activities may
seem overly mechanical—but perhaps it isn't, since Voyager was, after all, a robot executing computer commands.

Whether the chosen style works is, of course, a matter of purpose and taste.

Consider next the value of amplifying that lean story line with authorial commentary that constantly tweaks the significance of the narrative, much as Voyager's navigation team continually corrects the spacecraft's trajectory. The passage will have less straight narration and more reflection and attention to context. Most general readers will want to know what happened and why it matters, and will wish to share in the enthusiasms of the quest. Some technical references will help to anchor the text, as telling details generally do; but the prose must rush over them like a stream over small boulders. What the majority of readers will want is the drama of the flow and some cues as to what their intellectual and emotional reactions should be. Your task is to convey all this without falsifying what actually happened or deleting stuff that is relevant to those events.

Note that such an elaboration typically requires additional information or perspective that must be brought to the text from outside the original sources. Presumably such value-added prose will come from earlier portions of your larger manuscript or from descriptions in sources not cited directly (for example, Miner and Wessen in their preface say that "no other experience is likely to come close to matching the excitement of anticipation and discovery that accompanied the Voyager mission").[4]

> On June 5, 1989, more than 3.5 years after leaving Uranus, Voyager 2 entered its two-month-long observatory phase. This was the sixth time the Voyager Team had met a planet, but if the scenario had become partly ritualized, it had lost none of its wild alloy of awe, anticipation, and anxiety.

JPL sent Voyager three new blocks of commands. Two blocks—one at the onset and one at the close—would most excite the public because they involved cameras. The first was a series of regular, color images, shot five to each rotation of the planet, that would zoom in as Voyager approached and form a movie of Neptunian weather. The Great Dark Spot immediately captured interest. The second involved a search for new satellites. But mostly Voyager 2 would do what it did at each encounter: it would direct its instruments toward a full-body, geophysical scan of the planet. Specifically, it would measure properties invisible both to human senses and to popular enthusiasms.

It scanned for ultraviolet emissions that might identify atmospheric chemistry. It searched for radio signals birthed where Neptune's magnetic field met the solar wind, and for high-frequency radiation that could measure more accurately the opaque planet's rate of rotation. It measured the brightness of the Sun and of selected stars whose position could help the craft navigate through near-encounter events. It readied its infrared instruments by turning their flash-heater on and then off. It continued, as it had throughout its long trek across interplanetary space, to sample fields and particles, from time to time recalibrating its instruments by rolls and yaws that allowed researchers to account for the influence of the spacecraft itself. It commenced a series of occultation experiments, in which it would send radio waves to Earth through the planet's atmosphere.. And it searched for rings and satellites.

Those displayed images were what exploration meant in the popular mind: the revelation of new worlds. The Voyager twins had found a covey of them at Jupiter, Saturn, and Uranus, and there was every expectation Voyager 2 would discover even more exotic moons here at the outer fringes of the solar system. So its cameras imaged each side of Neptune, and in early July, Voyager found its first new satellite, unimaginatively dubbed 1989N1. That discovery gave the navigation team what it had most sought: a new coordinate by which to guide Voyager through near-encounter maneuvers. Other satellite discoveries soon followed. By the end of the month Voyager had detected four new moons, subsequently named after figures from Greek mythology: Proteus, Larissa, Galatea, and Despina. On July 30 it captured them all in a single, mesmerizing image.

On August 6 it left its observatory phase behind and raced toward full encounter. A world that before Voyager had had no sharper identity than that of a hazy blue smurfball, the third largest of the planets, now beckoned at 42,000 miles an hour.

Note the references to other encounters, which helps to situate this event within a larger narrative ("this was the sixth time"). The use of names for the discovered moons, which humanizes raw data and tethers the discovery to the sort of detail that a general reader can relate to. The introduction of a dramatic, visually enticing outcome ("Great Dark Spot"). The reference to a composite photo, which comes not from the original quoted text but from a captioned figure elsewhere in the source material. The fuller explanation of what the proposed instruments intended to do under the aegis of a topic sentence ("full-body, geophysical scan"). The framing of the entire episode through two sets of images, one of the planet's atmosphere and one of its moons. And throughout, indirectly by word choice and directly by commentary, cues as to why the reader should care ("wild alloy of awe, anticipation, and anxiety"; "beckoned").

This is certainly not the only way to rewrite that original material into a more accessible form. But it is one that shifts the style toward storytelling and interpretation so that the text will almost surely appeal to a broader readership—if that is your intent.

chapter 18

Figures of Speech

In which we speak plainly about elaboration, and consider the uses (and misuses) of figurative language, from allusive adjectives to informing conceits

Figurative language climbs all the rungs of the composition ladder, from individual words to phrases to a text's organizing design. Some aspects we have already discussed within the context of clichés, some under features of design; and some we've encountered simply in the ongoing flow of figurative expressions that have been used here to explain, illustrate, and animate remarks on various topics. Still, the theme deserves its own moment in the sun.

Prose minimalists, hostile to figurative language, often appeal to George Orwell and his call to sweep away windy clichés. What they forget is that he wanted to replace tired and tiresome expressions and fatigued phrases with fresh language and inventive imagery. Baroque language is typically clichéd language; it is stuffed with worn-out words, like a rag doll filled with scraps of discarded cloth. To say new things or to say old things anew requires a text still aglow with its creation. Figurative speech can—as with any other element of language—be used well or poorly. It can smother an idea or it can galvanize one.

Figurative language is generally characterized as rich,

and rich prose, like rich sauce, is not to everyone's taste. Figuration can bring a tang and saltiness that makes plain styles, by contrast, seem as appetizing as boiled cabbage. Those who like figurative prose can tolerate plain styles more easily than those who like plainness can stomach curried styles, so figurative language is likely to irritate and alienate a greater number of readers. Yet language itself is metaphoric and symbolic, so all writing is as well. Some types just show it more than others.

Begin with words. Many adjectives and adverbs merit oblivion because they add nothing: they are textual tapeworms sucking the lifeblood out of a noun or verb, adding nothing either to meaning or to rhythm. Not a few are oxymorons or tautologies, so thoughtless is their use ("armed gunman," "original copy"). But this is not to say that no good adjective or adverb could be used instead, or any of a host of allusive adjectives, analogies, images, metaphors, similes, or symbols.

An allusive adjective (or adverb) is a shorthand simile or analogy, useful for enriching a text without encumbering it in ways that might interfere with rhyme or reason. An allusive adjective functions rather like a hypertext link—that is, it doesn't simply trigger one definition or image but takes the word into another mental country. To call a prose passage "overwrought" suggests a restricted gamut of meanings; to call it "Faulknerian" is to launch into a far-off realm of connotations. The power behind the punch will vary: readers familiar with the alluded-to "link" will read the word with a richness more commonly found in a longer passage, while readers who miss the link can gloss over the word without losing much, or sensing that they missed anything at all. Packing too many allusions into a sentence, however, yields the opposite effect. It is likely to set off a storm of verbal popcorn in the reader's mind, all frenzy and little substance.

Figures of speech have a place to the extent that they boost meaning and enjoyment. They inform, they entice, they make you want to read on. They may be disposable or indispensable—an adjective-at-length or a conceit integral to the text's design. They may be abrupt, extended, or informing; they may be read in passing, one of several useful or striking allusions, little more than highway signs along the route; they may continue for several sentences, perhaps a paragraph, or reappear from time to time, clustering details for a discussion as if they were features for a portrait, or reminding readers and recalibrating the text; or they may frame the central organization of the overall text. In contemporary English, Homeric similes are no longer in fashion, having passed from the scene with the epic genre that birthed them; perhaps they came to seem an awkward length. (The equivalent of Homeric epithets, however, have flourished, eventually assuring ever-new generations of clichés.)

Yet in order to promote meaning, figures of speech must be grounded in something. So it's time we rooted this riff in some examples.

Disposable, One-Off Metaphors and Similes

Consider the following one-line figures, most apt when they connect their imagery to the subject at hand:

Driving through mining country: "In early slanting light, fields of prickly pears flashed like silver dollars."[1]

On access to off-budget funds for forest firefighting: "Like the wave of precious metals that flooded out of the New

World to the coffers of Spain, the emergency money momentarily enriched the economy and eventually impoverished the spirit of the Forest Service."[2]

Describing a TV character no greater than the sum of the pop culture he absorbs: "All the conversational lint that tumbles around the air-waves gets trapped on the blank mesh of his brain."[3]

Depicting the obsession of General Wolfe: "But as the needle, though quivering, points always to the pole, so through torment and languor and the heats of fever the mind of Wolfe dwelt on the capture of Quebec."[4]

On the paradoxical role of introduced flora: "The weeds, like skin transplants placed over broad areas of abraded and burned flesh, aided in healing the raw wounds that the invaders tore in the earth."[5]

On the supposedly rational professional baseball draft: "Eight of the first nine teams select high schoolers. The worst teams in baseball, the teams that can least afford for their draft to go wrong, have walked into the casino, ignored the odds, and made straight for the craps table."[6]

Explanatory Tropes and Organizing Conceits

Perhaps the most fascinating figuration uses tropes to shape a section of a text or even an entire manuscript; the figure of speech serves as an organizing conceit. The range of such figures, however, seems limited: rarely do they reach much beyond the essay or sketch. They may appear in a title (and often do so). But they're generally incapable of holding all the magnetized filings of a lengthy manuscript within a single force field. They inform by helping to establish meaning; they don't inform in the details of structure.

Still, a larger design built from smaller parts, each coherent in itself, can put the power of the trope-informed essay within a grander argument or narrative. Such pieces may each be organized around a conceit, and if well chosen and even extracted from the subject itself, such devices can enlighten the text significantly. As a rule, though, like gravity and radiation, the power of the trope seems to fall off with something like the square of the text's length. The examples that follow all apply to stand-alone essays.

Begin with Wallace Stegner's essay "Mormon Trees," in which he appeals to Lombardy poplars as peculiarly diagnostic ("the characteristic trees") of Mormon settlement, as "typical as English hedgerows." They demark as well as anything else the geographic dominion of Mormon settlements throughout the West. But Stegner also wants to see in some of the poplar's properties distinctive traits of Mormon culture. The analogy falters; and while Stegner wishes to make his points, he knows that his simile, like the Lombardy poplar itself, suffers from internal weaknesses and from shallow rooting unable to withstand too great a stress. Coyly, he makes his points while openly questioning, in a way that is completely unconvincing, the suitability of his chosen analogy.

> Perhaps it is fanciful to judge a people by its trees. Probably the predominance of poplars is the result of nothing more interesting than climatic conditions or the lack of other kinds of seeds and seedlings. Probably it is pure nonsense to see a reflection of Mormon group life in the fact that the poplars were practically never planted singly, but always in groups, and that the groups took the form of straight lines and ranks. Perhaps it is even more nonsensical to speculate that the straight, tall verticality of the Mormon trees appealed obscurely to the rigid

sense of order of the settlers, and that a marching row of plumed poplars was symbolic, somehow, of the planter's walking with God and his solidarity with his neighbors.

All those qualifiers ("perhaps," "probably") are tongue-in-cheek because it is clear Stegner does want to push the analogy even as he acknowledges its frailties. When he makes the leap directly, he does so with a double negative.

> Nonsensical or not, it is not an unpleasant thought. Institutions must have their art forms, their symbolic representations, and if the Heavenward aspirations of medieval Christianity found their expression in cathedrals and spires, the more mundane aspirations of the Latter-day Saints may just as readily be discovered in the widespread plantings of Mormon trees. They look Heavenward, but their roots are in earth. The Mormon looked toward Heaven, but his Heaven was a Heaven on earth and he would inherit bliss in the flesh.[7]

This bit of authorial sleight-of-hand may annoy as much as it delights, but few readers will fail to appreciate either the geography that Stegner's use of the trees reveals or its value as a way of refracting observations that, if stated baldly, might simply offend. Whether a less overtly manipulative phrasing might serve better is—no surprise, here—a matter of taste.

The easier strategy is to wrap the organizing conceit within a story, as George Orwell does in his classic essay "Shooting an Elephant." The story begins with Orwell's tenure as a member of the imperial constabulary in Moulmein, Burma, where he is "hated by large numbers of people—the only time in my life I have been important enough for this to happen to me." He describes his growing detestation of imperialism and his determination to "chuck up my job" and go elsewhere. Among his reasons are his dismay for the "dirty work of Empire at close quarters," his sympathy for the surly Burmese, and his sense that he is caught between "hatred of the empire" and "rage against the evil-spirited little beasts" who make his job impossible. But, he confesses, he can "get nothing into perspective." Then a minor incident occurs that becomes an epiphany.

He is called to deal with a male elephant that is suffering from "must" (or "musth"), a periodic state of aggressiveness, and is rampaging through the bazaar and has killed a man. By the time Orwell arrives, the frenzy has passed, the elephant is peacefully grazing in a paddy, and Orwell knows that the rational response is to wait for the mahout to show up and take the elephant away. This is, after all, a valuable animal, and no longer dangerous. Yet in the course of the pursuit, a large crowd has gathered. They, not Orwell, the imperial representative, will decide the course of action. "My whole life, every white man's life in the East, was one long struggle not to be laughed at." The crowd wants him to shoot the elephant, and so he does. It isn't pretty. The elephant refuses to die. Bullet after bullet splashes into him, yet he sinks into the mud, and lives, unable to rise, unable to expire. Eventually Orwell leaves, feeling that he cannot "stand it any longer." The elephant dies afterward.[8]

Like Melville's story of the white whale, the episode of the dying elephant lends itself to many interpretations. There is the meaning Orwell brings out explicitly: the scene illustrates the ambiguous power of imperialism, which depends on subject peoples. And there are subtler meanings, not least that the elephant symbolizes the dying empire. But what makes the text work is not the image alone, like a Sun holding all within its gravitational field, but the fact that the image unfolds as a story, which has its own narrative authority apart from its symbolic power.

One final variant, combining trope and story, was a form that I experimented with in one of my essays, which distills the fire history of India into a mere twenty pages. The piece takes as its organizing conceit a Hindu icon known as the nataraja: Shiva, the Lord of the Dance, holds a drum in one hand and a trident in the other, while a circle of flame surrounds him. This seemed to me a perfect expression of the monsoonal climate, with its alternating wet and dry seasons that power the endless cycling of fire through the Indian landscape.[9]

As the miniature history unfolds, the nataraja reappears to announce every new era, each time slightly altered but reincarnating the past in a ceaseless mandala of fire. In this way the essay tries to convey the persistence and pervasiveness of fire in India, not only on the landscape but in cultural consciousness. Instead of simply declaring that certain patterns endure (and offering illustrations), the overall narrative enacts those cycles, demonstrating in its very shape that the patterns are reborn over and over in a cultural form endemic to the society. It's a tricky exercise. Too much repetition, and the reader will become bored; too little, and the essay will lose its coherence. If the rhetorical artifice is too heavy-handed, the symbolic showing will become simply a clumsy telling. In Frost's parlance, the textual ice would no longer move by its own melt on the stove, but would try to carry the stove.

Titles

Titles are often figurative, and we may perhaps consider them a special subspecies. Because titles perform more work than figures do, the match is not always made in heaven. Titles inform: they say, in compressed form, what a book or essay is about. Titles entice: they can have curb appeal, causing a reader cruising through a journal or a bookstore to pause and perhaps sample the merchandise. Titles resonate: they can connote, either through their style or their wordplay, more than their component words say. (Most dissertation titles couldn't be mistaken for anything else. Most journalists who write books would regard an academic-sounding title as the kiss of death.) For each of these purposes, an appeal to figures of speech can work; and for each, too, such an appeal can fail.

Those who scorn academia often reserve special spleen for its widely favored two-pronged titles, in which a figure or phrase or quote is followed by a colon and a longer, explanatory subtitle. For (entirely bogus) example: *Barking up the Wrong Trees: Hunting Dogs as Contested Cultural Icons,* or *Banked Coals: The Hearth as the Domestic Antithesis of the Factory.* Some work, some don't. Some projects begin with a title; some crawl toward one only after the last revision. A well-chosen title, however, can add tang to a text, can help to define its boundaries, and, if present during the design stage, can sharpen the theme. Coining a title is an author's duty and an author's privilege.

But because a title is also a marketing tool, you won't have full say over what appears on the book's printed cover; you may, in fact, have no say at all. If you selected a title that doubles as a figure of speech, you may lose that figurative punch. (I wrote one book from start to finish under what I regarded as an inspired title, *Flame and Fortune,* only to have the marketing group toss it out as unsalable after the whole work was in page proofs. All the textual allusions that bounced off the old title had to be deleted.) Such experiences are common (I reckon only about half my books have the title I originally devised). Title changes are a part of the editing process.

Publishers want titles that inform, rather than titles that require a knowledge of the text before they can be appreciated. *A Great Engine of Research: The Life of Grove Karl Gilbert* was quickly scotched because the first phrase, while apt, didn't mean anything to someone who hadn't read the text. Reversing it to read *Grove Karl Gilbert: A Great Engine of Research*—the title that was eventually used—got Gilbert's name to the fore but added nothing, and may have dampened interest because it sounded so incurably academic. The phrase "great engine of research" (which Gilbert coined to describe the U.S. Geological Survey) should have been put in the preface. *Fire in America* came about after the book had already been advertised under another title altogether; the publisher pleaded for the shortest, most direct wording possible, and got it. If your working title serves as a figure or an implicit master metaphor for your book, casting a shadow of meaning over all that follows, be prepared to fight for it, and probably lose, and have a backup plan: you could place it prominently in a prologue or in the frontmatter, where it can do the same work in ways less liable to irritate marketers.

Figuration in-your-face and figuration by stealth: consider two authors, one renowned for his plain style, drubbed into him by his Presbyterian-minister father, and the other celebrated for his free-wheeling tropes, the academic as biker-punk.

First, Norman Maclean, explaining how the Mann Gulch fire conforms to classical tragedy:

> In this story of the outside world and the inside world with a fire between, the outside world of little screwups

recedes now for a few hours to be taken over by the inside world of blowups, this time by a colossal blowup but shaped by little screwups that fitted together tighter and tighter until all became one and the same thing—the fateful blowup. Such is much of tragedy in modern times and probably always has been except that past tragedy refrained from speaking of its association with screwups and blowups.[10]

The language certainly seems plain enough—all those simple words, the colloquialisms ("screwups," "blowups"), the overt parallelism between outside and inside worlds. But just how direct is the language? The passage is in fact deeply, if unobtrusively, figurative. Through the prism of Mann Gulch, Maclean refracts a classical theory of tragedy; his implicit figures boost the example into analogy, and prevent a sludge of scholarly jargon from drowning it. To the sensitive reader, such obvious colloquialisms signal that, in truth, something more profound is at stake.

Now, Mike Davis, sketching the nonlinear geography of Los Angeles:

It is still unclear, moreover, whether this vicious circle of disaster is coincidental or eschatological. Could this be merely what statisticians wave away as the "Joseph effect" of fractal geometry: "the common clustering of catastrophe"? Could these be the Last Days, as prefigured so often in the genre of Los Angeles disaster fiction and film (from *Day of the Locust* to *Volcano*)? Or is nature in Southern California simply waking up after a long nap? Whatever the case, millions of Angelenos have become genuinely terrified of their environment.[11]

And later:

Yet Southern California at least by Lyellian standards is a revolutionary, not a reformist landscape. It is Walden Pond on LSD. As in other Mediterranean and dryland environments, the "average" is merely an abstraction. Indeed, nothing is less likely to occur than "average rainfall." At Los Angeles City Hall, where the annual precipitation is pegged at 15.3 inches, that mark has been hit only a few times in the 127-year history of measured rainfall. Indeed, only 17 percent of years approach within 25 percent of the historical average. The actual norm turns out to be seven- to twelve-year swings between dry and wet spells. The graph of historical rainfall oscillates over the decades like a seismograph recording the successive shocks of a major earthquake. Sometimes the annual average rainfall is delivered during a single week-long Kona storm, as happened in 1938 and 1969; or even, incredibly, in a single twelve-hour deluge, as in Bel Air on New Year's Day 1934. During droughts, on the other hand, it may take two or even three years to achieve the mean.[12]

Each of the two writers is a master stylist with a unique voice; no one would likely confuse them. A closer reading, however, suggests that Davis is as much the plain-talking empiricist (though in disguise) as Maclean is a stealth trafficker in metaphors. Maclean's language is deeply allusive, the simple terms easily recognized as referring to unsaid Big Questions. Davis' pungent figures of speech are followed by hard numbers even as the metaphoric aura of his opening sentences lingers in the mind, extending over that landscape of cited quantities like a creeping fog. His text, however given to flights of rhetorical fancy, remains tethered in data.

The issue is not whether metaphoric language will come into play, but how, and at what scale. The fact is, numbers can be anecdotal, and figures of speech can acquire quantitative dimension.

chapter 19

Technical Information

In which we consider writing that demands not merely accuracy of fact but accuracy of understanding, and that often requires us to express extraordinary knowledge with ordinary language

How do you give an account of something that is complicated, depends on specialized information, or deals with topics not commonly known? Equally to the point, how do you present such material without distorting its complexity, stripping away its relevant detail, or mocking its seriousness? How do you incorporate it into your text without breaking the rhythms of the whole or altering your narrative voice? And what do you do when the technical information is not simply an aid to a larger topic but is itself the subject? The short answer is, you do it the way you do everything else in writing: by making those requirements integral to your design and voice.

A fuller answer is that, as always, many options exist and are worth studying. We've already explored some effective techniques, such as how to lift from a mass of sources the critical details for character, setting, and plot, or to abstract a usable symbol, or to otherwise place data in the service of the text. The task is so fundamental that almost any good nonfiction prose can serve as an example. Still, some authors shine where most only glow.

Master the Material and Restate It in Your Own Voice

Your persona in such cases might be termed the textbook omniscient narrator. You establish yourself as an authority, or at least you assume the literary role of one, and lay out the necessary material.

You might do it in something akin to a high style, as G. J. Whitrow does in *The Natural Philosophy of Time:*

> So far, in discussing universal time, we have concentrated mainly on the question of its nature—whether absolute or relational—and on the question of whether it has a natural zero or origin. In considering the question of duration, however, we are now confronted with the further problem of determining a satisfactory unit of measurement and of constructing a significant scale of time. As regards these problems, Newton's definition gives us no more assistance than does that of Leibniz. Moreover, both of these great thinkers seem to evade rather than to take account of, let alone resolve, the fundamental antinomy: that, whereas the concept of spatial measurement does not conflict in any way with that of spatial order, despite the sharp distinction which geometers have learned to draw between the metrical and the topological, the concept of succession clashes with the concept of duration.[1]

Here, Whitrow doesn't just let Newton and Leibniz describe their ideas in their own words, but restates those ideas within a framework of his own construction. While this particular passage is a bit meaty and magisterial (imbuing the subject with a sense of ultimate things examined with scholarly gravitas), the explanation is clear enough if read with the care it invites.

An omniscient narrator, however, may employ a lighter touch and gentler tone, even when the topic verges on the epic. Consider E. C. Pielou's *After the Ice Age,* which describes the recession of the last North American glacial era.

> The formation and disappearance of numerous temporary lakes strongly influenced the northward spread of land plants as the ice disappeared. The large lakes, especially, were barriers to migration, but whenever a lake drained, its exposed bed provided a tract of new land for colonization by pioneer plants. The frequent disruption and rearrangement of drainage systems had interesting biogeographical consequences. For example, many streams and rivers draining the eastern slopes of the Rocky Mountains in what is now Alberta flowed into the Milk River and thence into the Missouri when the lowlands to the east were ice covered. Now the same rivers drain into the Saskatchewan River system, which flows into Hudson Bay. This is only one of several such shifts that greatly affected the present-day distribution of aquatic organisms.[2]

In this passage the tangled history of stream origins and shifting drainage basins becomes a simple flow, made clear by the author's commanding vision and helped by the absence of jargon and cluttering details.

Or let Alfred Crosby try his hand at unraveling the power of weeds.

> We need a specific example: In primeval Australia the weeds called dandelions might have languished in small numbers or even died out, as the weeds the Norse brought to Vinland must have done. We shall never

know, because that Australia has not existed for two hundred years. When dandelions spread, they did so, in a manner of speaking, in another land, one containing and transformed by European humans and their plants, bacteria, sheep, goats, pigs, and horses. In that Australia, dandelions have a more secure future than kangaroos.[3]

Although this passage is voiced by an omniscient narrator, it doesn't read like a conventional textbook. Writing a formal parody of it in academese is an easy mark, akin to hitting the ground with your hat, but the exercise may remind us that clear and spritely prose is not easily achieved, nor is thudding prose more enlightening.

Australia furnishes a suitable example. The island continent may have held dandelions in its past, or not; the evidence is ambiguous and contested. Like most countries visited by northern Europeans, however, dandelions were brought to its shores. In some places they faded away because the environment was unfavorable. They succeeded in Australia, however, undoubtedly for a variety of reasons, but one cause was probably the simultaneous presence of many other species from Europe as well, for they could interact synergistically. The plant is now a permanent feature of the Australian landscape. The dandelion, that is, had an ecological agency, which granted it a future denied to other species.

Why does one text leap and the other lumber? Crosby uses a more personal "we" instead of an omniscient third person; he gives crisp details instead of abstract concepts; he relies on a specific comparison rather than generalizations; he avoids jargon either of words or of concepts ("synergistically," "agency"); he shuns a clutter of qualifying adjectives, adverbs, and conjunctions; he ends with an observation based on a counterintuitive contrast of particular species rather than a flaccid appeal to trendy language, which functions not so much to inform the audience as to identify author and reader as members of an intellectual caste.

Which is better? That depends on your purpose. Not everyone enjoys Crosby's figurative language and sardonic-tinged tone. If the purpose of the paragraph is to explain the technical success of the dandelion, to stuff the text with data, the second provides a firmer matrix. But if the point is to show how an exotic plant may emigrate successfully, and to undercut the bombast of many settler-society epics, then the ironic triumph of the dandelion is ideal. And to drive that point home may require a tack hammer rather than a sledgehammer. Crosby's textual hopping from one unexpected point to another is more effective at leading the reader into reconsidering well-worn conventional wisdom but requires, in turn, a spry voice to keep from falling. To repeat: the issue is not that one version is popular and the other scholarly, one springy and the other turgid; each may be a good or bad version of its genre. The issue is that each must think carefully about how to express its theme. The serious can be done nimbly, and the popular with a bludgeon.

Less elliptical but presenting a similar voice is Hans Zinsser's portrayal of the mouse and rat as they spread through Europe.

> From the time of its arrival, the rat spread across Europe with a speed superior even to that of the white man in the Americas. Before the end of the thirteenth century,

it had become a pest. The legend of the *Rattenfänger von Hameln,* who piped the children into the hollow Koppenberg because the town refused his pay for piping the rats into the Weser, is placed at or about 1284. By this time, the rat had penetrated into England. It had reached Ireland some time before this, where it was the "foreign" or "French" mouse, "ean francache." Our authorities tell us that in Ireland, even until very recent times, everything foreign was called "francach," or French. A little later, the rat was in Denmark, Norway, and the adjacent islands. By Shakespeare's time, the black rat was so formidable a nuisance that days of prayer for protection against its ravages were set aside, and rat catchers (see *Romeo and Juliet,* Act III) were important officials, probably calling themselves, as they would today, scientists or artists (or "rattors"—cf. "realtors" and "morticians").

For twice as long as the Vandals had their day in North Africa, or the Saracens in Spain, or the Normans in Italy, the black rats had their own way in Europe.[4]

The voice is witty, both charming and incisive, but what fleshes out the skeletal chronicle, otherwise too lean to hold a typical historical analysis, are the specifics of place and the many almost throw-away allusions that help mark the dates and duration: "(see *Romeo and Juliet,* Act III)," "for twice as long as the Vandals had their day in North Africa." The passage bursts with information that connects the data and also binds to the reader's general knowledge, all without apparent effort, and without lecturing, which is a mark of true artistry.

From which we may conclude: that while the omniscient narrator is the most common perspective from which to convey technical information, there is no single way to do the conveying. To this we might add a caveat, which might be termed the Third-Person Omniscient fallacy: either tell the story yourself or let others do it, but don't mix bits of each like a tossed salad of third-person presences. That is too often the dissertation-default style, and it is deadly.

Have a Character within the Text Explain the Technical Material

This is a favored tactic of journalists, and one that can do double duty when the character talking is also the focus of the larger project. Usefully, it also allows for irony (or, as those of us hungry for a post-ironic culture would prefer, for humor). But there is no reason that, through judicious quoting, historical figures or persons known through the literature might not serve as well.

Watch how Jonathan Weiner does the trick in *The Beak of the Finch*. The particular topic is the "principle of divergence." Weiner notes that "Darwin never actually saw it happen, though he argued that it could happen, had to happen, and had happened"; and he points out that Darwin cited pigeon breeders as examples of how natural variability could become, with selection, different varieties and, potentially, different species.

> In Darwin's view, natural selection too would tend to make nature "more & more diversified." Here the motor is not whim, taste, or love of novelty, as with the pigeon fanciers, but something more basic. The great thing is efficiency—or what economists of Darwin's day were already calling the "division of labor." "It is obvious," Darwin writes in *Natural Selection*, "that more descen-

dants from a carnivorous animal could be supported in any country" if some were adapted "to hunt small prey, & others large prey." Likewise with herbivores, "more could be supported, if some were adapted to feed on tender grass & others on leaves of trees . . . & others on bark, roots, hard seeds or fruit." In other words, as varieties and species ramify they will become better and better consumers of the world around them, like Jack Sprat and his wife, who between them licked the platter clean.[5]

Such quotations from the literature are common enough, but in this case the syncopation of original source and authorial commentary is exceptionally well done. Now consider the following, in which contemporary observers respond in real time to the query, "Is character divergence universal and powerful, as Darwin thought, or is it rare and weak, as some evolutionists argue today?"

"My own guess is, character divergence is likely to be quite common and important," says Peter Grant, "but I think of rather small magnitude, in terms of the quantity of the evolutionary shift."

"You mean . . . ?" asks Rosemary.

"Take two species that come together. Say they differ by 10 percent. They would need to be about 15 percent different to coexist without serious competition. There are two possible outcomes. One of the two may go extinct, or the two species may diverge until they are 15 percent different. That shift is not very great: only another 5 percent."

"I see. Okay," says Rosemary.

"Now if you agree with that, how easy would it be to

see the evolution of that 5 percent shift? The answer
is, not at all easy. You'd need a lot of detail. Character
divergence could be very common but simply not be
known."[6]

Instead of elaborating on the argument himself, Weiner
has his characters do it. The exchange is a bit stilted, almost
assuming the form of a Platonic dialogue, with Peter as So-
crates and Rosemary assuming the role of Phaedo, Protago-
ras, and Plato's other straight-men.

Nonjournalists rarely have this option, and can't manu-
facture an incident that they can then report on (say, by
arranging an interview). But the use of suitable characters
and selected quotations, edited, can produce something of
the same effect. Besides, if you are a historian, the ultimate
technical truth of the subject need not concern you: what
matters is how the characters in the narrative understand
it, and for this, judicious quotes and comparisons will do
nicely, as Richard Hofstadter demonstrates in summarizing
the perception of human nature held by America's Founding Fathers. "One thing that the Fathers did not propose
to do, because they thought it impossible, was to change
the nature of man to conform with a more ideal system."
Instead, they were "inordinately confident that they knew
what man always had been and what he always would be."

The eighteenth-century mind had great faith in univer-
sals. Its method, as Carl Becker has said, was "to go up
and down the field of history looking for man in general, the universal man, stripped of the accidents of time
and place." Madison declared that the causes of political
differences and of the formation of faction were "sown
in the nature of man" and could never be eradicated. "It

is universally acknowledged," David Hume had written, "that there is a great uniformity among the actions of men, in all nations and ages, and that human nature remains still the same, in its principles and operations. The same motives always produce the same actions. The same events always follow from the same causes."[7]

The past can indeed be a foreign country, as L. P. Hartley said, and the understandings of the world by its inhabitants can be every bit as recondite as the behavior of quarks and the molecular biology of the gene. What matters is not that you master the subject in its full complexity (although this helps), only that you appreciate how it functions in the narrative involving your characters and that you know how to let them portray the world as they perceive it.

A Variant: Restate the Information through In-Text Characters, If Not in Their Own Words, Then through Their Conceptual Inventions

Observe how Louis Menand sets up the discussion of chance in *The Metaphysical Club,* his group portrait of noted American Pragmatists. Each rival conception—determinism and indeterminacy—is allied with a character, and since the characters selected are a father and son, Benjamin and Charles Peirce, they represent a generational divide as well. Each idea, too, has its spokesman and symbol.

The pairings align like this. "The story of that difference —the difference between Benjamin Peirce's scientific generation and Charles's—is the story of two demons. The first made its public appearance in 1812 in Laplace's *Théorie analytique des probabilités.* 'We must . . . imagine the present state of the universe as the effect of its prior state and as the cause of the state that will follow it,' Laplace wrote." He then conjured up "an intelligence" that knows all the forces and all the positions of objects in the universe: "nothing would be uncertain for it, and the future, like the past, would be present to its eyes." Menand then personifies this concept. "This is Laplace's demon. It stands for the billiard-ball theory of matter, the belief that every event, including the actions of human beings, is the singular and inevitable consequence of a chain of antecedent events in which chance does not play a role."[8]

The second demon "proposed otherwise. This demon made its public appearance in 1871 in a work called *Theory of Heat*, by the Scottish physicist James Clerk Maxwell," who asked the reader to imagine "a being whose faculties are so sharpened that he can follow every molecule in its course." Maxwell's *Theory* was a disquisition on the second law of thermodynamics, a powerful Law of Nature that had seemingly given Laplace's demon a fire to tend. But "Maxwell's demon was invented to refute this version of the doctrine of necessity." What Maxwell "was trying to show was that the second law of thermodynamics is only probabilistic." The moral, "as Maxwell put it in a letter to a friend, is that 'the second law of thermodynamics has the same degree of truth as the statement that if you throw a tumblerful of water into the sea, you cannot get the same tumblerful of water out again.' Physical laws are not absolutely precise."[9]

One could discuss such ideas directly, as Whitrow does in contrasting Newtonian and Leibnizian conceptions of time. But Menand manages a multiple personification: the ideas are identified with demons, the demons with two rival philosophies, the philosophies with two scientists, the scientific conceptions with a father and son. This allows him to use quotations as something more than dead texts; they become a kind of conversation. He cannot muster the repartee recorded by journalists, but he doesn't have to. His task is to set up the symmetry. The demons can converse between themselves.

Let the Information Unfold within a Story

Another favored technique of journalists: let a narrative of some sort provide the frame to hold the information or quotations. The event might be the process of building something—say, a dam, a house, a field cleared and plowed. Or it might be a journey: a trek, a hunt, a search for a protein vital to cancer research. The problem of how to bind the shards of technical knowledge is solved by the inherent structure of the object created or by the act of creating. You need only devise the context within which all this will unfold. An example: imagine a pack trip through Banff National Park. The narrative begins at, say, the corrals of Ya Ha Tinda Ranch and ends at Banff townsite, and along the way the narrator can gather observations that link up together. A lot of technical information about trails, packing, horses, the warden service, wolves, fires, and forests can be stuffed into the panniers of that journey.

A good variant is to trace the history of how a certain knowledge or skill was acquired in the first place, and permit the technical items to drip into the text like a narrative I.V. You might, as Mike Davis does in *Late Victorian Holocausts,* open your understanding of the El Niño–Southern Oscillation by looking at the India famines of 1876–1878, which were brought about by the failure of the monsoons. Then turn to the evolution of an international weather network, assisted by the British Empire and the telegraph, and survey meteorologists' efforts to make sense of the torrent of new data: Henry Blanford and high-pressure systems in the Tropics, Sir Stanley Jevons and sunspots; Sir Gilbert Walker and the Southern Oscillation (SO), and other "strategic points of world weather" coded into breathtakingly complex regression equations; Jacob Bjerknes' linking of the SO with El Niño; Klaus Wyrtki and the physics of Warm Pools; and so on. Each argument for geophysical causation has its eerie echo in geopolitical theory. The information comes in chewable bites, with a degree of suspense and a focus on character. Explanation takes the form of a plot.

In the selection below, Davis contrasts Brazil with India, and, within Brazil, competing theories of cause and political consequence. The account is given a dramatic assist when Brazilian scientists and engineers "convened in a series of extraordinary meetings" at the Polytechnic Institute and later at the National Society for Acclimatization in Rio "to discuss the causes of the Grande Seca," and promptly "polarized into two acrimonious factions."

The "meteorologists," led by Guilherme de Capanema (author of *Apontamentos sobre secas do Ceará*), and visiting professor Orville Derby enthusiastically embraced the sunspot theory. Indeed, Derby excited the Indian meteorologists with a note in *Nature* summarizing the article he had published in *Diario Oficial do Brasil* in June 1878, which argued (after Hunter) that drought and flood records from Ceará strongly corresponded to sunspot fluctuations. In contrast, the "rainmakers," including the most eminent Brazilian engineers of the day, attributed the droughts to deforestation and backward agricultural practices, which they blamed on the racial "primitiveness" of the *sertanejos*. In line with Liberal Party fantasies for the development of the Nordeste, they advocated a

promethean program of giant dams, reservoirs and af-
forestation projects to "humidify" the climate. The two
camps would continue to battle one another for the rest
of the nineteenth century.[10]

The contrasts allow parallelism, which permits a good
deal of information to be compacted. As similar episodes
ramify throughout this era of globalizing science, they assume a kind of textual teleconnection akin to that of the
Earth's atmosphere. Links appear, dissolve, return, reincar-
nate, and eventually acquire something like scientific consensus, while the book tracks the unfolding saga.

Break the Text by Inserting an Explanatory Chapter
or Sidebar

Normal counsel is to keep the text flowing. It may merge,
pond, spill through rapids, or temporarily turn inward with
eddies; but the need to keep readers within the imagined
world, absorbed in the printed page, argues against anything that might jar their sense of immersion. So the sug-
gestion that you halt the flow of prose in order to introduce
some out-of-context material before returning to the text as
if nothing had happened may seem counterintuitive, not to
say wacky, and in many cases it would be. Better to slough
off that task onto graphs or to introduce a character to assist—anything other than pulling back the curtain on the
drama.

But the effectiveness of any technique depends on the
context, and there are times and places where one can do
more than inject tidbits of information, where the narrative
begs for a break of some kind, where the text needs a pause
or authorial time-out, where the reader wishes to regroup

before plunging ahead. Subsequent events, or an author's comments upon them, will be unintelligible without some dose of technical information enabling readers to understand why the cogs go with the gears in this way and not another, why this particular narrative will flow uphill rather than down. In a sense, this is another variant of the show-and-tell strategy; and in order to work, the out-of-sequence material needs to be integral to the design. It must have, as a break, some value apart from what the interruption permits by way of inserted information.

That, at least, was my intention when I wrote the essay "The Source," which opens with an evocation of the Great Fires that on August 20–21, 1910, roared through the Northern Rockies, overtaking and killing seventy-eight men in six separate incidents. The description of the fires begins abstractly, then swirls inward from a regional conflagration to the crews of the dead, tightening, finally, on one crew in particular.

> And then there was the crew cobbled together by Ranger Ed Pulaski. He had gone to Wallace for supplies and was returning on the morning of August 20 when the winds picked up their tempo and cast flame before them. He began to meet stragglers, and then a large gang spalled off from the main ridge camp. All in all he gathered forty-five men and with the smoke thickening in stygian darkness turned to race down the ravine of the West Fork toward Wallace. One man lagged and died in the flames. Pulaski hustled the rest over the trail before tucking them into a mineshaft. Then he hurried downcanyon with a wet gunny sack over his head before returning and herding the group into a larger tunnel, the

Nicholson adit, which had a seep running through it. Pulaski tried to hold the flames out of the entry timbers and the smoke out of the mine with hatfuls of water and blankets. But by now the men were senseless. They heard nothing but the din, felt nothing but heat, saw nothing but flame and darkness, smelled only smoke and sweat. As the firestorm swirled by the entrance, someone yelled that he, at least, was getting out. At the entry, he met Ed Pulaski, rudely silhouetted by flames, pistol drawn, threatening to shoot the first man who tried to flee.[11]

Now, with the tension nearly unbearable, the text stops and introduces a description of the contemporary American fire scene, most of which has evolved out of events surrounding the 1910 fires. The essay then returns to the mineshaft, and describes the immediate outcome: the bolter held, five men suffocated within the adit, Pulaski injured and blinded at its entrance. It concludes with the larger outcomes to Pulaski, the Forest Service, and wildland fire management.

At first blush, this seems to emulate the old-fashioned strategy in which a piece begins with a human-interest anecdote before doing any heavy lifting. But the pause is more fundamental to the design. The intensity of the passage, with its deferred climax, allows material to be inserted that otherwise might have fought with the narrative or been skimmed. The opening episode was not merely a hook; it was the line and sinker as well, because the essay returns to that incident to elaborate a conclusion, and by so doing says that the Pulaski story commands the text, that the rest fits within it. Had the larger themes been introduced and the Pulaski episode been inserted within them, the text would have said, in its design, just the reverse. The shock of the sudden pause permits that background information to get before the reader.

A good authorial intention (or aspiration). Readers will decide whether it works.

Rely on Graphic Materials to Carry Most of the Burden

Nearly from their origin, books have been illustrated. Word pictures can only do so much, and where quantities are involved, words and numbers can squabble like baby birds in a nest, begging for the reader's attention. Some illustrations are little more than decorative vignettes; some may do work within the text, supporting words; and some may be the book's very focus, an inverted illuminated manuscript in which the images are central and words entwine around them. Not only can pictures, graphs, tables, maps, charts, and diagrams convey information often not amenable to prose, but like the pilings beneath a bridge, they can bear enormous weight and allow prose to flow freely around them.

Such figures (not of speech) touch on topics that occupy whole books and professional guilds dedicated to graphic design. The actual message for our purposes, however, is much simpler, a few chips to place on the table as part of the ante to serious writing; for figures too have their genres, and the question you as a writer of prose must ask is: What added value does each type bring to a text? At what cost? With what new considerations for design?

Too often figures don't do the work they might. The reason may be that they aren't integrated with the overall design. They are treated like decorations, bas-reliefs on the façade, rather than arches and pillars. Especially where quantitative information is available, or where it is critical, graphics can unburden the text, allowing it a more limber shape and graceful cadence. They can transfer the weight of the numbers elsewhere and permit the text to concentrate on their meaning. They allow access to quantitative data that might otherwise be dismissed because they cannot be reconciled with words. Words and numbers don't often mix well, but each offers a comparative advantage in the economy of a text.

That's the first problem: the author's failure to think of graphic materials as integral elements rather than ornamentation, or to consider just how such figures will actually sit within the printed text. It's possible, for example, that they'll wind up on a page other than the one you've chosen, and hence may have neither the aesthetic appeal nor the informational punch you intend; page breaks obey their own logic.

So do designers. And that's the second issue: you must work with the designer or production editor who's assigned to your book at the publishing house. My own experiences with this relationship are overwhelmingly dismal. Designers generally do as they wish, with little regard for the text or my own attempts to synthesize text and illustrations. Maybe one of every five of my books has had the graphics I prepared, and rarely have designer and I agreed over their placement. There are picture books and there are text books, and publishers seem to regard hybrids as chimeras and monsters—another example, I suppose, of mixed genres that seem nifty in theory and that stumble in practice. But the potential payoffs are, to my mind, big enough that I keep placing my bets.

chapter 20
Questions of Scale

In which writings have proportions other than size
alone, such that a sentence is not a shrunken essay,
nor a book merely a bloated one

Agreed: style and substance must match. But what is the
right size of a project for a given theme? In truth, there may
be several possible sizes, according to the genre chosen. Essays are small, books large. Which is best? And what guidelines exist, what scaling laws, for moving an idea from essay to book or book to multivolume series, and back again?
Packaging, after all, is different from packing; building up
is not just bulking up, and downsizing is not the same as
distilling. An essay is more than an executive book-summary
with talking points, and a book is greater than an essay fat-
tened with examples and forced commentary, like so much
foie gras.

Size depends on purpose, as coded into the design. An
op-ed piece has space for a single point from a single perspective: it is an argument or opinion with perhaps some
context from recent news and some evidence, but it's fundamentally a statement. An essay is, as Montaigne proposed,
an assay of an idea, and demands more space because it develops and tests rather than states. An essay-type text may
stand by itself as a journal article, or join others in an anthology, or become a chapter in a larger project. The less it

stands by itself, the more it must reconcile with its sustaining context. The extended essay is a kind of nonfiction novella, a fuller treatment that allows for several strands of argument, character, and events to converge. In academic settings, this might take the form of a master's thesis or a tract on public affairs, a lengthy treatment but less rigorous and elaborate than a monograph. Within an anthology, it might function the way an anchor store does for a shopping mall, a destination in itself but also one that helps to hold the interior parts together.

And the book? The book we've already discussed at length. There is no mandatory size, though anything under 50,000 words would look peculiar (not a "real book"), and anything over 400,000 words would require more than one volume, and anything over 150,000 will cause publishers to squirm. Some designs are more elastic than others, and can expand and contract without fundamentally altering the power of style to explain theme. What size is right? Whatever meets your purpose, no more, no less.

Often books are published and then reissued, sometimes with little more than a new foreword by the author, but sometimes with substantial revisions. What is the relationship between size and revision?

In principle, the same considerations apply as with any text. There are occasions when the opportunity to revise means increasing the wordcount in order to shore up those crumbly arguments, plug those holes the critics poked, and account for new information and interpretations. Typically, economics argues for adding a chapter or two rather than recasting the entire manuscript; only the most significant and bestselling books in fields like history would warrant a complete rewriting. (Textbooks are another matter: here economics favors revisions throughout, both to keep the material current and to destroy the used-book market.) But there are points at which a text will no longer work if stuff is added or subtracted. The whole manuscript needs reconfiguring. This is rare, and it usually leads to a new book that builds upon the old, rather than one that's a reconstruction of the old.

As an example, ponder the four successive editions of an instant classic, Roderick Nash's *Wilderness and the American Mind*. The text began as a dissertation accepted in 1964, the same year the Wilderness Act was passed. Nash then rewrote the dissertation into a book that Yale University Press published in 1967. The politics of wilderness was aboil, and in 1973, as a response to evolving circumstances—particularly the growing environmental movement and the iconic fight over damming the Grand Canyon—he brought out a second edition, which added chapters on those topics. The brawl over Alaskan lands and the international export of the wilderness idea led in 1982 to a third edition with even more chapters.

Meanwhile, Nash became more deeply immersed in moral and philosophical questions relating to wild nature, and in 1989 he published *The Rights of Nature*. This, in effect, unburdened *Wilderness and the American Mind* from having to incorporate these themes in yet another edition. In truth, the book was becoming unwieldy; it no longer spanned just its original stream but covered the entire floodplain beyond. It was losing its structural integrity. The original had focused on three central characters—Henry Thoreau, John Muir, and Aldo Leopold—with their portraits equally spaced throughout the text. But the additional chapters did not include any further portraits, and the outcome started to resemble a bad run-on sentence.

In truth, too, another character was possible: Roderick Nash himself. The book had become a significant part of the history it continued to chronicle. In order for another edition to reclaim something of the original design, it would have to include a fourth personality, which might very well be Nash. Instead, he stepped back, let *The Rights of Nature* assume the heavy lifting of larger ideas, and returned to his role as author rather than activist. When a fourth edition appeared, in 2001, it added no further chapters and allowed the epilogue to serve as a valedictory for the entire enterprise. This gave the sequence of editions a kind of aesthetic closure.

Some projects are intended as a series of books from the outset, a suite of works by a single author on a common subject. The series may be ordered chronologically, each book laying claim to a particular span of time, though the order of publication may differ from the order of the timeline or geographic traverse they portray. Thus, Francis Parkman launched his magisterial seven-volume suite *France and England in North America* with *The History of the Conspiracy of Pontiac* (1851) and published the thematic climax, *Montcalm and Wolfe* (1884), before *A Half-Century of Conflict* (1892), which precedes it in historical material. (James Fenimore Cooper, whom Parkman admired, did the same with his Leatherstocking Tales.) Similarly, John McPhee's cross-section of North American geology, the five-volume *Annals of the Former World* (1978–1998), avoids following a strict geographic sequence. It begins with the Basin and Range Province, moves to New Jersey, leaps to Wyoming, crosses several geographic and thematic divides to California, and concludes with the deep geology of the continental craton that underlies the Great Plains, the order of appearance being driven by authorial opportunity and the evolving theory of plate tectonics, not strict geographic sequencing.

Alternatively, the suite may share a broadly related theme,

as Geoffrey Blainey's three-volume survey of Australia does, isolating three of that country's defining traits in *The Tyranny of Distance, The Triumph of the Nomads,* and *A Land Half Won;* or as William Goetzmann's trilogy on American exploration does, each volume absorbing its predecessor in a more general panorama, from *Army Exploration in the American West, 1803–1863,* to *Exploration and Empire: The Explorer and the Scientist in the Winning of the American West,* and finally to *New Lands, New Men: America and the Second Great Age of Discovery.* Or the series might form a literary triptych, like Ernest Samuels' three-volume biography of Henry Adams. The common requirement is that some order, however flexible, link the works into a whole which enhances the value of each component part.

As with book designs, a series may be tighter or looser—looser has real advantages—but integrating the volumes demands more than authorial Post-It notes. The books should be similar, yet different; they are, in a sense, a franchise, a kind of genre in themselves. Like the Brother Cadfael murder mysteries by Ellis Peters or Bernard Cornwell's Richard Sharpe novels set during the Napoleonic Wars, each subsequent book must carry the recognizable into new territory. There is good reason to avoid a too-rigid prescription; for when contemplating the eras and lands yet to come, you may suffer fatigue and your prose may go stale, as ideas become mute as mileposts and words become duties. Many series do not spring fully formed from the author's Zeus-like brow, but squirm and kick their way into the world as opportunities arise.

The grand historical cycle of an Edward Gibbon or a George Bancroft belongs to another era, one eager for epics but also one in which private patronage could support such costly ventures and a writer could expect a lifetime's employment. The present is more likely to see layoffs, scrambles for fellowships or grants, and public impatience with the long sweep. It leaves epics to fantasy and genre literature, and to space-opera movies. If you wish to write a multi-volume series, plan (paradoxically) on including spontaneity, allow the themes and prose to evolve, let the texts adjust to their (and your) circumstances. Think of the series less as a Golden Gate Bridge than as a San Francisco Bay in which a Golden Gate sits alongside a Bay Bridge and a Dumbarton and a San Mateo as well, each unique and each doing a particular task, yet in the end leaving the whole bay well spanned.

The point is, scaling involves more than size, in the same way that a dripping faucet and the Mississippi River are both running water but the dynamics of one is not simply the other with more volume. Writing does not scale in a linear way: genres invoke differences in kind as well as degree. The progression from a sentence to a library is no more a simple index of increasing words than organic evolution is a simple measure of increasing size from a molecule to a populated planet; there are distinct levels of organization (call them genres) in between. Boiling down a book-length work into an essay is not simple distillation carried to the concentrated dregs, but a process of identifying themes and reconceptualizing an autonomous piece. Similarly, a bigger work can carry more words, move more data, advance more ideas, sketch more events, settings, and characters, but does so at the cost of extensive redesign; and the author must recognize that a substantial portion of the new prose must go to support the weight of the added text. That is what distinguishes bigger from bloated.

Part III
Doing It

chapter 21
Theory and Practice

In which structure gives way to process, plotting moves to putting words on paper, and notes, schemes, citations, designs, and visions become prologues, chapters, forewords, bibliographies, essays, and profiles—in brief, a real manuscript

How to do it? Not how to plan and plot, not how to project spans and tinker with transitions, not how to experiment with voices, but how to get real words onto real pages. Students, writing-workshop participants, professors trapped in publish-or-perish, inquiring minds, all want to know. The questions are often oblique. Do you use a pencil or a laptop? Do you write in the morning or in the evening? Do you write all at once or in spurts? Do you crank out a full draft, or submit for editorial comments as you go along?

There are millions of answers, and no answers. The only meaningful advice is to find a method that works for you, devise a schedule that will allow you to apply it, and muster the discipline to hold to the drill. If you wrote a page a day, you could publish a book a year. The show-stopper is, that daily page has to draw upon all the preparations, all the scheming and designing, all the research trips and the mastery of sources, and most dauntingly all the time and money that you've needed to get that far. Advice is always suspect: it's as easy to spend somebody else's time as it is to spend their money. But here's the advice I give myself.

Follow Your Heart but Use Your Head

You have to care about what you are doing. Particularly if you are a student writing a thesis or dissertation, begin with something that truly excites you, not something that seems suitable or convenient to your supervising professors or that has an immediate funding source. You are committing a substantial fraction of your life to a consuming project. If you don't care, you won't get through it, or you will do hack work, which you will hate.

The career secret, as distinct from personal preference, is timing, timing, timing. The right subject at the right time. Some public fads last decades; some, no more than a handful of years; and scholarly fashions get quickly wiped out as career paths because the first wave gets tenure and shuts the hiring spigot. If, when you begin a major project or enter graduate school, you select a topic because it seems timely, the odds are that the fashion will have passed its prime by the day your text sees print. A dissertation idea, even if you adopt it the moment you sign your program of study, could easily take eight to ten years before publication. That's a long time for the academic equivalent of hula hoops or leisure suits, and if you selected the topic only for careerist reasons, thinking it would make you trendier and more saleable, you may find yourself outfitted with last year's fashion. The best strategy is to pursue what truly interests you. Besides, trends may turn your way by the time you finish.

Still, passion alone is not enough. Even apparently unbounded enthusiasm will exhaust itself if you squander it on poor planning, in trying to do something for which you lack the necessary resources, or if what you want to say can't find a mode of expression. Your heart may get you moving. But rely on your head to get you to your destination.

Time Is Money

The ultimate currency in writing is time. But since our society monetizes even calendars, you need to get money in order to buy time, or give up money in order to get time, or, if you have salaried employment (say, a university post), arrange your day job in such a way that you can carve out inviolate blocks of time in which to write. I've tried all three strategies. Having money is the simplest, but getting that money may be more onerous than the alternatives and may stall or shatter a project while you wait for your funding applications to go through. Perhaps the worst alternative is to hang around working at jobs that neither provide enough surplus cash to buy more time nor allow you sufficient chunks of discretionary time—being a graduate student without a comprehensive stipend, for example. The heart cannot remain unrequited forever.

Writing is about choices, and among the first of those choices is to assure yourself time to work. Otherwise you are writing a diary or a blog.

Writing Is the Art of the Possible

Like politics, writing is about doing what you can with the time, funds, sources, ideas, and talent available. Don't design a project that's simply impossible because you can't scrape up the travel money, or can't find adequate source materials, or can't finagle large blocks of time. Adjust.

Write your primary text during summers and holidays, and save the editing for after work or between classes. If you can't locate documents for a full-bore biography, write a profile instead. If you have an idea but can't bulk it up into a book because you lack travel opportunities, write an essay. Or write about the history of ideas regarding the topic, which you can do with the library materials at hand. If you can't muster the time or funding for a scholarly book, write something else until you can. Adjust your writing to your circumstances. But keep writing. Concert pianists don't practice only when they feel like it. Professional athletes don't wait for inspiration before they train.

Only Writing Writes

The North Rim fire cache (what wildfire firefighters call their fire station) had a sign that read: "If you don't get outta here, you don't get outta here." If you started the morning by hanging around the cache, you never got into the field. That's a perspective that translates well into writing. If you don't actually write, you don't get anything written. It needs saying.

The proposition has a corollary: simply by writing, you can solve many of the problems of writing and will come to understand better what you are doing—the ideas behind the text, the strength of the evidence, the resonance of your voice, the stability of your vision. Writing yields ideas, makes transitions, resolves plot lines. It continually prods and pulls vision and voice, the way digging up information in archives does. Ideas come from writing as much as writing comes from ideas. Writing is a means of understanding that ought to accompany research, not appear magically at its end. With practice, you will trust your ability to make the text happen. If you write, the words will come.

So stockpile phrases, outlines, sketches, and passages during your research phase. Just as no war strategy survives contact with the enemy, so no writing schema survives the shock of first-draft writing. That collision may mean tossed outlines and shredded drafts, a new design for a chapter, a chapter split, endless fussing and rearranging. It also means delight in seeing words fledge on the page, passages take flight, and ideas soar. None of this can happen without the duty and discipline of elbows-on-the-desk, derrière-in-the-chair writing.

Everyone goes about it differently—yes, of course. Every successful writer has some quirks of temperament and idiosyncrasies of technique that no one else has, or wants. But everyone has some routine, applies some craft to creating conditions that allow the mind to focus, and integrates writing into the rhythm of daily life.

These are mine.

STARTING

Don't wait until your research is done before you begin writing. Phrases, ideas, paragraphs, design features, all can be jotted down or put into (or deleted from) outlines, working texts, and so on. You should avoid writing before you know what you are writing about; but you won't know how to write up your results if you don't experiment along the way. Every shard of information should spark a concern about its expression. Where does it belong? How will it affect the design? How should it sound?

Don't get mired in introductions. One can imagine a joking injunction: Drop the first sentence of every paragraph, the first paragraph of every chapter, the first chapter of every book. Remember, the purpose of an introduction is only to introduce. Get into the text. Get to what it is that motivated you in the first place.

If you have written a previous book, try creating different circumstances to help distinguish the process of writing this book from your experience with the earlier one. Particularly if you have begun a new text while the prior manuscript is still wending its way through production, you need a reminder that you are not rewriting your last work. Fresh posters or maps on the wall, a new arrangement of the desk, a repositioning of the room—do something that will keep you from rewriting your last book into your new one.

Set realistic goals. Writing is an occasion for discipline, not dissipation. It's like an exercise program. Lift the right weights the right way, or you may tear something and be sidelined. Try counting: put numbers on each part of your outline, and on what you can expect to do in the blocks of time available. For example, limit your introduction up front to, say, five pages. A target length concentrates the mind as you shape whatever you want to say to the space allotted. Why five pages, and not fifteen? Because that is what your design says is proportionally right for this particular introduction so that it does not overwhelm the substantive parts to follow. Each unit—each chapter, each subchapter— will also have a rough proportion. If, say, you have six chapters and intend to write a manuscript of 300 pages, then each chapter will consist of about forty pages (including notes), with the rest committed to an introduction, conclusion, bibliography, and so on. In each chapter, adjust what you want to say to the forty pages available.

Likewise, determine a reasonable rate of production once you are committed to more or less full-time writing. Two pages a day, or three, or five? Analytical studies will usually proceed slowly, shoring up each advance with argument and evidence; narrative can fly. (My own rates vary from two to eleven pages daily, depending on design, especially the complexity of the evidence and the style of transitions. My maximum rate for analysis was three pages a day for eighteen weeks; for narrative, eleven pages a day for thirty-four days.) Every project will vary, but a working average rate should be part of your planning.

Why? Because you can then predict how much time you'll need to write a draft, or how lengthy a draft you can manage granted the time available. If you write three pages a day, then you will need more than 120 working days to complete a 350-page text. If you write five days a week, then you are looking at twenty-four weeks, or almost six months. Since writing is rarely uninterrupted, allow for 20 percent inflation, or almost eight months for shoulder-to-the-grindstone writing. How, then, do you propose to write this text over the next summer, or even to write a chapter over winter break? Or, to reverse the calculation, how many pages should the manuscript be if you have four months in which to write the draft? If you can manage only a 300-page manuscript, then you will have to modify your design, and everything else, accordingly.

A page a day, a book a year. That few nonfiction writers can even imagine such productivity suggests how easy it is to overestimate what you can achieve, and why you need discipline. Like calories, pages count.

PACING

The best way to sustain your pace is to write something you deeply desire. Nothing will deter you. You will find a way. Writer's block is unimaginable. The heart pumps.

But use your head to keep from stumbling. Whatever the will, the way may be hard if you have to cold-start every morning. Serious writers will have a means to get going and to keep going. Some will write in gushes, all at once, morning or evening. Some will write in dribbles all day long. Some will have a morning ritual of coffee or crosswords, or a walk. Some will dash directly to the desk, and let fidgeting fill the gaps when the mood sags. My own tricks of the trade (not to grace them with too high a gloss) include:

Keep the project always on your subconscious burners. Carry a pocket notepad so you can jot down ideas, which will come at odd moments. But have the upcoming task always simmering on the back of your mental stove so that you need only turn up the heat to set it aboil.

Break your outline into blocks of a length that you can write in one or two days. Each of the units requires immersion but has boundaries. They can be done in a measurable time; you see results; each segues into the next.

Leave a task overnight that can be done readily the next day. A section to edit, a narrative not quite completed, a patch of citation you have yet to clarify and insert—these become warm-up exercises that limber the mind and settle you at your desk for the job ahead.

Set small deadlines and targets, and celebrate when you reach them. The first chapter drafted, the first full draft (apart from those annoying notes), the first full revision with all the parts in place, the first shipment of text to a publisher—such moments break up a large project into do-able blocks and create a sense of accomplishment. It's happening. It will end. You're going to make it.

PERSISTING

Yet misgivings may remain; and as time goes by, as bank accounts erode, and as disappointments or outright rejections (perhaps) mount, those difficulties may slump into serious doubts.

There are ways to check that corrosion; every good writer will have a quiver of techniques. Most authors will rely on a daily routine and the discipline it imposes such that, like athletes or performing artists, they feel edgy and morose if they are not devoting themselves to their work. They know it's easier to continue than to start; they maintain momentum; they set a pace. Most good writers will enforce habits of writing, for it is the writing itself that often makes things happen. If you are blocked at one point, work at another. In firefighting, an indirect attack is a prudent strategy to keep from being overrun by flames; in writing, it can be a way of finding points of entry and flanking that allow you to keep at it. If that pesky survey-of-the-field chapter has you stalled, plunge into the core of the work—the stuff that got you excited in the first place. You can cycle back to preliminaries later, after you've said what you most wanted to say.

It's helpful to appreciate that the writer in the text is not you, at least not you in your entirety. That writer is a persona. It's the self as narrator. If that persona bores you, create another (a change of voice is the simplest way to do this). More extreme versions may involve the invention of a pseudonym. The struggles and rejections are happening to your persona, not to you. The persona does the experimenting. The persona takes the blows. It does no good to pretend that rejections are "not personal"; of course they are. But a persona can deflect the worst. A persona may fail. If you wish, you can devise another. Beginning authors may go through several. Accomplished authors may deliberately create various personae.

Mostly, persisting means having something you are determined to say and a way of saying of it. It means voice and vision.

But often questions regarding how to keep at it are not about persisting in a particular project; they're about persevering overall. They do not concern techniques and craft.

They are code queries for doubts about writing as a vocation. Such doubts cannot be shifted to a persona but fix on the self as a writer. On this, there can be no stock reply. Ambitions to succeed as a writer are, in some respects, no different from ambitions to play for the Arizona Diamondbacks, sing at the Metropolitan Opera, or win a Nobel Prize in chemistry. Only a few can garner public fame and fortune. At some point, the relentless wearing yields to weariness; other pulls attract prospective writers away from the need to keep pushing. Eventually we find a point at which our ambitions and our talents jostle into rough equilibrium.

When to push on and when to pull back? My own experiences are mixed. I know that doing all you are advised to do does not guarantee success, yet I've learned that not doing those things all but guarantees that you will fall short. The personal specifics behind that prescription are even more daunting; for in your drive to succeed, you can punish not only yourself but those around you. I can't, in good conscience, wish such experiences on anyone. Writing is about choosing. It's about constantly making calls regarding what is good enough. Assessing the unstable gap between what you desire and what you can do is the hardest call of all.

It is not something that can be taught, though you can benefit from a good teacher, good colleagues, or, as Joan Didion wonderfully put it in "After Henry," a good editor. The real role of an editor, she insists, does not involve changes to the text or matters of style, as usually understood. It is, rather, something both more vital and more ineffable. The editor ("if the editor was Henry Robbins") was "the person who gave the writer the idea of himself, the idea of herself, the image of self that enabled the writer to sit down alone and do it."[1] There are many routes to that sense of self, and they are not unique to writing. Yet it remains a delicate affair, between resolve and reason, with the self like an oil drop suspended between two charged plates of self-doubt and self-understanding.

Still, writing is different from other activities. It need not be a sole career (only a few people succeed at being full-time writers), and the range of possible writing is unbounded. Anyone who wants to write can. It is, as always, a question of aligning style with substance, of matching what you can do with what you want to say, neither of which is ever fixed.

ENDING

The important thing to remember about endings is that the project never ends. This is not a statement about textual revisions, which go on and on, beyond the point of nausea. It involves those minor matters—hunting for a lost citation, checking the bibliography, tracking an elusive photo—that belong in the realm of textual housekeeping. They never reach completion. Each demands many times more labor than you think it will. Revising the text doesn't complete the project; what does is finishing all the trimmings and impedimenta that turn a wooden frame into a completed house. Allow a lot more time than you expect, and anticipate a lot more frustration, tedium, and labor than you have time for. Bet on it.

Yet somewhere, somehow, the project does end: the manuscript gets into print. Expect a natural burst of pride as you fondle the book and a reflux of dismay if you deign to read inside it. By then, if you are destined for a career in writing, you will be well into another project.

chapter 22

Writing Lives

In which we examine the life cycles of books, of
book-based careers, and of bookish authors

Fewer books have been written about writers, or the life of
writing, than about writing itself, but not by much. Some
reasons are good, some suspect. The good cause is that writing is done by writers and cannot be segregated from the
writer's larger life. Writing is a hobby, a job, and for many a
vocation, not easily stripped out of quotidian existence. But
the "writing life" genre can also serve as a surrogate memoir that may have little to say about the art and craft of writing beyond personal biography. For some readers, that is
enough.

Life Cycle of a Book

Books are born, mature, and, while they can't be said to die,
get interred in libraries. The process of gestation and birth,
with its subsequent christenings and presentations to the
world, is well documented, and many are the published
counsels about how to move from conception to swaddled
book. Yet books live beyond that moment. How they do so
affects a writer's career.

A book's life cycle contains several epicycles. First, there is the epicycle of writing, which has largely occupied this text (as it does most writing guides). Second, there is the epicycle of production, by which the author-completed manuscript actually gets between covers and onto shelves. This process rarely lasts less than a year; fifteen to eighteen months is common. (For my books, the shortest production was eight months, and the longest, twenty-eight.) This significantly affects the overall rhythm of writing as a life. When combined with the post-publication review process, which for academic books can take one to two years, it means there are long pauses in the production of even one work. A serious writer will apply that downtime toward another project.

The third dominant epicycle concerns sales and shelf life. The ruling fact here is, most of a book's sales will happen in the first year, followed by an exponential decline. This reality holds whether the volume is a niche reference work or a scholarly thesis or a general-market trade book. The reasons are novelty and libraries. Novelty accounts for purchases by colleagues and general readers interested in the topic or in a new work by the author. This wave may last longer than a year, given the slow progress of reviews in disciplinary journals. Libraries buy for their varied readership, with research libraries purchasing around 300 titles annually. That does not seem like much in a nation of more than 300 million people; and it isn't. But academic books normally sell fewer than 1,000 copies, of which libraries might absorb as many as half. Trade books will target sales that are an order of magnitude greater, with public libraries again buying a substantial fraction. That libraries acquire fewer volumes these days has caused serious rents in the space-time fabric of publishing.

Once that flush has passed, however, a fall-off comes with shocking speed. The first wave will constitute perhaps 75 percent of total sales. The next year will account for 75 percent of the remaining sales; and so on. However enduring a book's contribution to scholarship or culture, its economic life is fleeting. If the book is successful, a paperback edition may follow as soon as the initial flush passes. For trade books, this will occur after a year; for academic books, typically longer. This rekindles sales, followed by the inexorable exponential decline. A robust used-book market will alter even these rates of sales, particularly if the book is destined for the classroom, while online bookselling may keep sales simmering past the time when publishers can afford to stock them on their shelves. But the numbers are small. Because trade publishers must pay taxes on inventory, they cannot afford to hold weak-selling volumes and will instead remainder them, dumping them on the market through various resale jobbers, or simply returning them to the pulp from which they came. (For sample trajectories of sales, see the graphs below.)

Is there no way to alter this logic? Unquestionably, the digital revolution is sending tremors through traditional publishing, but what will shake apart and what will rebuild when the quake subsides are unclear. A good guess is that the outcome will more resemble the past than prophets might expect. Online publishing, print-on-demand, web-based sales—the new technologies of manufacturing and distributing are shortening production, extending the long tail of sales, and making everyone a potential publisher. But for the near future the old verities will likely endure. Even doubling sales or increasing the production of printed books by an order of magnitude will not alter the fiscal fundamentals. Real value-added comes not from quickening the pace of actual printing but from editing, the lengthy process of sifting, editing, and judging, all of which will remain labor-intensive. And self-publishing may turn out to be the subprime economics of literature, inflating a world with books no one will read.

Within the existing landscape, however, it is possible through aggressive publicity to resist the often dismaying cycle of spike and collapse. This is a topic worthy of its own book (there are many on the market, testimonies to practicing what you preach). Here I will make only two observations.

One: sales will depend on media promotion—radio or, best of all, TV, and more recently websites; but all variants of self-promotion. If your book is topical, create a persona to publicize it, just as you did to write it. The varied media available now, and the diffuse niche markets, are driving sales-savvy authors to cultivate a "platform," of which the book is but a piece. Remember: the platform is you, not your book. Remember, too: publicity rages and passes quickly, like a fever. Publicists don't search book review journals; they watch what other publicists are doing. One appearance will lead to another, and another. And then it will end.

Two: another means of tweaking sales is to write a book that can be adopted for use in large lecture courses; then you should promote it as such. The sales add up. Remember, in this case, that you are selling not to the students but to their professors. The book has to fit their teaching needs. Even upper-level classroom adoption, a few classes of middling attendance, can keep sales percolating for many years, despite a vigorous used-book market. To renew the sales curve, you need to revise the text and publish it as a new edition. That economic logic becomes an argument for frequent revisions.

Now a bit of ground truth in the form of some real-world

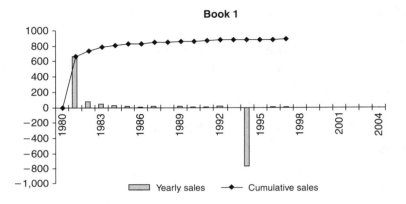

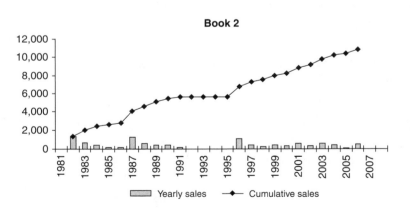

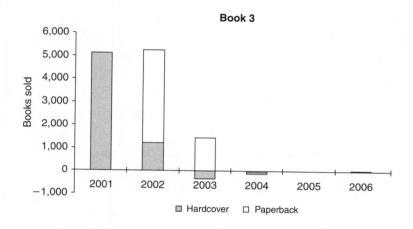

A tale of three books. Book 1 was a dissertation revised into a publishable book for an academic press. The collapse in sales was, in fact, a remaindering. Book 2 was a scholarly history that found a professional audience and went through three printings, each of which rekindled the sales curve. Book 3 was a trade book boosted by paperback sales after a year but still driven by the logic of annual decline. There are two important differences between Book 3 and the others. First, its initial sales were four times larger than theirs. Second, its publication in paperback a year after the hardcover edition had the effect of smoothing its decline, though nothing could disguise the unmistakable trend in its sales. And third, the curious negative sales were the result of that peculiar practice known as "returns" by which books are shipped to stores and, if unsold, returned to the publisher. Organized along a calendar year, this can yield books that are nominally sold in one year but which might be returned the next year.

data. Consider a sample of twenty books from a single author but various publishers, a sample drawn from a source I can rely on (myself). The average length of time from conception to print was 5.6 years. Of that period, probably a year or a year-and-a-half was spent in writing, depending on how extensive the revising became, and a year-and-a-half in production (editing, typesetting, printing, binding); the rest of that period was devoted to applying for money, organizing my time, doing research, and allowing all or parts of the manuscript to undergo some sort of critical vetting. On average, a book appeared every eighteen months, but that included some brief books for which I was able to rummage through or cannibalize old materials, or which assembled essays I'd written after short travels over several years. A more reasonable average rate, based on a more or less full-time writing schedule, would be one book every two years. The explanation for why a thirty-year career in writing has yielded twenty books rather than five is that several books, at various stages, were always taking shape simultaneously.

But whether your book is academic or trade, written for scholarship or aimed at a general audience, big or little, sales will shrivel to a nubbin within two years—the minimum time required to write a book of this kind, assuming you do nothing else. Writing for a living means fighting against this Malthusian logic.

Life Cycle of a Writing Career

Many kinds of books, many reasons for writing them, many kinds of lives for writers: no single career path can absorb them all. Books may be a hobby, a form of self-entertainment, intended for only limited circulation. They may be art, an expression primarily of an author's aesthetic understanding of the world. They may be referential, social, or political, concerned with encapsulating data, conveying observations about society and culture, or advocating policies. They may be a business. Fewer than 5 percent of the Authors Guild, however, live primarily on their income as writers, and this figure includes those with lucrative movie rights, overseas translations, and so on. (For other media, sales figures are comparable. For music, 10 percent of recordings make a profit; for movies, 6 percent of all releases keep studios solvent.) A few writers do succeed financially; most must find another way to pay for their habit. They will have a day job, often at a university, and they will write because this is required by their profession, which provides them with the necessary opportunities (notably discretionary time, and access to research grants and fellowships). For this group, writing—creating books—is a career.[1]

The data set of twenty books we examined above can help to explain some of the traits of such a professional path. Two relevant trends in particular fall out. One: the shelf life of each of those twenty books averaged 5.5 years. The span was longer for books published by university presses because, as nonprofit operations, such presses are not taxed on their inventory. But to some extent their in-print titles make a deceptive index because the publishers are likely to dump large quantities of unsold copies onto the remainders market and to raise the price of the small number of books they retain, which helps to keep the title on the shelf amid ever-dwindling sales. Two: for those scholars who publish primarily book-length works, these cycles resonate eerily with the rhythms of academic life—that is, the cycle of sabbaticals and the cycle for promotion and tenure. The life cycle of academic or academic-trade books thus comes as no surprise to anyone whose primary job resides within a university.

But whether or not you work for a university, the Malthusian fact persists that books grow arithmetically and die exponentially. Barring terrific sales—which point to a book about a celebrity or by a well-known author, or one that instantly finds widespread classroom adoption, or, even less likely, one with saleable motion-picture rights—the financial constraints of career publishing argue for a single book, or one book with an echo. For most scholarly writers, this will be a revision of their dissertation, which was initially drafted while they remained students and had time (if not money). If you wish to publish routinely, you need outside income (or lots of discretionary time, which is nearly the same thing), and you need to fill the hiatuses in the production of one manuscript with the writing of another.

The Life of a Writer

Not least, there is the existential issue: writing as a way of living.

It has its perils. You will likely not live by words alone; you will have to marry well, have access to private income, or depend on grants, fellowships, and contracts, all or part of which you can apply to the writing you wish to do. Truly popular writers on massively popular themes can command substantial advances against royalties, but few university presses can extend financial aid. (Most university presses live off subsidies or endowments of various kinds; their sales do not cover all their expenses.) For those writers who produce regularly, there are also hazards associated with their accumulating body of work: they may begin to self-cannibalize and recycle, rather than creating a new corpus, and this may lead them into a stale voice or even self-reference, if not self-parody. It's hard enough to publish routinely; it's even more difficult to keep changing themes, refreshing voices, evolving styles. Industriousness is easier than innovation, for the latter can run hard against an intellectual curve of diminishing returns.

Yet writing has, of course, its pleasures. It is a supremely creative act; it projects knowledge, ideas, and self before society; it allows you to participate actively in the civic life of the culture. For all the digibabble that clogs cyberspace, the book endures as a token and totem, and as an intrinsically satisfying artifact. For the serious scholar, writing can advance a career. Publish well and you will rarely perish. The system may not be fair or reasonable, or even rational, but it will, over time, recognize and reward the kind of productivity that writing represents, and for many fields the book remains the coin of the realm. Like baseball teams, which can always be relied upon to find a place for someone who can hit, universities will find a niche for someone who can write.

That relationship may be more reciprocal than is commonly recognized. My own trek through Academe may be relevant here, for even as my academic career has allowed me to write, so writing has permitted that career. Books got me hired, more books got me promoted, and still more got me promoted again or allowed me to transfer to another post. My academic career is fundamentally a record of writing. As measured by book sales, it has undergone four waves and troughs; at every trough I moved, and I moved only during the troughs. It is not sales per se (the royalties, the reviews) that matter. It is the action. When I'm not writing, I'm bored, I'm morose, I'm restless. The moment I realized that, I knew I had become a career writer.

One final note. For the serious author, writing is a vocation that contains its own order. It can shape a life as much as it does a day's routine. It demands a duty and discipline that can be indistinguishable from a moral code and that can similarly satisfy, a purpose applied to create something tangible that you can lay before others, a universe of meaning. A life as art: reconciling what you want to do with how you do it. Not a bad prescription for living.

notes

index

notes

2. Art and Craft

1. Quoted in Rachel Donadio, "Truth Is Stronger Than Fiction," *New York Times Book Review* (7 August 2005), 27.
2. Quoted in John B. Thompson, *Books in the Digital Age* (Cambridge, Mass.: Polity, 2005), 152.
3. Wallace Stegner, "On the Writing of History," in Stegner, *The Sound of Mountain Water* (New York: Penguin, 1980), 205.
4. "Le style, c'est l'empreinte de ce qu'on est dans ce qu'on fait." René Daumal, "Dialogue du style" (interview with Lanza del Vasto, ca. 1941), in Daumal, *Essais et notes, II: Les Pouvoirs de la parole,* ed. Claudio Rugafiori (Paris: Gallimard, 1972), 265. I thank Maria Ascher for bringing his marvelous reference to my attention.

4. Nonfiction as Writing

1. Antjie Krog, *Country of My Skull* (New York: Three Rivers Press, 1998), 43.
2. Jack London, *The Call of the Wild and White Fang* (New York: Barnes and Noble Books, 2004), 353–354.
3. For a very thorough (and fair) review of the controversy, see Philip L. Fradkin, *Wallace Stegner and the American West* (New York: Knopf, 2008), 252–272. Fradkin left me with the impression that Stegner kept so much of the original material that he is indeed open to charges of plagiarism, an odd outcome for a writer of fiction.
4. Wallace Stegner, *Beyond the Hundredth Meridian: John Wesley Powell and the Second Opening of the West* (New York: Penguin, 1992; orig. pub. 1953), 94–95.

5. Voice . . .

1. Hans Zinsser, *Rats, Lice, and History* (New York: Bantam, 1971), 80.

2. Carl Ortwin Sauer, *The Early Spanish Main* (Berkeley: University of California Press, 1969), 17, 142.

3. Samuel Eliot Morison, *The Great Explorers: The European Discovery of America* (New York: Oxford University Press, 1978), 474–475.

4. Simon Schama, *Citizens: A Chronicle of the French Revolution* (New York: Vintage, 1989), 875.

5. William H. Goetzmann, *New Lands, New Men: America and the Second Great Age of Discovery* (New York: Viking, 1986), 154–155.

6. See William Cronon, "A Place for Stories: Nature, History, and Narrative," *Journal of American History,* 78, no. 4 (1992), 1347–1376.

7. Patricia Limerick, *The Legacy of Conquest: The Unbroken Past of the American West* (New York: Norton, 1987), 32. Much as I personally long for a post-ironic culture, it won't happen in my lifetime.

6. . . . and Vision

1. William James, *A Pluralistic Universe* (New York: Longmans, Green, 1909), 20.

7. Designing

1. George Orwell, "Politics and the English Language," in Orwell, *A Collection of Essays* (New York: Harcourt, 1981), 158–159.

2. Mike Davis, *The Ecology of Fear* (New York: Holt, 1998), 7, 10.

8. Plotting

1. Tom Wolfe, "Two Young Men Who Went West," in Wolfe, *Hooking Up* (New York: Farrar Straus Giroux, 2000), 63.

2. Norman Maclean, *Young Men and Fire* (Chicago: University of Chicago Press, 1992), 143.

3. Ibid., 144.

4. Simon Schama, *Landscape and Memory* (New York: Vintage, 1995), 3.

9. Transitioning

1. John McPhee, *Encounters with the Archdruid* (New York: Farrar Straus Giroux, 1971), 28–29.

2. Eric Rolls, "More a New Planet Than a New Continent," in Rolls, *From Forest to Sea: Australia's Changing Environment* (St. Lucia, Australia: University of Queensland Press, 1993), 170.

3. Ibid., 170.

4. Mike Davis, *The Ecology of Fear* (New York: Holt, 1998), 127.

5. P. J. O'Rourke, *All the Trouble in the World* (New York: Atlantic Monthly Press, 1994), 194–195.

10. Dramatizing

1. Wallace Stegner, "On the Writing of History," in Stegner, *The Sound of Mountain Water* (New York: Penguin, 1980), 203.

2. John Gardner, *The Art of Fiction* (New York: Vintage, 1983), 65–66; William James, *The Writings of William James,* ed. John J. McDermott (New York: Modern Library, 1968), 647–648.

3. John Barry, *Rising Tide* (New York: Simon and Schuster Paperbacks, 1977), 157.

4. Ibid., 191.

5. Ibid., 192.

12. Prose

1. George Orwell, "Politics and the English Language," in Orwell, *A Collection of Essays* (New York: Harcourt, 1981), 170.

2. George Dangerfield, *The Era of Good Feelings* (New York: Harcourt, Brace, 1952), 14.

3. William H. Goetzmann, *New Lands, New Men: America and the Second Great Age of Discovery* (New York: Viking, 1986), 88.

4. Wallace Stegner, *Beyond the Hundredth Meridian: John Wesley Powell and the Second Opening of the West* (New York: Penguin, 1992; orig. pub. 1953), 9–10.

5. Felipe Fernández-Armesto, *Pathfinders: A Global History of Exploration* (New York: Norton, 2006), 298–299.

6. Ibid., 274.

7. Francis Parkman, *France and England in North America,* vol. 2 (New York: Library of America, 1983), 856.

8. John McPhee, *The Control of Nature* (New York: Farrar Straus Giroux, 1989), 203.

9. Stephen J. Pyne, *Fire in America* (Seattle: University of Washington Press, 1995), 274.

10. Catharine Parr Traill, *The Backwoods of Canada* (Toronto: McClelland and Stewart, 1989), 158–159.

11. George Stewart, *Names on the Land,* 4th ed. (San Francisco: Lexicos, 1982), 183.

12. Gerard Helferich, *Humboldt's Cosmos* (New York: Gotham Books, 2004), 337.

13. Leigh B. Lentile et al., "Remote Sensing Techniques to Assess

Active Fire Characteristics and Post-Fire Effects," *International Journal of Wildland Fire,* 15 (2006), 320.

13. Character

1. Barbara Tuchman, *The Guns of August* (New York: Ballantine, 1962), 423.
2. David Howarth, *1066: The Year of the Conquest* (New York: Penguin, 1981), 107.
3. Ibid., 110.
4. Ibid.
5. Ibid., 110–111.
6. Wallace Stegner, *Beyond the Hundredth Meridian: John Wesley Powell and the Second Opening of the West* (New York: Penguin, 1992; orig. pub. 1953), 304–305.
7. Joan Didion, "James Pike, American," in Didion, *The White Album* (New York: Farrar Straus Giroux, 1979), 52.
8. Ibid., 57–58.
9. George Dangerfield, *The Era of Good Feelings* (New York: Harcourt, Brace, 1952), 4.
10. Ibid., 10–11.
11. Ibid., 7–8.
12. Ibid., 14.
13. Michael Lewis, *Moneyball: The Art of Winning an Unfair Game* (New York: Norton, 2003), 6–7.
14. Ibid., 34.
15. Bernard DeVoto, *The Year of Decision: 1846* (Boston: Houghton Mifflin, 1942), 60.
16. Stephen J. Pyne, *Awful Splendour: A Fire History of Canada* (Vancouver: University of British Columbia Press, 2007), 20.
17. Ibid., 127.

14. Setting

1. John McPhee, *Rising from the Plains* (New York: Farrar Straus Giroux, 1986), 26–28.
2. Ibid., 79.
3. Simon Schama, *Landscape and Memory* (New York: Vintage, 1995), 554.
4. Ibid., 555.
5. Jill Ker Conway, *The Road from Coorain* (New York: Vintage, rpt. 1990), 8.

6. Norman Maclean, *Young Men and Fire* (Chicago: University of Chicago Press, 1992), 43.

7. Ibid., 43–44.

8. Ibid., 45–46.

9. Garrett Mattingly, *The Armada* (Boston: Houghton Mifflin, 1959), 70–72.

10. Ibid., 72–73.

11. Ibid., 73–74.

12. Bruce Catton, *This Hallowed Ground: The Story of the Union Side of the Civil War* (Edison, N.J.: Castle Books, 2002), 386.

15. Point of View

1. Henry Adams, *The Education of Henry Adams* (Boston: Houghton Mifflin, 1961), 6, 121.

2. William Germano, *From Dissertation to Book* (Chicago: University of Chicago Press, 2005), 106. Original quote about Fremont from Bernard DeVoto, *The Year of Decision: 1846* (Boston: Houghton Mifflin, 1942), 222.

3. Alfred W. Crosby, *Ecological Imperialism: The Biological Expansion of Europe, 900–1900* (Cambridge: Cambridge University Press, 1986), 42.

4. DeVoto, *The Year of Decision*, 42.

5. Ibid., 169–171.

6. John McPhee, *Assembling California* (New York: Farrar Straus Giroux, 1993), 156.

7. Ibid., 198.

8. Ibid., 24.

9. Walter A. McDougall, *Let the Sea Make a Noise . . . : A History of the North Pacific from Magellan to MacArthur* (New York: Basic Books, 1993), 1–2.

16. Showing and Telling

1. Mark Fiege, *Irrigated Eden: The Making of an Agricultural Landscape in the American West* (Seattle: University of Washington Press, 1999), 205.

2. John M. Barry, *Rising Tide: The Great Mississippi Flood of 1927 and How It Changed America* (New York: Simon and Schuster Paperbacks, 1997), 189.

3. Barbara Tuchman, *The Guns of August* (New York: Ballantine, 1994), 82–83.

4. Wallace Stegner, *Beyond the Hundredth Meridian: John Wesley Powell and the Second Opening of the West* (New York: Penguin, 1992; orig. pub. 1953), 17.

5. Bernard DeVoto, *The Year of Decision: 1846* (Boston: Houghton Mifflin, 1942), 280.

6. Ibid., 281.

7. Alfred Crosby, *Ecological Imperialism: The Biological Expansion of Europe, 900–1900* (Cambridge: Cambridge University Press, 1986), 7.

8. William H. Goetzmann, *New Lands, New Men: America and the Second Great Age of Discovery* (New York: Viking, 1986), 89.

9. Joan Didion, "7000 Romaine, Los Angeles 38," in Didion, *Slouching toward Bethlehem* (New York: Farrar Straus Giroux, 1968), 69, 71.

10. Ibid., 71.

17. Editing II

1. Alexander von Humboldt and Aimé Bonpland, *Personal Narrative of a Voyage to the Equinoctial Regions of the New Continent,* abridged and translated from the French by Jason Wilson (New York: Penguin, 1995), 24–25.

2. Ellis D. Miner and Randii R. Wessen, *Neptune: The Planet, Rings, and Satellites* (Chichester, U.K.: Praxis, 2002), 171–172.

3. The authors refer to a "professional text": Dale Cruikshank, ed., *Neptune and Triton* (Tucson: University of Arizona Press, 1995). They contrast that work with their own, which aims "to present a more coherent account in a language and style more accessible and understandable to the 'non-expert'" (Miner and Wessen, *Neptune,* xix).

4. Ibid.

18. Figures of Speech

1. John McPhee, *Assembling California* (New York: Farrar Straus Giroux, 1993), 157.

2. Stephen J. Pyne, *Fire in America* (Princeton: Princeton University Press, 1982), 277.

3. Tad Friend, "The Paper Chase," *New Yorker* (11 December 2006), 98.

4. Francis Parkman, quoted in Simon Schama, *Dead Certainties* (New York: Farrar Straus Giroux, 1991), 64.

5. Alfred Crosby, *Ecological Imperialism: The Biological Expansion of Europe, 900–1900* (Cambridge: Cambridge University Press, 1986), 170.

6. Michael Lewis, *Moneyball: The Art of Winning an Unfair Game* (New York: Norton, 2004), 112.

7. Wallace Stegner, *Mormon Country* (Lincoln: University of Nebraska Press, rpt. 1970), 23–24.

8. George Orwell, "Shooting an Elephant," in Orwell, *A Collection of Essays* (New York: Harcourt, 1981), 148–156.

9. Stephen Pyne, "Nataraja," in Pyne, *World Fire: The Culture of Fire on Earth* (Seattle: University of Washington Press, 1997), 149–170.

10. Norman Maclean, *Young Men and Fire* (Chicago: University of Chicago Press, 1992), 92.

11. Mike Davis, *The Ecology of Fear* (New York: Holt, 1998), 8–9.

12. Ibid., 16.

19. Technical Information

1. G. J. Whitrow, *The Natural Philosophy of Time,* 2nd ed. (Oxford: Oxford University Press, 1980), 42.

2. E. C. Pielou, *After the Ice Age: The Return of Life to Glaciated North America* (Chicago: University of Chicago Press, 1991), 25–26.

3. Alfred Crosby, *Ecological Imperialism: The Biological Expansion of Europe, 900–1900* (Cambridge: Cambridge University Press, 1986), 292.

4. Hans Zinsser, *Rats, Lice, and History* (New York: Bantam, 1971), 148.

5. Jonathan Weiner, *The Beak of the Finch: A Story of Evolution in Our Time* (New York: Vintage, 1994), 143.

6. Ibid., 156.

7. Richard Hofstadter, *The American Political Tradition and the Men Who Made It* (New York: Vintage, 1948), 7.

8. Louis Menand, *The Metaphysical Club: A Story of Ideas in America* (New York: Farrar Straus Giroux, 2001), 195–196.

9. Ibid., 197–198.

10. Mike Davis, *Late Victorian Holocausts: El Niño Famines and the Making of the Third World* (London: Verso, 2001), 221.

11. Stephen Pyne, "The Source," in Pyne, *Smokechasing* (Tucson: University of Arizona Press, 2003), 103.

21. Theory and Practice

1. Joan Didion, "After Henry," in Didion, *After Henry* (New York: Vintage, 1993), 20.

22. Writing Lives

1. Figures on other media from James Surowiecki, "The Science of Success," *New Yorker* (9 and 16 July 2007), 40.

index